STUMBLING IN THE HALF-LIGHT

JOHN D. SARGENT

FriesenPress

Suite 300 - 990 Fort St
Victoria, BC, V8V 3K2
Canada

www.friesenpress.com

ISBN
978-1-5255-1666-5 (Hardcover)
978-1-5255-1667-2 (Paperback)
978-1-5255-1668-9 (eBook)

1. BIOGRAPHY & AUTOBIOGRAPHY

Distributed to the trade by The Ingram Book Company

Dedicated to:

John David Sargent Sr.
Who found Bahá'u'lláh and passed on this
priceless legacy to his decendants.

Contents

Acknowledgments

First of all, I would like to thank all those who have been a constant source of encouragement for me to write down these stories. Especially my sister Tanja Sargent and my daughter Celeste. Second, a big thank you to my wife, Anne, for putting up with all my anxiety over this project and for being the alpha and omega (first and last) editor of these stories. Special thank yous to Reggie Newkirk for his wonderful Foreword and to Kim Naqvi for coming up with the perfect title for this compilation of stories. Next, I would like to thank those who reviewed the rough draft of the manuscript and offered their many helpful suggestions: Sandra Maitland, Karen McKye, Reggie and Cindy Newkirk, Wendy Rosen, Celeste Sargent, Nathan Sweeney and Patricia Verge. And especially MJ Oakes, who meticulously went through the manuscript to correct the multitude of capitalization, punctuation and tense agreement errors.

I would also like to take this opportunity to mention four mentors that served as guides and role models for my life: my father, whose selfless service so inspired me; Angus Cowan, who championed me in my work with the First Nation Peoples; Charles Grindlay, who helped with the development of my career; and Jameson Bond, whose aid was invaluable in helping me get back into the First Nations teaching work after my return from Africa.

Foreword

Reggie Newkirk

As I read the first few stories of *Stumbling in the Half-Light* I was reminded of a comment made by William James in his *Varieties of Religious Experience*. He wrote "Knowledge about life is one thing; effective occupation of a place in life, with its dynamic currents passing through your being, is another."

Stumbling in the Half-Light is a collection of stories that explores a life lived by the author that can resonate with anybody who strives to find and effectively occupy their own place in life. The active agents in these stories are: humility, intellectual honesty, authenticity, companionship, courage, and the workings of a deep and abiding spirituality.

Telling his own story the author serves as a sojourner guide through tests and difficulties, joy and sorrows, and periods of doubt. However, the difficult times were resolved through prayer, deep reflection on the Revelation of Bahá'u'lláh[1] and informed obedience to the institutions of the Bahá'í[2] community—the anchors that stabilize our life experience and strengthen the soul (an ineffable and mysterious entity). A case in point was when his dad wanted to marry a First Nations[3] woman. There was little support in his family for inter-racial marriage. One major concern the family had was that an inter-racial marriage would produce half-breed children. Returning from his tour of duty during WWII, John Sr. "… headed straight back to Buffalo and so it was that the black sheep (John Sr.) and the noble savage (John Jr.'s mother) were married."

Stumbling in the Half-Light is a series of vignettes on the author's life, education, service and the many interesting people he met along the way. His stories demonstrate the learning and experience gained during his travel teaching/consolidation efforts in many localities including First Nation and Native American reservations in Canada and the United States and localities in Rhodesia (now Zimbabwe) where he and his father pioneered. Adapting to differing cultural views and practices was a hallmark learning experience and this learning continues to the present day.

Stumbling in the Half-Light provides Bahá'í youth with an object lesson that they too can learn to rely on God in their personal lives and careers, and in their service to the Cause of Bahá'u'lláh.

The author has an uncanny sense of humour that comes through the stories. The reader will experience a range of

---

1   See Glossary

2   See Glossary

3   Canadians refer to the original inhabitants of North America as First Nation peoples.

emotions: laughter, joy, sadness, surprise or perhaps even the feeling that she or he "has been there before."

John describes his journey towards faith. This gradual acquisition of knowledge, backed up by actions and deeds, is described in such a way that the reader can identify with their own journey. He has a profound ability to describe the inner journey in a way which is both exciting and comforting. Whether the reader is young or old, the path from blind imitation to true faith is strewn with obstacles of all sorts: doubts and perplexities, vain imaginings and desires. The more light upon the path the safer the journey. *Stumbling in the Half-Light* is a book filled with light and compassion for the fellow wayfarer.

Reggie Newkirk 2015

The Preface

Since I was little I loved the art of storytelling. My grandfather, Samuel Anderson, relished this Haudenosaunee tradition. In addition, he had been a school teacher at a time when memory work was an important part of education. The students memorized poems and dramatic prose and took part in contests where selected students presented these memorized works to rapt audiences (their parents). My grandfather would often be asked to recite a poem at family events. My personal favorite was 'The Cremation of Sam McGee' by Robert W. Service. Often after Sunday dinner the family would gather and anecdotes were shared (and embellished) by various members of the family. We were especially interested to hear from friends and family visiting from far away.

From a very young age I would often repeat these family stories as well as make up new ones on the spot—much to the annoyance of my parents and grandparents who wanted the quick answer to: "How did this vase get broken?" As I grew older and became actively involved in the proclamation and consolidation work with the Bahá'í friends in First Nation communities, I found that story telling was a good way of presenting the history and verities of the Faith. I used this technique in firesides and public presentations as well.

*Samuel and Minnie Anderson with two of their
children, Six Nations Reserve, c1917*[4]

Oral storytelling connects the heart of the storyteller with
the hearts of the people listening and, when the story is done,
it disappears into thin air, except for what the hearer takes
away with them. There is a sacred connection made in personally telling and receiving stories so, of course, I kept no written
record of them. Although I didn't stop people from recording
them, I was not particularly happy with that because I was

---

[4]   The Canadian Museum of History – Photo Collection

afraid they could be used out of context. Also, I would always watch the faces of the audience and use sound effects and hand and facial gestures to emphasize or dramatize certain aspects of the story to keep the listeners engaged. I would have no control over this with written or recorded versions of these stories. Furthermore, when you write it down there is always someone (usually your wife) who says, "I remember that incident differently." This is why, when my sister and daughter would ask me to write them down for posterity, I was averse to do so.

However, a couple of incidents caused me to reconsider. I was saddened to hear that my mentor, Jamie Bond, had been unable to finish his memoirs before he passed. Fortunately, some of the Friends, most notably Don Brown, stepped in to complete this work. Also, when I read 'Return to Tyendinaga,' I discovered that my old friend, Evelyn Watts, was suffering from severe health issues. This almost prevented her from telling the story of her parents' amazing pioneering work. However, Patricia Verge was able to come in and help her finish it. These incidents prompted me to reflect—if I was going to set anything down on paper I should get a move on while I still had some sense left. (Some say I'm already well past my 'Best Before Date.')

So I finally decided I would write these stories down. I gave the book the working title 'Centum Fabulae' which is Latin for one hundred stories. I thought I could write a story a day for one hundred days and my book would be finished. Ha, ha. After two years had passed I realized that there was no way I was going to get to one hundred stories. I started off writing random stories just as they came to mind. This introduced the problem of repetition as I had to explain background information to clarify each story. At that point it occurred to me to place the stories in chronological order, thus enabling the reader to keep the context in mind without me having to reiterate it. At the same time I realized that this was a very eclectic collection. Part family history, part autobiography, part humorous anecdote and part stories of the importance of reliance on God. I was then unsure who the audience for such a book might be. In the end I decided to publish it 'as is' and trust it will find its own audience.

Finding a title for this collection was also problematic as it was obvious that the working title was not going to fly. I had a notebook with a list of potential titles, but I wasn't really fond of any of them. One day I mentioned this to Kim Naqvi, who had read a number of the stories, and she immediately suggested '*Stumbling in the Half-Light*' as a potential title. This was a reference to a quote by Shoghi Effendi[5]—"Amidst the shadows which are increasingly gathering about us we can faintly discern the glimmerings of Bahá'u'lláh's unearthly sovereignty appearing fitfully on the horizon of history. To us, the 'generation of the half-light,' living at a time which may be designated as the period of the incubation of the World Commonwealth envisaged by Bahá'u'lláh, has been assigned a task whose high privilege we can never sufficiently appreciate, and the arduousness of which we can as yet but dimly recognize."[6]

I was ecstatic! This was the perfect title for this collection. There have been many books written about the saints and heroes of the early days of the Faith but few about the halting efforts of us ordinary Bahá'ís trying earnestly to move the Faith forward but sometimes managing only to flub things up.

Throughout the book I have made reference to individuals and terms that may not be familiar to all readers. It might be

---

5   See Glossary
6   Shoghi Effendi – *The World Order of Bahá'u'lláh*, p.168

helpful to read the Glossary at the back first and then place a marker on it so you can quickly refer to a brief explanation of these individuals and terms.

Finally, a word to the readers of these stories: several times I refer to quotes from the Sacred Writings of the Bahá'í Faith and offer my understanding of what they mean to me. The reader should not take this as an authorized interpretation but rather should refer directly to the published works of The Báb[7], Bahá'u'lláh, 'Abdu'l-Bahá[8], Shoghi Effendi, and the Universal House of Justice[9] for an authorized understanding of the teachings of the Bahá'í Faith. More information can be obtained by visiting the website of the worldwide Bahá'í community at <www.bahai.org>

---

7   See Glossary

8   See Glossary

9   See Glossary

Stumbling in the Half-Light

Here is a collection of stories from my rapidly deteriorating memory. They are roughly in chronological order but some stories may jump forward or backward in time, and some have no time at all.

I've always been a story teller but when my daughter asked me to write them down for future generations I was averse to do so. More than half the fun of the story is in the telling and I was not sure that I could capture that fun in writing. Be that as it may, here they are in written form. Keep this book by the bedside and let me tell you some bedtime stories. We'll start with some early family history. Enjoy!

1. Wilderness Prophet

When I was a young child, my Grandfather Anderson used to tell me the stories of The People and that I should be proud to be a Mohawk of the Turtle Clan and how the Haudenosaunee (Who-den-o-shaw-nee, the People of the Longhouse) came to be.

Back in the dark days before the League of Peace, the Mohawk, Onondaga, Oneida, Cayuga, and Seneca tribes lived in the land of the Finger Lakes in what is today Upstate New York. While they tried to share the land and its resources, more often than not these interactions led to competition and conflict. Over time these conflicts became more savage and nearly continuous. There was no peace or security, and all the people lived in constant fear of raiding parties. Many villages whose food supplies were stolen or destroyed would starve to death during the long winters. These wars of attrition made the tribes small and powerless, and surrounding tribes would prey upon them and push them out of the good hunting grounds.

Soon the cry of the people reached up and touched the heart of the Great Spirit. He sent a messenger to a young girl across the great water in Huron Territory (near Tyendinaga Reserve today) to tell her that she would give birth to a special child formed by the Creator to bring peace to the people far to the south. She was to call the child Deganawida. (My grandfather always called him 'The Peacemaker' as his name is so holy it shouldn't be used in general conversation.) However, the girl had a premonition that her child would bring great evil upon her own people in the future and she tried three times to drown him,[10] but each time the child bobbed to the surface unharmed. Eventually, she accepted her responsibility, and her son grew up strong, handsome, and spiritually powerful. His only imperfection was that he suffered from a speech impediment. When the time was right, the Creator revealed to 'The Peacemaker' his great commission—to go to the warring tribes across the great water and bring the Law of Love and Peace. At first 'The Peacemaker' was reluctant to take on this role and complained that his speech impediment would just make him a laughing stock. The Creator reassured him that through the power of the Holy Spirit all things were possible, that He would raise up a 'mouth piece' who would speak on his behalf, and to be not afraid of anything as He was always with him. The Creator then raised up out of the lake a fine stone canoe that 'The Peacemaker' could use to travel to the tribes in the south.

When 'The Peacemaker' reached the southern shore, he happened to land in Mohawk territory. The chief of this area was a much feared, fierce warrior who ate the hearts of his enemies to capture their strength and courage. His name was Hiawatha, and he was amazed to see 'The Peacemaker's' stone canoe and fearlessness, and invited him to his camp to find out why this stranger had come to his territory. 'The Peacemaker' told Hiawatha that the Great Spirit had sent him because he had heard the cry of the people and that it was His desire to see peace and trust restored among the tribes. "Has your constant warfare made you stronger? No, it has only

---

10   Some traditional story tellers say she used several methods to try to destroy the child including burial or throwing him in the fire. The end result was that no harm came to him. However, as his mother had foreseen, the Huron and the Haudenosaunee struggled for dominance of the Eastern woodland for centuries.

made you weak and fearful," 'The Peacemaker' explained. "The law of the Creator is love and peace; this is the source of strength and prosperity. He wants to see all the tribes living together under one 'League of Peace.'" Hiawatha was much impressed by 'The Peacemaker' and his powerful message and indicated that he could get the Mohawks to agree to work toward peace. Hiawatha even agreed to go with him to the other tribes to speak on his behalf.

Iroquois Chief, c1710

'The Peacemaker' and Hiawatha travelled to the other tribes and tried to convince them to come together under the Creator's Great Law of Peace. Because of the generations of conflict, many said it was a good idea, but they didn't trust the other tribes to uphold the law. However, 'The Peacemaker' was able to show signs and miracles to convince them of the truth of the Creator's words, and many agreed to give it a try. All the time they traveled together, 'The Peacemaker' taught Hiawatha to memorize the Great Law of Peace and how the structure of the League was to be organized.

The last holdout was Thadodaho, the hate-filled chief of the Onondaga, who was a powerful shaman and put a curse on 'The Peacemaker' and Hiawatha. Thadodaho lived alone in a cave and let hate and desire for vengeance so fester in his heart that his physical appearance changed to that of a distorted monster. When Hiawatha returned home he found that all three of his daughters had died under mysterious circumstances, and he was convinced it was because of Thadodaho's curse. He became despondent and felt that all their efforts were in vain. It seemed that all was lost, but, eventually, 'The Peacemaker' rekindled Hiawatha's faith in the Creator's plan and helped him to forgive Thadodaho's evil curse. Together they travelled back to Thadodaho's cave and talked calming words and sang sacred songs to him for days. Eventually, Thadodaho's countenance began to change, the evil spirits of hate and vengeance left him, and his face became radiant with smiles. So changed was Thadodaho that he became the most ardent supporter of 'The Peacemaker' and Hiawatha, and was, eventually, named Grand Chief of the League and hereditary keeper of the Council Fire.

With all the tribes willing to try, 'The Peacemaker' convened a Council Fire and brought all the chiefs together. He said that the three main principles of the Great Law of Peace were: that through consensus the people should agree on the hunting grounds allocated to each tribe; they should reduce their weapons to those required for hunting; and, if any one tribe were to rise up against any other tribe, then all the other tribes should intervene to stop the aggressor. He then pulled up a young white pine tree and, below the root ball, a hollow area containing a small stream opened up, and he asked the war chiefs to throw their war clubs and hatchets into the hollow. After this, he replanted the tree and said that as they applied the Creator's Great Law their peace and prosperity would grow like this white pine. Four white roots of peace would grow out from this spot into the four directions and, eventually, an eagle would build a nest in the top of the tree as a symbol of the all-protecting eye of the Creator over them.

He then tied five arrows together in a bundle and asked each of the chiefs to pass it around and try to break it. The bundle went around the circle, but none of the chiefs were able to break it. This, he said, was symbolic of the League; as long as the chiefs held fast to the Great Law they would be unbreakable like the bundle. Then he cut the bundle apart and easily broke one of the arrows. "If you turn aside from the Great Law you will each become like this one arrow and be easily broken." He added, "I tell you this: there will come a time in the future when your descendants will turn back their heels on the Great Law. This will bring a time of great trouble, your people will be broken, you will become strangers in your own land, and the trees will begin to die from the tops down, as a sign. When this time comes," he continued, "I will return and re-establish the Peace—this time not just among the five but among all the nations."

After the Council Fire, he left the chiefs in the hands of Hiawatha and Thadodaho, got into his stone canoe, and paddled off to the west, never to be seen again. The nations remained united, and the organization of the League brought peace and security.

Years later, when I heard that Bahá'u'lláh[11] had come from God to establish peace among all the nations, I remembered this story of 'The Peacemaker' told to me by my grandfather. Then, when I read Bahá'u'lláh's Writings about the Lesser Peace[12], I was really amazed. He said the three main principles of the Lesser Peace were that the nations should, through consensus, fix their boundaries with one another; they should reduce their armaments to those required for internal security; and if any one nation were to rise up against another, then all the nations should rise up to subdue that aggressor. I realized then that Bahá'u'lláh fulfilled, within Himself, the prophecy of 'The Peacemaker' that he would return and re-establish the Law of Peace among all the nations of the world.

---

11   See Glossary
12   *Gleanings from the Writings of Bahá'u'lláh*, p.249. Also, see Glossary

2. The People of the Longhouse

Anthropologists and archeologists aren't exactly sure when the Haudenosaunee formed the 'League of Peace' but about 1360 CE is the most likely date. Most people today know the Haudenosaunee as the 'Iroquois' (Black Snake People) which is the derogatory name given to them by the Huron who, historically, had been their principal rivals. Back in the days before the League of Peace the Haudenosaunee were the Mohawk, Onondaga, Oneida, Cayuga, and Seneca tribes living in what is now upstate New York. In those days they spent most of their time in internecine warfare. However, with the development of the League these conflicts soon ceased. This organizational framework, together with the perfecting of an agricultural methodology known as 'The Three Sisters' (corn, squash, and beans) quickly made this League one of the most powerful and prosperous in the eastern woodlands.

The development of this League enabled the Haudenosaunee to expand their territory which pushed to the Gaspé Peninsula and New Brunswick in the east, Virginia and Kentucky in the south, Illinois in the west, and most of the Niagara Peninsula in the north. This put pressure on the surrounding tribes to develop confederacies of their own and began a period of rapid nation building throughout northeastern and central North America. The boundaries between these various tribal groups were constantly changing and, with the arrival of the European colonialists with their own conflicting interests, it was like adding three or four more tribes to the mix.

European first contact with the Haudenosaunee

The French linked up with the Huron and developed a lucrative fur trade. The Haudenosaunee wanted in on this trade and tried to set up their own treaty with the French, but the French double-crossed them. They captured the fifty chiefs sent to negotiate with them and shipped them back to France as slaves. This was not a good idea, however, and instantly the full wrath of the Haudenosaunee fell on them, shutting down the fur trade and almost driving the French out of the New World. In the end, the French returned the thirteen surviving chiefs and agreed to enter into a treaty. Even so, the Haudenosaunee remained deeply suspicious of the French, and it wasn't long before they sided with the British against the French interests in North America.

With the American Revolution, the Haudenosaunee continued to support the British Crown, this time against the
American colonists. George Washington was furious and
demanded that his generals not just defeat the Haudenosaunee
but utterly wipe them out. Not all the founding fathers were
so harsh, however. In fact, Thomas Jefferson and, particularly,
Benjamin Franklin were fascinated by the organizational
structure of the League and incorporated many of its features
into the United States Constitution. After the British lost the
war, most of the Haudenosaunee fled to Canada where King
George III granted them large tracts of land to resettle.

One of the largest of these was the Haldimand deed. It was
to extend ten kilometres either side of the Grand River, from
its head to its mouth, a length of about 280 km (5600 km^2).
Today this grant is known as Six Nations Indian Reserve #40
and has shrunk to ten km by sixteen km (160 km^2) on one side
of the Grand River near Brantford, Ontario. This dramatic
reduction has been the result of a labyrinthine mix of land
deals, many of which are still in dispute to this day. It is from
this reserve that my mother's family comes and where I spent
my early childhood.

3. **Down on the Rez**

Back at the turn of the Twentieth Century, Six Nations Reserve was an agricultural based society, or at least it was up until World War I. After the Great War, mechanization became a major influence in farming, but Indians were not able to buy capital equipment on credit. As a result, the Indian farmers could not compete, and the agricultural base of the reserve (rez) collapsed. Most of the farms either went fallow completely, or were leased out to white farmers from off the reserve. All over the rez there were large farm houses with huge, now dormant, barns out back—that was the way our farmstead was.

This change didn't affect my grandfather (Samuel Anderson, born April 10th, 1882) too much as he was a bit of an enigma in many ways. He was more of an intellectual than a farmer. He loved to tell stories and recite poetry, particularly by Robert Service and others of that era. He was an elementary school teacher and taught at Six Nations School House #10. He really enjoyed this work and was very influential in the early life of many children on the rez. Unfortunately, his career was cut short. In those days teachers were not allowed to speak in their Native language in the classroom. He had a number of students who were Cayuga and they couldn't speak English very well, so he kept them back after school to give them English lessons. One day the school inspector came in and found him helping these kids with their English. However, as he was speaking to them in Cayuga, he was summarily fired from his job. After this he went to work as an industrial labourer in Brantford for, I think it was, the Massey-Harris or the Cockshutt Plow Company as a common labourer. But it was not really in line with his spirit. He loved activities of the mind and I think he felt diminished because he wasn't able to serve in the capacity of an educator.

Grandpa Anderson with students in front of #10
School, Six Nations Reserve, c1923

My grandmother (Minnie Anderson, née Miller, born February 8th, 1896) was a hardworking mother and house-keeper as were most women of that time. She had twelve kids, well, she had ten of her own, plus Laurel and me. (I'll get to more about Laurel and me a little bit later.) As you can imagine, with ten kids, they're spread over quite a length of time. In fact, that's the way most women did it in those days—they bore children and served the family and, in Grandma's case, also served the community. Like many of the women on the rez she belonged to the Anglican Women's Society. They would meet regularly and sew clothes and bed quilts for anyone who might have had a fire or flood and needed blankets and clothing. Every Tuesday they had their 'bee' where they all gathered around to talk, share lunch, and sew for the community weal.

Anderson homestead on Six Nations Reserve

My grandparents were married on the rez April 13th, 1913 and lived in a two-storey log cabin about three-fourths of a kilometre East of St. John's corner. When I say a 'log cabin,' I'm not talking about some sort of rough shack by a stream. It was quite an impressive structure. The logs were roughly squared with mitred ends like a cabinetmaker might make. The walls on the inside were lath and plaster and wallpapered. It was a big house with four bedrooms upstairs. There was one master bedroom and then the other three bedrooms were just packed with beds for all the kids. There was no running water, electricity, or indoor plumbing. Things were as they had been for centuries for a lot of people who lived on farms.

With the loss of commercial farming my grandparents only planted a garden big enough to supply their own needs, but they would go about the usual farming routines of getting the horses rigged up for whatever equipment was required for the day's work. They had chickens and a pig, and several types of fruit trees out along the back fence. As each crop became ripe, grandma would gear up her canning operation and everyone would pitch in to harvest, cut up, cook, and can the crop. So that was pretty well what their life was like. Later, my grandfather gave the farm to Maynard, his second oldest son, and he and Grandma, along with the three youngest kids, set up a small country store at St. John's Corner. The living quarters behind the store were simple and cramped, but for me it was like paradise, living behind a big room full of pop and chips!

My grandparents were very pious people. My grandfather thought a lot about religion. He would not only attend the Anglican Church on Sundays, but also the Longhouse ceremonies (which are part of the traditional religion of the Haudenosaunee). He was familiar with the traditions and the legends of the Haudenosaunee and did quite a bit of reading and thinking about First Nations[13] issues. Many a summer's evening, he used to sit on the front porch of the store with other old men of his generation talking about the old days and what's wrong with the youth today.

---

13   The Aboriginal Peoples of Canada refer to themselves as the First Nation Peoples.

My Uncle Maynard was an avid horseshoe player, so he rigged clothesline wire from the store to the trees out by the road and hung two incandescent gas mantle lanterns between two parallel horseshoe pitches. This turned out to be a great idea and the store was kept busy late into the night selling cigarettes, tobacco, pop, and potato chips to the people who came to pitch horseshoes or just to watch. In my memory, these were magical nights of good fellowship and community unity.

When the agricultural industry collapsed on the reserve, my grandfather gave a great deal of thought to the changing structure of Canadian society. He was particularly concerned about his children's future. He came to the conclusion that professional, career-based opportunities were what they needed to prepare for. He determined that his children should get a university education or technical training at least. So he encouraged his eldest daughter, Marjorie, to go to university, where she got her degree in French Literature. His eldest son, Arnold, became a nuclear physicist. He received a special commendation from President Truman for his work on the Manhattan Project. My mother was the next eldest daughter and she became a registered nurse. His second son, Maynard, was not academically inclined, so he turned the old farmstead over to him. The next daughter, Luella, became an optical physicist. She was the project lead of the team that developed soft contact lenses at Bausch & Lomb. And so on down the line to the youngest daughter, Carol, who got a master's degree in social work. Grandpa really tried, as much as he could, to make sure his children had a good education, because he could foresee that this would be required to make a successful life in this rapidly changing world.

The Haudenosaunee have a reputation as hard, stoic people who never forget and are slow to forgive injustice. But among themselves they love humor, unity, and equanimity.

They form close, loving families where seldom a harsh or loud word is spoken. As my grandfather used to say, "A true human is concerned for his responsibilities and the rights of others, not the other way around. In the end, the Creator sets the balance aright."

4. Green Mountain Boys

The Sargents have been kicking around the New World for a long time. My grandfather on my father's side, Roy Sargent, traced the Sargent family line back to William Sargent, who was born to a Richard Sargent in England in 1602[14]. However, family historians have discovered several Richard Sargents with sons named William living in England at about this time, so there is no certainty as to where the line leads backward from there. We know that William was trained as a seaman, under Captain John Smith, in his youth. Later, on one of his trips to 'New England,' he became enamoured of the beautiful country around Agawam in the Massachusetts Colony.

William married Elizabeth Perkins, the daughter of a British colonist, in 1633 and they initially settled in Agawam, but moved to Salisbury New Town (Amesbury) in 1655. Many generations of Sargents lived in Amesbury, Massachusetts, and the local cemetery is well stocked with them. My Great-Great-Great-Great-Great Grandfather Timothy Sargent Jr. (1725-1754) was a Captain in the British Reserves. Trouble had been brewing for some time between Britain and France over their New World colonies and a dispute over control of the Allegheny River in 1754 led to all-out war. Timothy was mobilized to Nova Scotia. No details of his death are known,

---

14 The information I have about William comes from Grandpa Roy's research and the book *Sargent Record* by Edwin Everett Sargent, published by The Caledonian Company in 1899.

only to say that he drowned in the Bay of Fundy late that same year. By the time of the American Revolutionary War, my line of Sargents were living way back in the Green Mountains of Vermont. Timothy Jr.'s son, Phineas Sargent, was sort of the original hippy. He believed in making love, not war. Even though local patriot Ethan Allen organized the Green Mountain Boys and captured Fort Ticonderoga from the British, Phineas managed to dodge the Revolution and stayed on the farm way up in the hills and sired twenty-five kids!

Corinth, Vermont

Phineas Lafayette Sargent, the grandson of the 'original hippy,' was of a more patriotic bent. When the Civil War broke out, he enlisted with the Green Mountain Boys, who were renamed the 1st Vermont Infantry Regiment, and fought on the side of the Union.

By the time my grandpa Roy was born, our line of Sargents were living in Corinth, Vermont, and the Sargent family still owns the farmstead there. The hills behind the main farm are covered in spectacular, old-growth maples, and my great grandfather, Nathan Sargent, was a major supplier to the 'Vermont Maid' maple syrup company. This little town is stunningly beautiful and is one of the most photographed locales in New England. When I was a little boy, I several times visited my grand-uncle James in Corinth.

For centuries, the Sargents were New Englanders and shared many of the qualities of those people. These were sturdy and steady people—patriotic, faithful, and loyal; modest, moderate, and sincere; dutiful, hardworking, and disciplined. I am grateful to trace my lineage to this line of people.

5. Ma and Pop Sargent

My grandparents, Laura and Roy Sargent, didn't start out as Ma and Pop Sargent, but through the years their sterling, caring characters and tireless community service made them everyone's favourite ma and pop. Laura was born Laura Estelle Hursey in Dillon, South Carolina, on March 29, 1899. She attended Bowen MacFeat Business College in Columbia, South Carolina, and went to work for an insurance company in that city. During World War I, she volunteered for the Red Cross making bandages, distributing leaflets, and recruiting volunteers to help the war effort. After marrying Roy on March 29, 1920, they moved to Windsor Locks, Connecticut.

In 1924, she resumed her work for the Red Cross, which was, at that time, part of the Visiting Nurse Association. She dedicated herself to the blood donor clinics, for which she continued to work for an astonishing sixty-three years! This, together with her volunteer work for the American Cancer Society, the Muscular Dystrophy Association, and the Leukemia Society, earned her the nickname `Florence Nightingale of Windsor Locks.' At the same time, she was active in the Baptist church and raised three energetic boys. My father, John David, was born January 18, 1923; Robert Hursey June 25, 1927; and Wesson Phineas May 19, 1937.

Roy Ezra Sargent was born in Groton, Vermont, on March 17, 1896. After high school he traveled to Salina, Kansas, where he graduated with honours from the Wesleyan Business College in 1916. The First World War was on, so Roy enlisted and was deployed to Camp Jackson, South Carolina. When the brass found out that he'd been a camp cook for the Forest Service, as summer work through college, he was made a camp cook and worked at Camp Jackson for the remainder of the war. It was while he was stationed there that he met Laura. He served two years and was honourably discharged in 1919. In 1922, he went to work for the Dexter Paper Corporation in Windsor Locks, Connecticut, first as a bookkeeper, then as a purchasing agent, until his retirement in 1961. During this time, he continued his education through part-time studies in business administration at Northeastern University, and graduated with honours in 1943. He was also a member of the National Purchasing Agents Association.

Laura and Roy Sargent, 1920

It wasn't long before Laura had roped him into helping out with the Red Cross, and, for decades, he was an active first aid instructor with that organization. With three active sons, it was only natural that he became interested in the Scouting movement. He helped organize Windsor Locks Boy Scout Troop 84, and served as its scoutmaster for twenty-five years. He was also active in civic affairs and served on the Board of Education, was a member of the public school building committee for twelve years, a member of the Windsor Locks Rotary Club, and secretary of the Windsor Locks Chamber of Commerce.

Roy was a devoutly religious man and served his Lord every day of his life. He was a charter member of Grace Baptist Church in Springfield, Massachusetts. He, Laura, and the boys attended there until he was able to help build the Calvary Baptist Church in Windsor Locks, for which he served as a deacon, Sunday school teacher, and member of the building committee. He started his own correspondence Bible ministry and was able to touch thousands of people through the Word of God.

As a result of his civic, Red Cross, Boy Scout, and church works, he was able to positively affect the lives of a vast number of the youth in Windsor Locks. By the time I came to live with Grandma and Grandpa Sargent in 1955, everyone called Roy 'Pop.' I remember, even men that I thought were near his own age would say to me, "So you're Pop Sargent's grandson." At first I thought they may not have known what his first name was, but I came to realize that, just as you would never call your own father by his first name, out of a deep sense of respect, people would never think to call Grandpa by his first name.

6. Of Black Sheep and Noble Savages

My Uncle Robert was the second oldest Sargent son, but he was a chip off the ol' block. He looked and talked just like my grandfather, had the same straight-arrow character, and even succeeded him in his job at Dexter's paper mill when grandpa retired. My dad was completely different—a real black sheep—or rather, as my grandfather thought, a black stain on the reputation of an otherwise fine upstanding Windsor Locks family. Right from the get-go he was a curious free thinker, who questioned every convention and was suspicious of tradition and authority. He absolutely saw no difference in people and would meet king or pauper with the exact same open, friendly manner.

He was, also, very rebellious. He did many of the things that a son of a fine Baptist family should not do—tried smoking, played cards, would take girls to dances, and all those terrible things. He would even go to movies, oh my gosh; he was on the slippery slope to hell as far as his parents were concerned! They determined to straighten out their wayward son and sent him to Mount Hermon School for boys at Gill, Massachusetts. This was a Christian preparatory school, founded by the evangelist Dwight Layman Moody in 1881. Opinions are divided as to whether they straightened him out, or whether he bent them completely out of shape.

The school had made national headlines a few years before my dad went there, when the previous headmaster, Elliott Speer, was gunned down in his study by an unknown assailant. The trustees were now anxious to keep an extremely low profile so as to rebuild the confidence of the benefactors and parents that the school was a safe place to send their children. Then my father arrived.

One fine spring day my dad and Jerry Bryson, his roommate, were bored and decided to sneak off school grounds and go exploring along the banks of the nearby Connecticut River. After all, who was going to know, right? The ice pack on the river was rapidly breaking up under the pressure of the rising spring freshet, and, somehow, the boys became stranded on a piece of ice careening down the river. One of their schoolmates heard their cry for help and ran off to tell the headmaster, who quickly organized the grounds crew to take the truck and ladders down to the river. He then called the local police. Meanwhile, passers-by also heard the boys, and a growing number of would-be rescuers were running down both sides of the river wondering what to do.

When the police arrived, the boys were still too far from either shore to attempt a rescue, so they radioed the State Troopers to get a rescue boat to the river as soon as possible. Eventually, the makeshift ice raft neared the shore and a rope was thrown to the boys who grabbed on and dove into the freezing water. When the two drowned rats were hauled ashore, they were ushered through the throng of groundskeepers, police, state troopers, spectators, and, of course—the press. How my dad managed to talk his way out of not being expelled from school that day is a mystery.

My father graduated from Mount Hermon into an unsettled world. Europe was engulfed in war, and on December 7, 1941, the Japanese attacked Pearl Harbour. The next day the United States Congress declared war. After graduation, my father was enticed by the stories of flying aces like Richard Bong and Thomas McGuire, to enlist as a fighter pilot with the Army Air Corps.

My mother, Edith Anderson, was born on Six Nations reserve on July 25, 1919. As opposed to my dad she had a much more conservative nature. She was named after her Aunt Edith Montour (née Anderson), who was the first Aboriginal Canadian to become a registered nurse. Ms. Montour went straight from nursing school to World War I, serving in the military hospital in St. Vital, France. When she returned home from the war, she regaled her nieces and nephews with her exciting adventures in Europe. My mother would listen to these stories with rapt attention, and so, from an early age, she desired to follow in her aunt's footsteps and become a nurse herself. After graduation from high school in Caledonia, Ontario, she was accepted into the Edward J. Meyer Memorial Hospital School of Nursing in Buffalo, New York.

Edith I. Anderson, 1944

Although my mother had grown up in the rough farming conditions on Six Nations Reserve, she had a natural, refined, regal aura about her. She was always elegantly and immaculately dressed, and I remember, from when I was a child, she had a far-off attentive gaze like a bird of prey who had heard a tell-tale rustle in the underbrush—still, unflinching, expectant. Like her father, she had a love of poetry, literature, and the arts, and even did a little writing herself. After she received her registered nursing certificate, she went right to work at E.J. Meyer Memorial Hospital.

Meanwhile, my father was stationed at Hendricks Army Airfield in Florida, where he went to flight school. He was not trained as a fighter pilot, as he had hoped, but as a bombardier on the flight crew for the B-17 'Flying Fortress'—the legendary heavy precision bombers used in the European theatre. After his training, his crew took the train up to Buffalo, New York, where they were to take command of their new bomber and head off to England. When they arrived, however, their plane was not ready and they were given a few days leave. My dad and two of his buddies decided to 'do the town' and set off for the bright lights of Buffalo. That evening they had supper in a fairly fancy restaurant. Although they all ordered something different, they all had the chicken noodle soup to start, and by morning all three of them were in E.J. Meyer Memorial Hospital with food poisoning.

One of their nurses was my mother. The three young soldiers were, of course, cheeky and flirtatious, but something about my mother caught my dad's serious attention. Although she was friendly, kind, and attentive, she had an unreachable calm and nobility that set her apart from the other women he had met. He asked her to dinner when he was released from hospital and she accepted.

John D. Sargent, 1944

Because they were sidelined by their misadventure, the three airmen had missed the B-17 crew to Europe. Instead they were hastily retrained for the brand new B-29 'Superfortresses' that were going to the Pacific theatre. That meant that they had to stay in Buffalo another month, and my dad spent all his free time with my mother. After a short while, my dad was so taken by her that he asked her to marry him, and she agreed. Thanksgiving was coming up, so he took her home to meet the family. Then all hell broke loose—their son was dating an American Indian!

Edith and John Sargent, 1947

Oh, this was not going over well. An interracial marriage? The boy has no sense. What was he thinking of? To his parents, this was the typical stupid thing that my father would do. He had always been rebellious, always taking these screwball actions. Now he wanted to marry an Indian! My grandmother was so distressed she called her brother, who was manager of a hotel in Florida, to come up and tell her son about the facts of life. So Uncle Jessie came up and he explained the impracticality of marrying someone of a different race—and a lot of the things that he explained were true at that time. For example, he said, "You marry an Indian, you know, in thirty-four states of the Union, you can't stay together in the same hotel. You could be arrested if you stayed together in the same room, assuming the hotel would even let you stay there. You could be arrested even if you were caught crossing state lines together in the same vehicle. What are your children going to be like? They're going to be half-breeds, biracial. They won't be accepted by anybody. It's going to be a disaster. Think about it for a moment: to marry somebody of a different race, you're just asking for trouble."

Well, if you know my dad, having the family unite against him like that was just a further inducement to go through with it. After his retraining, my dad left for Tinian in the Pacific, but he and my mother kept up an active correspondence throughout the remainder of the war. When he got back to the States, he headed straight to Buffalo, and so it was that the black sheep and the noble savage were married.

7. The Scars of War

In all the years of my growing up, I never heard my dad talk about the war and his time in the service. Much later, I realized that my father was wounded in the war, not physically, but psychologically.

He was stationed on the Pacific Island of Tinian with the 313th Bombardment Wing. This strategic island was at the centre of a 2500 km arc that included Papua New Guinea, Indonesia, the Philippines, Taiwan, and Japan. It was the largest air base in the world at that time and housed 40,000 personnel. From here large flights of B-29 Superfortresses would carry out saturation bombing of Japanese military installations and heavy industry. Rather than the low level night-time bombing favoured by the British, the American Army Air Corps preferred high altitude daylight raids. However, if they misjudged the low-level wind patterns, they could easily take out whole residential sections of cities rather than the strategic targets they were aiming for. Also, it was from Tinian that the two atomic bomb raids that ended the war were launched.

The one time I did hear my dad talk about the war was the day before Anne and I were married in Albuquerque, New Mexico. We were visiting the atomic bomb museum (I guess to take our minds off the upcoming wedding), and my dad mentioned that he had flown cover for both those missions and had seen the flashes, although they were many kilometres away. His whole flight of B-29s took off for another target with the 'Enola Gay'[15] tagging along. At the appointed time, she slipped away from the pack. The rest of the flight continued on to a secondary target to lead the Japanese air defences away from the real mission objective.

B29s lined up on Tinian, 1945

I think my dad enlisted as a young, eager youth with dreams of glory to be an ace fighter pilot, but he came home again an older, wiser man, sobered by the realities of war. I only came to this realization years later when his younger brother, Wesson, got a Congressional medal for his work during the 'Desert Storm' war in Iraq. He was the project manager on the Apache

15   The Enola Gay was the name of the B29 that was specially fitted out to carry the two atomic bombs used to destroy Hiroshima and Nagasaki.

Weapons Platform, those silent helicopters that accurately bombed targets, in the middle of the night, from kilometres away. He led the development of that weapons system. My father wrote him a letter, in which he said, "I'm glad to see that I'm not the only mass-murderer in the family." When I heard that terse, bitter comment, I suddenly realized he had been a bombardier sent to destroy the industry in dozens of Japanese cities. He knew he'd killed hundreds and hundreds of men, women, and children in their homes, because of the inaccuracy of bombs in those days. Being a sensitive person, it seriously affected him. As a result, he came back from the war psychologically scarred, like so many of his generation.

8. Uncle Arnold and the A-Bomb

As I mentioned earlier, my mother's eldest brother, Arnold, was a nuclear physicist, but this was not really true. Arnold was very interested in everything; he had a very active and curious mind. After leaving high school, he went to McMaster University to study chemistry. To support himself, he took a job with the city transit as a streetcar conductor. In his third year at school, he married Elsie, his university sweetheart, and, before long, my cousin Skipper was on the way.

It soon became obvious that he could not support a family and university studies on a streetcar conductor's salary, and he began to look around for other employment. He noticed an advertisement for a foreman for one of the chemical divisions of Union Carbide. This looked very interesting to him, even though the basic requirement was for a master's degree in chemical engineering. He applied anyway, claiming he had a master's degree from the University of Buffalo. To his surprise, he was hired.

Arnold had excellent people skills and was a natural manager, and before long had developed a reputation within the company as a young 'up-n-comer.' Even though he was doing his job well, he realized that he still needed to keep studying to bring his chemical knowledge up to the level required, so he subscribed to all the latest chemical journals. The 'new thing' that everyone in these industry journals was talking about was 'nuclear chemistry.' Later, it became obvious that this was not really chemistry but physics and the field is now called 'nuclear physics.' Arnold would bore the heck out of everyone at coffee breaks and lunch time talking about the 'real scientific alchemy' that these breakthroughs represented. New metals, ceramics, and polymers fashioned from made-to-order isotopes, with new and fantastic properties!

World War II was raging and soon the United Sates was involved. World War I had shown how important scientific research was to winning these conflicts, and everyone was frenetically searching for the bigger, better stick to take into battle. Leó Szilárd, a leading nuclear chemist, wrote to President Roosevelt indicating that a fission reaction could release many orders of magnitude more energy than any known chemical reaction, and got Einstein to back up his theory. The war department decided to 'go for it' and quietly put out the call for anyone who knew anything about nuclear chemistry. When the higher-ups at Union Carbide got the call, they scratched their heads and said, "We don't have anyone involved in that kind of work—do we?" Then someone said, "Wait a minute, there's that Arnold Anderson down in the Tonawanda Chemical Division; he knows all about this stuff." So, before he knew what was happening, Arnold was packed off to the 'Manhattan Project.'[16]

There were a number of difficult technical problems to be overcome to make Leó's device a reality. One was making enough of the fissionable U235 isotope of uranium needed to make the bombs. U235 and the much more common U238 were almost identical in atomic weight, so separating them was going to be difficult. Several teams were set up to tackle this problem and Arnold was on one of them. He thought best while he was walking, so one cool autumn afternoon he went for a walk, leaving Elsie at home to make supper. Soon there came a

---

16   The US army's code name for its effort to develop an atomic bomb.

weak knock on their front door, and when Elsie opened it she saw a small, old hobo standing there. It was her practice to give a meal to passing hobos in exchange for a little yard work, but, because of this man's strange appearance—he looked a bit like an escaped inmate from a mental institution—and the fact that Arnold was not home, she said, "Sorry, I have nothing for you today," and started to close the door. But the old man quickly inserted, "Good afternoon, Elsa. Is Andy home?" The close approximation of their names caught her attention and she said, "No, he has some thinking to do so he's out for a walk." He then flatly stated, "I vill vait. He is expectink me, I think," and walked in. Elsie was nervously making some tea when Arnold came home. "Dr. Einstein, you're early," he said, "I see you've met my wife." Elsie nearly fainted.

Aunt Elsie, Uncle Arnold and 'Skipper'

Unfortunately, all these teams were successful in overcoming these many technical problems and the atomic age was upon us—ready or not. After the war, Arnold received a letter of gratitude from President Truman, and he gave it to his dad (Grandpa Anderson) who kept it in the pocket of his vest, so that it was handy to proudly show to any and all who crossed his path.

However, not long after the war, the Russians detonated their first atomic bomb and everyone said, "Okay, who let the cat out of the bag?" Obviously, there was a spy in the organization, and the FBI was called in to investigate. They went through all the personnel files to make sure everyone was who they claimed to be. And they were—except for that Canadian guy who claimed to have a master's degree in chemistry from the University of Buffalo. The University's records showed no degree of any kind awarded to an Arnold Anderson. The jig was up, and he was hauled in for questioning. The situation was serious, and Arnold spent a couple of bad months trying to prove his innocence. In the end, the investigation established that the real spy had been Klaus Fuchs, a member of the British contingent working on the project.

After Arnold was cleared of the spying charges, he returned to Union Carbide, but, as he didn't have a master's degree in chemistry, he no longer qualified as a foreman in the Tonawanda Chemical Works. The company had no choice but to promote him to senior manager in the R&D division, where he continued to work until his retirement.

9. Darwin and the Evolution of Black Sheep

After my mom and dad were married, they settled down in Buffalo. My mother continued as a nurse at E. J. Meyer Memorial Hospital, and my dad decided to go to university on the GI Bill, which provided returning service men tuition and a stipend to finish their education. He wasn't really sure what he wanted to do, but finally decided to get his degree in bio-chemistry. One of the available electives was paleontology, which he really got into. In his second year, he switched his major to geology and continued with courses in paleontology. It was in his third year, while on a field trip, that he discovered and published a paper on a new species of trilobite (which was named after him). After completion of his bachelor's degree in geology, he continued on to get his master's degree in geo-chemistry.

Often, on the major holiday breaks from school, my mom and dad would travel to Windsor Locks to see his folks. As my father's mom and dad got to know my mother better, they began to get used to the fact that she was an American Indian, and their fears about an interracial marriage began to fade. In fact, they could see that my mother was a positive, civilizing influence on their wayward son. His casual, 'rough and ready' apparel became clean and pressed, and she even picked out a couple of nice suits and ties for him to wear to school. He was slowly, but visibly, becoming a respectable gentleman. Having cleaned up so well, his parents were actually beginning to feel a bit relaxed to be seen with him among their friends and at church. This was a mistake.

One Sunday, the minister gave his homily on the creative power of God's Word. Unfortunately, he used the story from chapter one of Genesis in his talk. At this, the newly minted Bachelor of Geology got up and said, "Excuse me, but the scientific evidence indicates that the earth was not created in six days, but is in a state of constant change, always has been, and always will be. Furthermore, the geologic strata built up over billions of years shows that today's plants and animals have progressively evolved from more primitive forms over that time."

John Sargent (centre) with his university buddies

A stunned silence fell over the church, and all eyes turned and looked straight at my grandmother and grandfather, who sat transfixed in their pew, as if they had just been struck by lightning. The minister straightened his vestments, smiled and replied, "This is the House of God. Those who seek fellowship here believe in Him, His only begotten Son, and the Holy Bible. Those who do not believe in these things needn't attend here."

Disfellowshipped?! Their son had been disfellowshipped! And they—charter members of Grace Baptist Church in Springfield, Massachusetts. My grandparents were, of course, heartbroken. But what could you expect? The child had lived on the slippery slope all his life. And now, the inevitable had happened. My dad, on the other hand, was not the least perturbed, and stated flatly, "I believe in God. I just don't believe the earth was created in six days 6500 years ago. There must be another understanding for that story, but for the life of me I can't think what it might be." My father was perfectly happy to continue to go to church with his parents, but everyone was extremely careful not to invite him back.

Years later, when I went to live with my dad's parents, my grandfather would often, spontaneously, tell me a parable and explain what it meant to him. One of his favorites was the parable of the 'prodigal son.'[17] It is one of my favorites too; but at that time I wasn't able to understand its particular importance to my grandfather.

---

17   *King James Bible,* Luke 15:11-32

10. The Halcyon Days

After my dad graduated from university, his first job was as the Curator of Geology at the Buffalo Museum of Science. The museum had a large collection of minerals, but most of them were poorly organized in the warehouse, and the public display area was shabby and timeworn. So my dad set, as his first priority, the refurbishment of this area of the museum.

He first had to get a budget for this from the directors. He made a pitch that this was a neglected area of the museum and that he was sure that a proper mineralogical display would be a great draw for the general public to visit. This change was not accounted for in the museum's development plan, but, in the end, the directors reluctantly agreed. So he set to work with the museum's display designer to completely redesign the mineralogy area. During the time this section of the museum was closed for renovations, my dad worked on cataloguing the museum's collection.

While preparing his catalogue he made two important observations. One was that the collection included hundreds of kilograms of some minerals, but was completely lacking in others. He thought that all museums must be having the same problem, so he started the *Museum Mineral Exchange Newsletter*, which showed all those minerals that his museum had a surplus of, and indicated that he was willing to exchange samples of these for samples of minerals lacking in his collection. This idea caught on and is still in use today, but, of course, it is now a web-based exchange site. The second observation was that he found a carefully wrapped sample of an exceedingly rare mineral. These beautiful crystals were extremely sensitive to water, and even exposure to the humidity in the air would quickly destroy them. He decided to have the cabinet makers design and build an argon-filled, sealed display case just for this specimen. This would be the centrepiece of the new mineralogy area.

Buffalo Museum of Science, Buffalo, New York, c1950

When all the work was done, the museum set up an ad campaign to invite the public to see this newly renovated area of their museum. My dad waited expectantly and excitedly to show the public his new creation—but nobody came! So my dad wrote an article for the paper highlighting the museum's beautiful specimen of the exceedingly rare mineral in their collection and that this was a special opportunity to see this mineral up close—but nobody came. What was my dad to do? He had sold the directors on the idea that, if they spent the time and resources on updating this area of the museum, the general public would turn out in droves, but nobody was coming. Then my dad had a brainwave. He wrote a letter to the paper claiming to be Professor Heimer-Schmidt[18] of the geology department of Utrecht University. He said, in this letter, that the rare mineral, which the museum claimed to have, was a fake! This mineral could not possibly survive long once exposed to the air. The next day, my dad, as himself, indignantly responded to this charge! Newspaper articles flew back and forth about this specimen. Soon there were long lineups of people clamouring to see this new controversial exhibit. His renovation had been a success!

In fact, the interest generated was so great that the local TV station gave the museum a prime time, half-hour slot once a week, and my dad was often on, showing various mineral specimens and explaining their formation. Whenever this story was told around the dinner table, my mother always had to comment how embarrassed she was because, "Johnny never cleaned his fingernails before showing his samples on public TV."

The new mineralogy exhibit caught more than local atten-tion. A visiting Raja, who was patron of a local museum in India, heard about it, and wanted to visit. The museum direc-tors were all excited, but they worried about the proper proto-cols and potential racial difficulties they may have to contend with. But wait—wasn't John Sargent's wife an Indian? The Sargents could escort the Raja and his entourage around while they were here. Slight misunderstanding, but still . . .

_____

18   He chose the name from the children's song 'John Jacob
     Jingleheimer Schmidt.'

My father said "sure," and he and my mother went to the train station to greet him and his attendant/body guard. The Grandee was wearing a long, grey overcoat against the early autumn chill and a white turban with a magnificent ruby ornament. When my mother first saw him, she spontaneously gasped, "What a beautiful ruby!" Immediately, the Raja reached up and began unpinning it to give it to her. My mother was horrified, realizing her faux pas, and a battle of wills broke out—the Raja insisting she take it and my embarrassed mother absolutely refusing to accept it.

Apart from this shaky start, the visit went very well. My dad and the Raja's sense of humour complemented each other, and they had a grand time visiting the museum, the university, Niagara Falls, and many other sights in the Buffalo area. They had meals together and the Raja even said that, if my dad wanted to move to India, he would be welcome to work in his museum. The visit was a great success, and, a few days after the Raja's departure, a package arrived in the mail addressed to Mrs. John David Sargent. When she opened it, there was a beautiful silver and cut crystal necklace, bracelet and earring set, along with a magnificent star sapphire of an unusual plum colour. A ring made from this sapphire has become a family heirloom, and has been handed down from generation to generation. It seems that, in the end, the Raja had won the contest of wills.

In addition to the success that my dad was having with his budding career, life was generally good for the newly married couple, and they went camping and hiking with Dad's former university friends. They attended lectures and seminars on various topics of current interest, and even took up oil painting. Things were going so well that thoughts began turning to having a family of their own, and soon I was on the way.

Edith and John Sargent. The Halcyon Days, 1948

But then clouds appeared on the horizon, portending that these beautiful halcyon days were coming to an end. My mother caught a cold, which turned into a chronic cough. It was soon discovered that she had caught tuberculosis from her patients at the hospital. Because there were no antibiotics for tuberculosis in those days and, with the naïveté of her First Nation's genome,[19] she had virtually no resistance to the disease. It spread quickly, destroying large portions of her lungs. The doctors realized that the diseased portions of her lungs had to be removed urgently, but they didn't want to perform the operation while she was pregnant. So they suggested she terminate her pregnancy. However, I think my mother instinctively knew that this was going to be her only chance to have a child, so she determined to see the pregnancy through to term.

As soon as she gave birth, my mother had a major operation and was immediately placed in a sanatorium. Before antibiotic treatments existed, the rationale for sanatoria was that a regimen of rest and good nutrition offered the best chance that the sufferer's immune system would 'fend off' pockets of the tuberculosis infection. Her recovery was slow, but she seemed to respond well to this regimen.

My Grandma Anderson had come down to live with my parents during this difficult time and, as soon as I was born, she took me back to Six Nations Reserve to live with her. So it was in the midst of all this turmoil that I began my great adventure.

---

19 While tuberculosis was a general scourge at this time, First
    Nations people were particularly susceptible to this and other
    European diseases.

11. He's a Little Fella

When I first came home from the hospital, I went to live with my maternal grandparents in the old family homestead on Six Nations Reserve. By the time I was old enough to remember anything, we had moved three-quarters of a kilometre up the road to St. John's Corner. Grandma and Grandpa had set up a little corner store there. Across the road, to the north, was Schoolhouse #10, where grandpa had taught many years before. Across the road, to the west, was St. John's Church and community hall. Many generations of Andersons were buried in the graveyard out back, and my grandfather used to mow up and down the neat rows of headstones. In the middle of them was a large rectangular area marked by four whitewashed stones. This was one of the mass graves for the victims of the 1918 flu pandemic. Nearly one- third to one-half of the people on the reserve died during that swine flu outbreak, and Grandpa told me how everyone thought that flu was the White Horse of the Apocalypse and that the Day of Judgement had arrived.

The store was in the front half of the structure. Behind this was the living/kitchen area with two bedrooms to the east. Grandma, my Aunt Carol, and Laurel used one bedroom and Grandpa and I were in the other. Carol was the youngest of my grandparents' ten kids and she was eleven or twelve when I came to stay. Laurel had been dropped off at grandma's by her second youngest daughter, Elaine, who had found the baby abandoned at a potato farm where she was working as a migrant farm worker. Elaine initially thought she could look after the baby on her own, but soon discovered she was unable to. My grandparents took the baby to the Indian Agent in Brantford, but, in those days, there were no child services programs on the rez, so he just looked nonplussed and said, "What do you want me to do about it?" We never knew when her birthday was, but grandma assumed she was about four months older than me. Although my grandparents never formally adopted Laurel, we all considered her another kid in the family.

Grandpa was usually first up and he made fire in the wood stove. This provided heat for cooking and to heat the whole structure. He would boil water for tea and sit listening to the radio. We had no electricity, so his old, red, Bakelite radio ran on a car battery which Uncle Maynard had hooked up for him. The local Brantford station he listened to had this little, moralistic jingle that talked about Johnny-go-right and Johnny-go-wrong. Johnny-go-right always made the right choices in life, while Johnny-go-wrong always made the wrong choices and ended up in trouble. When I heard this jingle playing I would wake up and wander into the kitchen, rubbing my eyes. My grandfather would exclaim, in mock surprise, "It's Johnny-go-right! He's a little fellow, don't you know?" and I would go running to him and climb up onto his lap.

Other than my grandfather's humorous allusion to 'Johnny-go-right,' I was always called Jackie, even though my name was John David Sargent Jr. (after my father). In later years, the Anderson family took to calling me 'John-David,' similar to the southern practice of using double-barreled names like John-Boy Walton or Billy-Bob Thornton. I really don't know how that developed.

Grandma would cook breakfast, which always followed the same routine. During the week and Saturday, we would have toast with oatmeal, cornmeal, or Red River cereal. On Sunday, we had pancakes with back bacon. We would make the toast by throwing slices of white Wonder bread directly on the wood stove, wait ten seconds and flip them, wait another ten seconds and toss them on a plate for buttering. This gave us a fine lacework of completely carbonized bread on each surface and warm, but still spongy, bread on the inside. I loved it! You just can't get toast like that these days.

Andersons Place store at St. John's corner, 1950

After breakfast on Sunday, we would get all dolled up and head across the road to the church. Grandpa was the custodian, so, in winter, he would start fires in the two potbelly stoves at the front and back of the main hall, or, in summer, would open a few windows to freshen up the air after a week of being shut in. We had only one minister for the three Anglican churches on the reserve, so services in St. John's wouldn't start until eleven-thirty, when the minister arrived in his car. Very few people on the rez had cars in those days, so it was quite exciting when he drove up. Almost all of the families arrived in horse-drawn carriages.

Most of the goods that were delivered to the store also arrived in horse-drawn wagons. I particularly enjoyed the ice man's weekly deliveries. We had an insulated pop cooler. The drinks were mostly immersed in a tub of cold water, and the ice man would set a block of ice on the side of the cooler and expertly chip it into small chunks in a matter of seconds. Grandpa also kept the milk and butter in this cooler. The bread and vegetable man came every other day, and his name was Alexander, but I used to call him Mr. Axe Handle, which he loved, and he would give me a horse ride on his knee. The milk delivery was the only one I remember that came by truck.

Being a little person, there were two big, possible danger spots around the store. One was the well and the other was the outhouse. The well had a wooden framework at ground level, and a board was laid over the opening. Grandma would always warn Carol to put the cinder block back on the board after getting water, so the little kids wouldn't fall down the well. I was the most concerned about the outhouse. I'd have a screaming fit every time my grandma tried to set me on the hole. "I'm gonna fall in! I'm gonna fall in!" I'd shout. But my grandma would say, "Stay still, I've got you. Just stop squirming or you will fall in!" Eventually, my grandpa cut a smaller hole in a separate board for Laurel and me to use. But then there was the problem of the flies down the hole. "There's bees down there," I would complain. "They're gonna bite me on my bum!" Grandma would say, "Stop it; there are no bees down there. Bees like flowers, only flies like poo!" I remember that, at first, the Eaton's and Sears catalogues were printed on newsprint and made good toilet paper. Later, the catalogues went to a shinier bond and that didn't work so well. It was then that our little corner store started selling toilet paper for the first time. I guess it must have been the same for rural stores right across Canada.

Life on the rez was fun for us kids. Our aunts and uncles lived throughout this area of the rez, so there was always a gang of cousins hanging around. We would go running off through the woods with our dogs, and at whatever house we happened to be near at lunch time, we had the standard tomato soup and baloney and mustard sandwiches. The only house I feared was Uncle Maynard's. He had a mean rooster who never seemed to bother the other kids, but it was his one joy in life to chase me around the farm yard. One time, he chased me right into the kitchen and we ran round and round the central table sending pots, pans, plates, and people flying in all directions. One Sunday soon afterward, Maynard invited his parents and us kids down for a special chicken dinner. Nothing was ever said, but I never saw that old rooster again.

After her operation, my mother's health began to slowly improve, so my parents would be able to take day trips up from Buffalo to see me at grandma's house. However, they were strangers to me and, if they tried to take me too far from Grandma, I'd put up such a battle that they had to either bring me back or take grandma with us. Slowly, however, over the years, I got to know them better, as they would come up, or Grandma and I would go down to Buffalo to visit. By the time I was five, my dad had a new job with the United States Bureau of Mines in Washington, D.C. and they had bought a home in Falls Church, Virginia.

I was getting to be school age, and my parents thought that the one-room schoolhouse on the rez was not the best educational opportunity for their son, so my dad hatched a plan to have me go live with his mom and dad in Windsor Locks,

Connecticut. Thus ended my happy early days on the rez and began a new and troubled period in my young life.

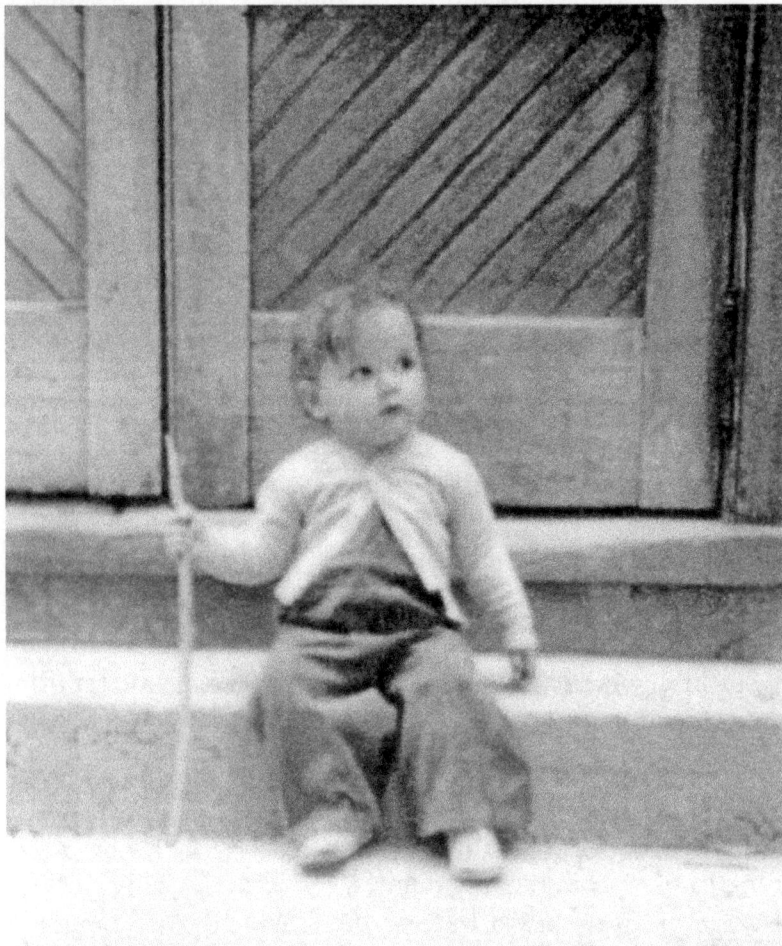

Jackie on the steps of St. John's church, 1951

12. Early Religious Questions

My dad's parents began to change their attitude towards my mother and they became quite favourably impressed with her. She had come from a family that was well-educated and were not the 'stereotypical savages' that their minds had imagined. So she became a bit of a novelty, you know, here was that one good Indian.

As I mentioned, my father did not think the education on the rez would be as good as American education, so he tried to convince his parents to look after me. That way, I would receive my education in the United States. Eventually, they agreed and I went to stay with them. But, for me, this was an incredible change from life on the rez! I can't remember this time so well, myself, as I was only about six years old, but my grandmother Anderson talked about it often. Here I was, growing up on a reservation. I had all kinds of first cousins, and we were just completely free to run riot, you know, through the woods and up the roads—whooping it up and running around with our dogs—I mean, it was really great growing up on the rez. But then they took me away from my grandma and all that. To me, Connecticut was a completely different world.

My dad's parents were very staid and solemn, religious and upright, very disciplined and proper. There were only a few television shows that we could watch. Playing cards, going to the movies, or acting silly were not allowed. It was, what I would call, a very strict Baptist home. Now, I was all alone with these older people. I did make some new friends at school, and often my grandparents would allow them to come over after school or on weekends.

Two perfectly respectable gentlemen. Roy Sargent and Jackie, 1954

Now, I do not want to give the impression that my grandparents were unkind or cold to me—quite the opposite, but the change was dramatic and difficult for me to adjust to. I loved my paternal grandparents, especially my grandfather, who I thought was a saint or an angel. He was always quoting stories and parables from the Bible for me to learn, and he spent the first half hour of every day in prayer in his den. I would sneak downstairs in my pajamas and, from outside the doorway to his den, listen to him pray. I think he knew I was there, as he would always end with a slightly louder, "And God bless little Jackie and his mommy and daddy."

However, I soon started getting colds easily and began to miss a lot of school. These colds would often develop into pneumonia, and the doctor was frequently at our house. My grandparents began to worry, and grandma had grandpa move the television upstairs to my room, so that, when televangelist Oral Roberts was on, she could place my hand on top of the set while he prayed. One morning, I woke up to discover that I could not move at all; I couldn't even get out of bed. I called out frantically to my grandparents, who flew into a panic because they thought I had poliomyelitis, which was epidemic in those days. The doctor came again and reassured them that it was not polio, but, having come so many times recently, drew my grandparents aside and said, "This is a classic case of 'failure to thrive.' This kid has got to get back to his grandma's in Canada as fast as possible." So, as soon as the school year ended, I was packed up and sent back to my grandma on the reserve and to life as I knew it.

The one thing that was a positive help in my life, during this stay in Connecticut, was my early religious education. We went to church every Sunday morning and Wednesday evening. The Sunday school was very good and we learned many of the biblical stories, which my grandfather systematically reinforced. He had his own correspondence Bible study program, and was always imparting wisdom from Proverbs, Psalms, and the parables of Jesus. I didn't know it then, but it is amazing how a thorough knowledge of these stories helps in understanding many of the allegories used by Bahá'u'lláh[20] in His Writings.

All was calm in my spiritual life until one Sunday evening as we sat watching the Ed Sullivan Show on TV. The Korean War was raging and there were a lot of children being orphaned by the fighting. As a result, there was a real humanitarian need for aid to all these orphans. So some of the aid agencies working with these kids set up a children's choir to raise money to support their mission work in Korea. They toured the United States and they were very good. So good, in fact, that they got on the Ed Sullivan Show. (My grandparents always watched the Ed Sullivan Show because, normally, it was good, clean fun.) The Korean Children's Choir sang several songs, very nice; everyone was really appreciative of that. But one of their final songs was 'Buddha Laga Lami' ('Buddha Loves Me' sung to the tune of 'Jesus Loves Me'). As soon as they began to sing that song, my grandmother couldn't get out of the couch fast enough. She zoomed across the room, turned off the TV, and said, "Buddhists are going to hell!"

That was a profoundly disconcerting moment for me, as a child, because, here were these children who'd lost everything, their mothers and fathers and everything, to this war. Now, was God going to send them to hell just because they were Buddhist? Somehow, a God like that just didn't jive with what my concept of God was, and particularly of Jesus. I was taught of His great love of children. But I didn't say anything; I was only six years old, and I wasn't going to enter into a

---

20   See Glossary.

theological debate with my grandparents. I just quietly sat there with this crisis of faith. That was likely my first religious questioning, but it wasn't going to be the last.

13. Up and Down, Back and Forth

As soon as I was finished with first grade, I went back to the rez to live with my maternal grandparents again. The little corner store supplied enough for the family's immediate needs, but provided little extra for savings. My grandparents were getting on in years and dreamed of getting a new DIA[21] home with plumbing and electricity. They would need a two thousand dollar down payment and to sign a rent-to-own agreement for the remaining four thousand. Two thousand dollars was an incredible sum in those days and, with their meagre savings, it didn't seem possible. My grandfather would dream about it constantly and I could hear him mumble as he napped, "Where can I get six thousand dollars?"

Meanwhile, my mother's health was improving rapidly. She was released from the sanatorium and, as I mentioned, my parents bought a home in Falls Church, Virginia, to be near my dad's work in Washington, D.C. My father's new job, at the Bureau of Mines, was to determine the secure supply of rare earth and radioactive materials for the national strategic stockpiles. This primarily involved research from his office in Washington, but also involved some travel, particularly to the western states, where new supplies of uranium were being discovered.

With things going so positively, my parents thought it was time to unite the family, so I moved down to Virginia to live

---

21   Canadian Department of Indian Affairs

with them. Grandma came down with me for a month to ease the transition and we passed that summer together, planning that I would attend the elementary school in Falls Church that September. However, that was not to be. In the early fall, my mother developed a chronic cough, and it was soon discovered that the tuberculosis was back and progressing rapidly. She had to return to the hospital and I went back to the rez once more.

At last, a nuclear family—for a while, 1955

Then my dad suggested that Grandma and Grandpa Anderson move down to the States so I could go to school there. As an adult, I can't believe his impertinence with this request, but they moved to Rochester, New York, and

Grandma found work as a domestic/nanny for a rich Italian family. This turned out to be a blessing in disguise because, although her hours were long, she was paid minimum wage, which, together with Grandpa's Old Age Security, was enough for them to set a fair portion aside as savings. So I spent my second and third grade years in Rochester.

During this time, on a business trip to Colorado, my dad heard of a new program at the National Jewish Hospital in Denver, trying to develop antibiotics that would fight tuberculosis. When he returned to Washington, he discussed this with my mother's doctors, and they applied to have her enrolled in the program. They felt that, even if the treatments were ineffective, the drier climate would at least help. Soon my mother was accepted into the program and moved to Denver. The trips out west were difficult and expensive, so my dad left his job in Washington and set up his own independent geochemical consulting laboratory in Casper, Wyoming, which was, at that time, the centre for the '50s uranium rush.

During the summer and winter school breaks, Grandma and I would fly out to Denver and visit with my parents. My mother had had a further operation to remove the newly diseased portions of her lungs, which reduced, even more, her energy level and respiratory capacity, but the cocktail of new drugs appeared to be working. After a couple of years, she seemed to be in complete remission and was released from the hospital. I was nine, by this time, and pretty much able to look after myself, so my parents thought it was time to try re-uniting the family again, and I moved out to Casper to be with them. Thus, for me, the period of being shuffled around came to an end, and a period of near normalcy began.

My grandparents moved back to the rez and, with the money they had saved while in Rochester, were able to get the DIA home they had dreamed of—sort of. Actually, it

was a repossessed home that had been trashed by the previous tenants, so they were able to buy it at a much reduced
cost. Fortunately, a work crew of uncles and nephews came
together, and the place was shipshape again in no time.

Grandma Anderson plants a garden in front of her DIA home, 1959

14. Hell Freezes Over

My dad had written a paper about 'Geologic Isostatic Oscillation and its relationship to the Viking Exploration in North America.' As it happened, the XXI Geological Congress in 1960 was taking place in Copenhagen, Denmark, and he was invited to present it there. Because he had had a recent run of good luck with his business, the whole family was able to go with him to Europe for about a month, travelling around and camping. We really enjoyed Denmark and went to Tivoli Amusement Park and Elsinore Castle, and my dad took part in an archeological dig. From there we visited Sweden, Germany, Belgium, the Netherlands, and France. It was, I would say, the one time that our newly re-established family unit had a really good bonding experience—an exciting adventure together.

This trip had been a high point for all of us. However, Europe, being very low, very damp, was not good for my mother's health. After we came back, our family situation worsened. My dad's business began failing, my mother's health became very precarious, and I had a little trouble adjusting to my new family situation. My dad was becoming increasingly stressed, and I guess he was feeling very at sea in a stormy world. Since he had been thrown out of the Baptist Church, my dad hadn't sought membership with any denomination, although he attended the Episcopal Church (the American version of Anglican) from time to time with my mother. It was about this time that he joined the Unitarians. The Unitarians are a Christian fellowship, but they don't have a set dogma and let the individual members search for truth on their own, and that suited him well.

Edith and Jackie beneath the Arc de Triomphe
on the Champs-Élysées, Paris, 1960

He was attending the Unitarian Church quite regularly simply because his life was hard, and he was turning to God more and more in prayer—for solace. It so happened that, at this time, the Unitarians in Casper decided that they wanted to put on a series of talks to explore the differences between all the major religions. By all the major religions, I think they meant all the major Christian denominations like Catholic, Methodist, Baptist, Lutheran, that sort of thing. But, for some reason, I don't know how, they added the Bahá'ís[22] to the list. Maybe they thought it was some kind of Christian denomination.

Anyway, they invited the Bahá'ís to come and speak, but my dad was not there to hear it. When he came back to church the next Sunday, everybody was abuzz about what the Bahá'ís had said, and my dad was asking, "Ba-who? Ba-what? What are you talking about?" But his fellow church members just brushed off his enquiries saying, "Oh, never mind, you missed it." But what they were saying sounded fascinating to him, so my dad looked up the Bahá'í number in the phone book and asked if he could hear about this faith of theirs. Well, if you know anything about the Bahá'ís, you'll know that if someone calls up out of the blue and says, "I want to hear about the Bahá'í Faith," the Bahá'í will just about fall out of their chair and scramble to get over there right now!

So, this Bahá'í invited my dad over for coffee. And my father listened to him for about an hour, drinking his coffee, and, finally, he said, "You know, you seem like an intelligent, sane person and you're trying to tell me that Christ has returned and nobody knows about it?" And the guy thought for a moment and said, "Yeah, that's just about it." So my dad exclaimed, "Well, it'll be a cold day in hell before I join an outfit like that!" And he left. But it continued to bother him. He thought to himself, "This is so ludicrous. It should be absolutely easy to disprove this nonsense. This whole religion is based on nothing. I'm going to write a paper, or a tract, called *'The Case Against the Bahá'ís'*."

He realized, however, that you can't just write a tract against something without knowing anything about it, so he called

---

22   See Bahá'í Faith in the Glossary.

the guy back, and asked, "Do you have any books on this subject?" Now, that's another question that you don't want to ask a Bahá'í, because you'll end up walking home with a whole stack of books! And so my dad did; he went home with all these books, and began reading them. He started seriously researching the Faith, and he began writing down a list of contradictions and ridiculous statements that he found in the Bahá'í Writings. Every time he would come across something he found contradictory to the Bible, or rather contradictory to common beliefs about the Bible, or something that was just plain too hard to swallow, he would write it down on his list. And his list was growing and growing.

Two lonely bachelors, 1961

One day, as he was reading, he came across a quote of Bahá'u'lláh[23] and he said, "Oh, you know, I get that. I understand that." So one of the points on his list he had to cross off because he understood what the Bahá'ís were saying, and he didn't disagree with it. At this point, he realized, "You know, I'm looking at the Bahá'í Faith through Baptist eyes, not through rational, impartial eyes. I have to look for internal consistency, not for consistency with others' interpretations of reality." He began looking at his list with these new eyes, and, before long, instead of his list of objections getting longer and longer, it started getting shorter and shorter. It slowly began to dawn on him that Christ had indeed returned "as a thief in the night," just as He had foretold.

Time was going by, probably a period of about two or three years, during which things became very difficult for him. My mother passed away, his business went bankrupt, and he became a substitute teacher at the school and did a few odd things just to keep body and soul together. This was, I would say, probably the most stressful and difficult time in his life. He would often say to people that Casper was his private hell.

At this same time the Bahá'ís' Ten Year World Plan[24] was coming to an end. One of the goals of the plan was to have a local Spiritual Assembly[25] in every state, and there wasn't one in Wyoming. The National Spiritual Assembly[23] sent Amoz Gibson[26] to Casper, which needed only one more Bahá'í to have their Assembly. He suggested that the community have

---

23   See Bahá'u'lláh in the Glossary.

24   See Tablets of the Divine Plan in the Glossary.

25   See Bahá'í Assemblies in the Glossary.

26   Amoz Gibson was a member of the National Spiritual Assembly of the United States at this time. He was later elected to the Universal House of Justice.

a prayer campaign. He asked if there were any contacts that they felt were close. Someone said, "There's John Sargent," but somebody else said, "He's been studying the Faith forever. I don't think he's ever going to make up his mind." Amoz said, "Here's what we'll do—let's everyone remember him in our prayers every day." And so the prayer campaign began.

My dad was unaware of these events, but a few days after the campaign began, a blizzard hit Casper and the temperature fell way below zero. He was driving back through these treacherous conditions when his car slid on the ice and crashed through the railing of an overpass and onto the railroad tracks below. At that moment, he called out, "Bahá'u'lláh!" and, although his car was demolished, he escaped completely unharmed. As he sat there recovering from his fright, he realized that he was a hypocrite; that he'd been sitting on the fence all this time, and only when the chips were down would he admit that he actually really did believe. So he asked if he could meet with the local Bahá'í community to declare his faith in Bahá'u'lláh. I believe that night set a new record low temperature for Casper. At any rate, the guy that had initially introduced him to the Faith put his arm around my dad and said, "You know what, John? It really was a cold day in hell when you joined this outfit!"

15. All I Want for Christmas is True Understanding

One unseasonably warm October day in Casper, when I was about eleven, I had a strange mystical experience that was to have a profound effect on me for the rest of my life. This story, like a number in this collection, is hard to tell, because it transcends normal consciousness and seems to take place in a realm of hyper-reality. I have not studied mystical thought, so I'm not clear on how this works, but it seems 'normal reality' is a subset of a greater reality that can be sometimes glimpsed in a dream or during prayer—or it can just suddenly appear. In this case, it was occasioned by the arrival of the Sears 'Wish Book' catalogue.

A group of us boys was sitting around on the porch of my friend's house just chatting about all the neat stuff in that year's 'Wish Book,' when someone said to me, "What do you want for Christmas?" I said, "Well, I hope Santa brings me a Shootin' Shell rifle." Then all the guys began to mock me, saying, "You don't still believe in Santa Claus, do you?" I turned red and said, "No, no, I don't believe in Santa Claus. I'm just saying, I hope someone gives me a Shootin' Shell rifle for Christmas." They all laughed. Then one of the guys said, "Do you still believe in God?" Now, after having just made myself appear naive, I didn't want to look stupid or childish, so I was about to say no—when, all of a sudden, fear gripped me. I had the uneasy feeling that my answer to this question would have a profound impact on my future well-being. In an instant, it went from that kind of silly childhood banter to a much more serious question. But, as I sat there, confused about how to answer, 'normal reality' seemed to dissolve and I entered this 'hyper-reality' state, and the question zoomed right down to the core of my being and confronted me. Inexplicably, in that expanded space, I could see plainly and certainly the true nature of reality. Yes, God exists! And not only does God exist, but, to my surprise, I instantly realized: God is the only thing that does exist! Everything else is contingent, ephemeral. All things, including me, existed only in the mind of God. The only reality I had was as a thought in His mind!

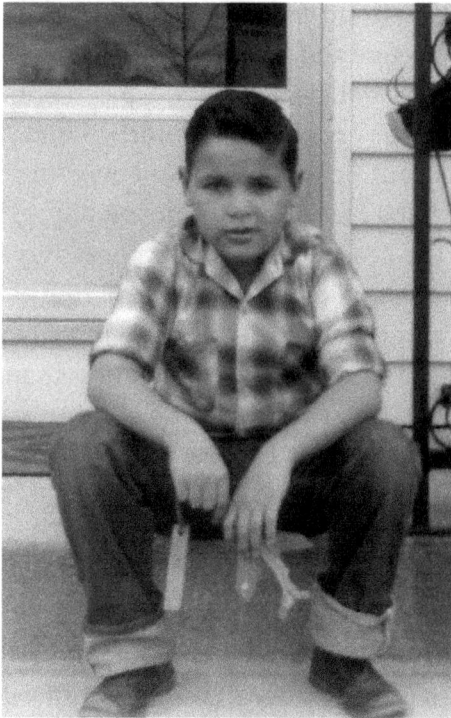

I hope Santa brings me a Shootin' Shell rifle

I don't remember what I did or said after that. I just remember looking around with this new understanding and marveling at God's omnipresence and attention to every detail. It was, for me, a whole new creation—not cold, accidental, and impersonal but in the constant care of His loving providence. As Bahá'u'lláh says: "*O son of man! Veiled in My immemorial being and in the ancient eternity of My essence, I knew My love for thee; therefore I created thee, have engraved on thee Mine image and revealed to thee My beauty.*"[27]

Although I was unaware of it then, this happened during the time my dad was studying the Bahá'í Faith. I was not attending church, Sunday school, or any other religious activities during this time, but then, one day, my father came to me and asked, "Would you like to go to Bahá'í Sunday school?" I'd never heard of Bahá'í before and I really didn't want to go to a Sunday school of any kind, but, because of the uncertainties in my early life, I had become a very obedient child. So I said, "Sure, I'll go."

As it turned out, it was just about Ayyám-i-Há time (the period on the Bahá'í Calendar for hospitality, gift giving, and charity) and the teacher was making an Ayyám-i-Há tree. (Now, I'd never heard of an Ayyám-i-Há tree before, and I've never heard of an Ayyám-i-Há tree since, but anyways...) This Ayyám-i-Há tree consisted of a dried branch stuck into a bucket of sand. The teacher got us all to sit down, and she handed out mimeographed sheets of paper with the religious symbols of all the major faiths. On one sheet, there was the cross of Christianity, on another the crescent moon and star of Islam, the Star of David of Judaism, and so forth. We all had a different religious symbol that we were to colour, and, after we coloured them, we were to cut them out, put a string on them, and hang them as decorations on this Ayyám-i-Há tree. Well,

---

27   Bahá'u'lláh – *The Hidden Words* - #3 from the Arabic.

guess which one I got—the Buddhist prayer wheel. Now, I didn't know much about different religions, but I did remember that incident at my Grandmother Sargent's—"Buddhists are going to hell!" So I said to myself, "Now what's my father gotten me into?" However, as we coloured, the teacher explained the process of progressive revelation:[28] that God periodically sends Messengers to humanity to progressively lead man forward in our spiritual development; that each Messenger reaffirms the previous Messengers and foretells the coming of future ones. At once, the process seemed absolutely clear to me. I would say this was my next religious epiphany.

Before, when I looked at all the different religions of the world, I saw what looked like warring factions, each its own castle with high walls, in opposition to the others. However, as the teacher spoke, all these walls seemed to crumble away and all became part of the same Faith, under one God. It just became so obvious and so beautifully elegant and clear, and this wonderful understanding pervaded me. Religions aren't in conflict, and God doesn't send Buddhists to hell. It's all part of the same process. So, for me, I can remember leaving that class having discovered this most wonderful thing, and I would say that, perhaps, I was a Bahá'í from that moment. Now, in those days, you couldn't become a Bahá'í until you were fifteen, so no one asked me if I was interested in becoming one. But I was, from that very first class; I understood this principle and wanted to be part of this Faith.

I began reading a book called *Release the Sun* by William Sears, which tells the story of how the Bahá'í Faith began. As soon as I read about the early exploits of the followers of The Báb[29], I immediately considered myself one of them—a 'Dawn

---

28   See Progressive Revelation in the Glossary.
29   See Báb (The) in the Glossary.

Breaker'! A soldier in the army of light battling the forces of darkness! I must have bored every one of my friends to death telling them the story of The Báb, how a new age had dawned, and how the whole world was changing as a consequence of His appearance in Persia a hundred years earlier. Well, of course, the other kids couldn't figure out what the heck I was going on about. Religion was the last thing on their minds. So, gradually, I became more circumspect about how and to whom I broached this subject, but I felt like I had this amazing secret and was exploding to tell everyone about it.

In high school, one of my classmates did show interest: Barbara Zidarski. We would talk about the Faith for hours, and she would come out to various Bahá'í events. Barbara had had a hard life. She, her sister, and brother lived with their mom who, for some reason, kept attracting violent alcoholics as companions. Yet, despite the fear and stress this caused at home, Barbara had a sunny, positive disposition, and she had a peculiar laugh consisting of four or five ha's ascending in tone that sounded vaguely like a question. Eventually, she wanted to become a Bahá'í, and wrote a letter to the local Spiritual Assembly asking for enrolment.

Her house was on my way to school, and often I would stop by her place and we would walk to school together. However, soon after she became a Bahá'í, I went to her house and was told that Barbara didn't live there anymore and I wasn't to call there again. Her mother had burned her Bahá'í books and sent her to live with her aunt in Colorado. It looked like that was the last I would ever see of Barbara, and I worried about her spiritual wellbeing.

Nearly eleven years later, I was attending the North Pacific Bahá'í Oceanic Conference held in Anchorage, Alaska, and I was walking across the gym when I heard someone shout, "Jackie!" I just kept walking, but the same person shouted again, "Jackie Sargent!" I stopped and whirled around. "Jackie Sargent?" Nobody had called me that in over a decade. There stood a pert young woman with a broad smile, but I had no idea who she was. She saw that I was drawing a blank, so she quickly put her hand over her name tag to prolong my befuddlement. However, as she did, she uttered this ascending question mark of a laugh, and I instantly recognized her—"Barbara? Barbara Zidarski?"

Barbara Zidarski, Anchorage, Alaska, 1976

Not only had Barbara remained a Bahá'í despite the disapproval of her family, but she had also taught her sister the Faith. Barbara had married a young air force officer, had two sons and was living in Seward, Alaska. It was a source of real thankfulness to me to know that the first person I had introduced the Faith to had remained firm in the face of trials and was herself a teacher of the Cause.

16. Changing Times in Indian Country

After my father had become a Bahá'í, I noticed an immediate change in our pattern of activity. It was early 1962. As I mentioned before, the Ten Year World Plan was coming to an end and the teaching work was in full gear. He threw himself into the Faith so wholeheartedly that it wasn't long before I got swept up in the process too. Because of my father's fascination with, and love for, the American Indians, the work that we threw ourselves into most vigorously was teaching the Faith amongst the First Nations people of North America. We began to go to the various reservations, talking about the Faith, but not with a lot of success in those early days.

Bob and Carol Manuelito were Navajo Bahá'ís living in Laramie, Wyoming. After work on Friday, they would leave Laramie and arrive in Casper at about nine o'clock at night. My dad just opened his house to them. They knew they could come in, throw their sleeping bags on the living room floor, and be ready for an early start. Then, early in the morning, Carol would stick her head into my room, and say, "Junior." (People had taken to calling me Junior, which I preferred over Jackie.) "Junior, we're goin' Injin' huntin.' You wanna come?" I'd say, "Sure," and go with them up to Fort Washakie or one of the other reservations in Northern Wyoming. Virtually every weekend, my dad and I would travel to the various reserves from Wolf Point in Montana down to Pine Springs in Arizona. We met a lot of nice people, and, eventually, many of these communities were opened to the Faith, but the work was very slow.

John Sr., Carol Manuelito, Paul Schwartz, Junior, Marie and Nelson Lee at Window Rock, Arizona, on our way to the Pine Springs Bahá'í Council Fire, 1962

Across the border in Canada, however, it was another story. Angus Cowan was teaching in Saskatchewan and Alberta and meeting with overwhelming success. Angus was a really sweet, pure-hearted person who just loved the First Nations people, and who the First Nations really loved in return. As a result, they started becoming Bahá'ís in vast numbers. So much so that he couldn't handle the follow-up work. He wrote to the National Spiritual Assembly (NSA) of the Bahá'ís of Canada, asking them to send some reinforcements out to help him. They, in turn, sent out the call to the Canadian

Bahá'í community; the Irwins, the Rosses, and a few others responded and came out to give a hand, but they were still too few. So the secretary of the Canadian NSA wrote to the NSA of the United States and said, "Have you got any Bahá'ís experienced in working with the First Nation peoples that could come up and give us a hand?" As the NSA of the United States had heard about the work that my dad was doing on some of the reserves in the West, they asked him, "Could you go up to Canada and help out because things are really poppin' up there?" So we went up and started working with Angus. I went with him that summer, but I had to return to school in the fall. We went from reserve to reserve, from the summer of '62 through to the summer of '65. That was the time of mass teaching of the Bahá'í Faith on the Canadian Prairies.

It is just my opinion, but I feel the First Nation peoples were more spiritually attuned then than they are now. A lot of people would say not, but I think materialism has dulled the spiritual senses of many individuals globally. We couldn't see it at first, but big changes were beginning to fuel turmoil within Indian Country. On top of the developing 'Indian Residential School Crisis,' militant nationalism and particularly the increasing flow of alcohol onto the reserves were starting to tear families and communities apart. But, when we first came to Saskatchewan, in the summer of '62, the full consequences of all these things were still in the future, and the power of the spirit was moving as a palpable force. Everywhere we went, we found the people in a state of expectation. It was almost as if they knew we were coming with a message from the Creator and they were eager to embrace it. The following example, I think, may give you some feeling for what was happening in those days.

Most people in the European tradition filter their beliefs through their minds first. Any concept must meet certain intellectual conditions before they open their hearts to the idea. The First Nations people seem to do the opposite: they test an idea with their hearts first, and, if it feels right with their spirit, they are then willing to spend the intellectual time and effort to learn all the details. The following incident may demonstrate how this works. It took place many years after these mass teaching efforts, when I had returned to Canada from pioneering[30] in Africa. I was trying to do consolidation of the teaching work we had done years earlier and was not being all that successful.

Andrew Kay was an elder on Poorman Reserve[31] in Saskatchewan—he was a spiritual leader for the community and well respected in Indian Country. I came up to his house unannounced and knocked on his door. We had visited his home many years before, but he didn't recognize me, of course, because I was ten years older. So, instead of thirteen, I was a twenty-three-year-old young man. He invited me in and offered me tea and biscuits, and I charged into a long-winded explanation of the importance of the Faith to the First Nation peoples and how we had to read the Writings and pray every day. He listened patiently for some time, and then gently said, "I think you should stop talking now." It was not a threatening comment, and actually I could feel, in my heart, he was right—but I still felt defeated because I so desperately wanted the Faith to enter properly into the lives of the First Nations people, so that they and their families could benefit from the blessings it bestows. We just sat there quietly for some time until finally I asked, "Andrew, how is it you became a Bahá'í?" He thought for a moment and said, "Come with me."

---

30 See Pioneer in the Glossary.
31 This reserve is known as Kawacatoose First Nation today.

We went into his bedroom, and over his bed he had his medicine bundle and pipe hanging on a nail, and, to my surprise, behind his bundle he also had the Greatest Name hanging there. (The Greatest Name is 'O Glory of the All-Glorious' in Arabic calligraphy.) He took his pipe and his medicine bundle, sat down in the living room, set out all his paraphernalia, and together we smudged and smoked his pipe. When we had finished, he said, "One day, I was praying under my tree."

I should tell you a bit about this tree. I had noticed, when I arrived, that just outside of his house he had this magnificent, old, broken-down, cottonwood tree. When these trees get old, the great limbs crack and break off. They lay down in confusion on the ground. They're ugly, but they've got a certain dignified character. This one was covered with rags. I mean covered with rags! These were the prayer cloths that Andrew had been putting up there for years and years. Some were brand new and had only been put up maybe days or weeks before. Some had been put up years before. They were faded and tattered, and they looked more like Spanish moss than colourful prayer cloths.

Anyway, he said, "I was out under my tree and I was praying. I must have dozed off, because a spirit guide came to me and said, 'Andrew, follow me.' And so I went with the spirit guide and we got up on a knoll on the prairie, and he looked way across, and he said, 'Look over there across the prairie. What colour is that?' And as I looked way across the horizon of the prairie, I saw that it was blue, and I said, 'It's blue.' Then he said, 'Andrew look over here, and tell me what you see.' And I looked over there and saw Quill Lake. And he said, 'What colour is that?' I said, 'It's blue.' And then he said, 'Look over here and see the hills in the distance. What colour are the hills?' And I said, 'Blue.' And then he said, 'Look at this.' And I looked up in the sky, and there was this strange symbol, the symbol of the Greatest Name, in the sky. And he said, 'What colour is this?' And I said, 'It's blue.' Then he said, 'Remember this, Andrew: to the Creator all things are one. In four days, a very important messenger will come to your door, and you must listen to what he has to say.'" So Andrew woke up from this vision. Four days later, he got up in the morning; he put the kettle on, set out the table for two, and got biscuits ready in anticipation of this important messenger. About mid-morning, he heard a knock. He went to his door, opened it and there's Angus Cowan standing there.

Angus Cowan, Fort Qu'Appelle, Saskatchewan, 1964

17. Hooray! Now What?

The teaching work was going so well in Canada, and the number of Bahá'ís helping were so few, that my dad dedicated most of his time to this effort. I would go up whenever I could, during the summer and during the winter break, but I spent the school year staying with Al and Sue Foreman, a Bahá'í couple living in Casper. Our teaching method was to go from reserve to reserve and do 'home visits.' In winter, this could be hard as the roads into the reserves were usually not ploughed; and, sometimes, access was closed due to the reserve being quarantined. I'm not sure quarantined for what? But, still, we were not allowed in. However, when we did go in, the people were so highly receptive it was, as I mentioned before, as though they were in a state of expectation. Here are a couple of stories that may illustrate the nature of the teaching work at this time.

A man on one of the reserves got drunk one night. He walked out of the house, without a coat on, without his shoes and socks on, and fell asleep in a snowdrift. It was extremely cold that night. When they finally found him, the next day, he was near death from hypothermia and they rushed him to the hospital. The frostbite was so severe that they had to amputate some of his fingers and toes; and it was touch and go as to whether or not he would survive this exposure. While he was in bed and unconscious, suddenly the door opened, and

'Abdu'l-Bahá[32] walked into the room. He walked up to this guy and said, "Ben, what have you been drinking?" Ben hung his head, and said, "I've been drinking alcohol." 'Abdu'l-Bahá responded, "What is wrong with the pure, clear water that we have created for you?" Then he added that a visitor would come soon to help him. With that, 'Abdu'l-Bahá disappeared.

A few days later, my father came to visit him in the hospital. My dad had met his family on one of the reserves we were visiting, and they asked if he could say some prayers for their uncle who was critically ill in the hospital. When he got there, Ben was conscious and awake, but still not in good condition. My dad asked, "Is it all right if I say some prayers with you?" Ben said, "Yes, please. Thank you." My father opened his prayer book and, as it happened, he had a picture of 'Abdu'l-Bahá as a bookmark. Ben suddenly bolted up against the headboard of the bed, his eyes wide, pointed to the picture and said, "That's him! That's him!" My father was puzzled and asked, "What do you mean, 'That's him'?" And Ben said, "That's the man who came to visit me a couple of days ago in my hospital room!"

Another time, when we were doing home visits on a reserve, we came to this particular house. Back in those days, the Department of Indian Affairs houses were very cheaply built. The internal partitions were just 2x4 framing with one-eighth inch plywood panelling on both sides. I mention this because Patricia Verge, in her book *Angus – From the Heart*, repeats a story of a family who tore down a wall to make more room for one of these home visits. As it happened, I was there that night. Angus, my dad, and I went to that house at random and unannounced. We were going to go around the reserve over the next couple of days and visit the people. This was our usual modus operandi. It was a very cold, clear Saskatchewan night. The temperature

---

32   See 'Abdu'l Bahá in the Glossary.

was well below zero and the stars shone spectacularly overhead in the clear moonless sky. As we were visiting, they put on some tea and opened a tin of biscuits for us. We weren't there long before there was a knock on the door; somebody came in and sat down. So now there were more of us. Soon, there was another knock, and there were still more of us. People just kept coming, and coming, and coming, until there was no more room for us. And so, they had to tear the wall down between the living room and the bedroom to make room for all the people that were coming. Now, I'll tell you what: I don't think anybody left that room to go out to tell other people that they needed to hear this and be there. Who knows how they got there? Why they all came there? Why they felt they needed to be there?

Teaching team (left hand group), including Junior (with his hand in a can of wild blueberries), home visiting with Shorty Whitecalf and family (right hand group), Rocky Mountain House, Alberta, 1963

And, to be part of it, you know, you could feel the power of the Holy Spirit. It fills your veins with life. I can't remember how many days we stayed or where we slept: in the car, on the floor, or wherever, it didn't seem to matter. We only wanted to be with the people, and the people wanted, eagerly, to hear this message. The Spirit was just flowing, and everybody knew it; everybody could feel its power. And they seemed to just come to us. Wherever we went, the Spirit drew them. The more the people came, the stronger the flow of the Spirit, which, in turn, attracted even more people. We were amazed by what was happening.

Hundreds and hundreds of people were accepting the Faith—more than a thousand, spread across the Western Provinces. We had never seen anything like it. We were only a handful of teachers, and we were all so excited. However, it slowly began to dawn on us—how can we ever hope to consolidate (deepen in the teachings and help them begin to function as a Bahá'í community) so many new believers? The whole situation was fraught with difficulties—logistical difficulties. The primary one was that there were just plain not enough Bahá'ís with enough spare time to really consolidate such a large number of new believers. Secondly, even if the Bahá'í community could devote the necessary time, there was no methodology or plan or material developed to cope with this large an influx of new believers. The third problem was that of basic education—basic literacy skills, as well as basic administrative skills—that just did not exist in the First Nation community at that time.

Some felt that the adult generation was 'lost' anyway, and that all our energy and scarce resources should be directed into children's classes. Others, like my dad, felt that some effort had to be made to help deepen the adults, and he began to go out regularly to the reserves and hold study classes with them. He would read to them for hours from *The New Garden* by Hushmand Fatheazam.

Sometimes, he would come back so hoarse that he could hardly speak. While the friends tried their best, the situation was just too overwhelming, and, one by one, they began to burn out.

Ultimately, I don't know the real meaning and value of that earlier work or the spiritual benefit to those that were involved. I guess we'll only know that in the next world. But the House of Justice[33], in their essay 'The Century of Light'[34], called this work essential to the learning necessary for advancing the process of entry by troops.[35]

33   See Universal House of Justice in the Glossary.
34   Century of Light p 103
35   One of the anticipated steps in the development of the Bahá'í Faith. See Tablets of the Divine Plan in the Glossary.

18. Miscegenation Redux

My dad's uncle, Jessie Hursey, who had come all the way up to Windsor Locks, Connecticut, from Florida to talk my dad out of marrying an Indian, had one son and three daughters. The whole family lived in the hotel he was managing. Uncle Jessie thought his son, who was approaching twenty-one and had lived all his life on the beach of a tourist trap, was becoming somewhat of a sissy. So he loaded him up on a Greyhound bus and sent him out to my dad in Wyoming, 'with an implied note attached to his lapel, saying, "Make a man of him."'[36] So it was that my second cousin, John Hursey, came to live with us in Casper. As my dad had 'John' tied up and I took on 'Jackie' or 'Junior,' that left 'Little Johnny' for the third John in the household.

My dad was owner of Sargent Geochemical, a small, independent mineral exploration company with a staff of three or four fieldworkers. So my dad took Little Johnny on as one of his field hands. They spent most of their time taking samples out in some of the most remote and rugged parts of the American West. The lead hand during this time was Rustom Kerawala. Rustom came from Southern India and was very black. He was a PhD student at the University of Arizona, where he was studying geochemistry. I don't know if my dad purposely put Little Johnny in to bunk with Rustom as a dig at Johnny's father's attempt to thwart my dad's marriage to

---

36   Not literally, of course.

an American Indian or not, but he did. Little Johnny, however, thought some kind of game was being played on him, and boldly asserted that he'd have "Rustom polishing my boots in no time." This was going to be interesting to watch. Not only was Rustom a gracious and kind individual, but his intellect was light years ahead of this little beach bum that had been put under his charge. As it turned out, the two became fast friends over the summer and Little Johnny was quickly shedding the last traces of racial prejudice that had been trained into him.

To my dad's surprise, Little Johnny was a natural, rugged outdoorsman, and he loved the work, particularly roughing it out in the field. The whole 'live off the land' mentality was right down his alley, and he was spending all his spare time and money getting the latest 'survival gear.' I loved that, in his free time, he would often take me camping. He wasn't much into fishing, but he was an excellent orienteer and would take a topographic map and a Brunton compass and get us just about anywhere and back again. One time, in the spring, we were hiking early in the morning, when he trod on a ball of rattlesnakes, causing them to disperse. I was walking a few paces behind, and by the time I got there, it seemed that the whole area was crawling with them. I screamed, "Rattlesnakes!" and couldn't figure out which way to jump, as they seemed to be all around me. Suddenly, I heard blam, blam, blam as Little Johnny had pulled out his .44 Magnum and was shooting wildly at them. Now rattlesnakes were the least of my worries, as I started jumping around and shouting, "Don't shoot! Don't shoot! You're going to shoot my foot off!"

When my dad's business went under, Little Johnny got a job with the Sinclair Oil Company. As my dad was studying the Bahá'í Faith at this time, he would share some of his insights with Little Johnny, so it wasn't long after we became

Bahá'ís that Little Johnny also joined the Faith. I don't know if there was anything special about the name John, but we three Johns were the only Bahá'ís in our family at that time.

Junior, Little Johnny, Edith and John Sr. in front of
Sargent Geochemical, Casper, Wyoming, 1960

About this time, we started going to the Bahá'í Summer School in Geyserville, California. It was not long after Little Johnny declared that we set out for Geyserville and took him with us. It seems that, soon after a person declares his/her belief in Bahá'u'lláh, there is a honeymoon period when the power of the Holy Spirit is particularly powerful. My dad stopped for gas in Salt Lake City. We continued west on old Highway 30 through the Bonneville Salt Flats, when the car engine started missing and hesitating. My dad grumbled that the gas we got must have had ground water in it. Little Johnny, as a joke, waved his hand mystically at the gas gauge and said, "Evil gas be gone." Almost immediately, the gas gauge started plummeting toward empty, and it was all we could do to make it to the next gas station. Apparently, the line from the fuel pump had cracked, and we had pumped the bad gas right out of the tank. After everything was fixed, my dad chided Little Johnny to be careful what he wished for so soon after becoming a Bahá'í.

As we had to pass through San Francisco on our way to Geyserville, we decided to see the 'Hippies' that we had heard about on the news, so we headed up to the Haight-Ashbury area for lunch. We got quite a kick gawking at all the long-haired weirdos with their funky sunglasses, beads, and tie-dyed T-shirts. We could not have guessed, at that time, the impact this little band of counterculture rebels would have on the youth throughout the world.

The only way we could afford to go to summer school was to go for two weeks: the first week we worked as staff, and that enabled us to attend the school for the second week for free. In many ways, I preferred the first week, when I worked as a vegetable cutter, busboy, and dishwasher. Serving the friends brought a great feeling of joy. Those two weeks, every year, at Geyserville, were like heaven in my memory: the talks in the evening by Hands of the Cause, Auxiliary Board members, and members of the National Spiritual Assembly; sitting under the 'Big Tree'[37] by day or late into the night discussing

---

37   In the centre of the school campus was a hundreds-of-years-old fir tree. In its youth, the top of the tree had been torn off in such a way that three main trunks shot up from the common base. The lower branches had been trimmed, picnic tables were set out all around the main trunk, and lighting was suspended from the lower branches.

various issues concerning the Faith; and browsing in the old library. One of my favourite teachers at the school was Amoz Gibson, for he was, like me, himself a half-breed (half Black/ half American Indian), and it was also through his prayer campaign initiative that my dad had accepted the Cause. Another highlight was Hand of the Cause William Sears, who came up one night a week and gave a talk, which was always entertaining and inspiring. These much anticipated days at Geyserville were a special treat after a year of hard but rewarding teaching work on so many western reserves in the United States and Canada.

During this time, we became especially close to the Navajo friends Bob and Carol Manuelito, and Marie and Nelson Lee. We went on teaching trips, to conferences, and visited isolated believers together. What I didn't know was that Carol and Marie's younger sister, Maggie, was also there a lot of the time. This was because Maggie was so shy that she would hide under a tarp in the back of the Lee's pickup truck for hours, and we didn't even know that she had come along. One day, as a joke, Carol asked Little Johnny to get something for her out of the back of the Lee's truck. Next thing, we heard screaming and a commotion coming from outside. I don't know who got the biggest surprise, but it seems it was 'love at first fright,' and soon the two were going out together.

After a short while, Little Johnny confided to my dad that he was getting serious about Maggie, and he was going to ask her to marry him. At that point, my dad just shook his head and said, "Good luck with that." He then proceeded to tell Little Johnny the story of how his dad had tried so hard to talk him out of marrying my mom because she was an American Indian—now his own son wants to marry a Navajo! As a Bahá'í, Little Johnny would have to get his parents blessing for the marriage. He couldn't disregard his parents' wishes as my dad had done all those years ago. This was going to be problematic, so we all said some serious prayers, and Little Johnny wrote to his parents for permission. He waited on tenterhooks for over two weeks for their reply. I don't know if it was our prayers or if my mother had cleared the way by her good example or, as Bob Dylan sang, "The times they are a-changin'." Perhaps it was a little bit of each, but his parents sent their permission for him to marry Maggie.

One obstacle overcome, they still had several to go. Bahá'í marriage was not recognized in Wyoming at that time, but they could resolve that by having two weddings—one Bahá'í and one civil. However, while they were filling out the application for a marriage licence, they noticed that there was an anti-miscegenation law in Wyoming, and they had to certify that they were both of the same race. They stared at the form in dismay. At that time, interracial marriage was still illegal in many states. The clerk looked at it and said, "Just ignore that. The law has just been struck down by the State legislature." So it was that John Hursey and Maggie had one of the first (if not the first) legal bi-racial marriages in Wyoming.

19. The Time of Man

Then can I walk beside you?
I have come here to lose the smog,
and I feel just like a cog in something turning.

Well maybe it is just the time of year,
or maybe it's the time of man.
I don't know who I am,
but you know life is for learning.

We are stardust.
We are golden.
And we've got to get ourselves back to the garden.

—Joni Mitchell - *Woodstock*

Sociologists have proposed every theory to explain the sudden rise in social activism that swept the youth of the western world in the sixties. For those of us who were a part of it, it just materialised, suddenly, as a palpable force. By 1960, the North American Bahá'í community had aged considerably, and the next generation of youth were just not getting involved. But the tides of social consciousness are always churning, and, out of nowhere, rogue waves can suddenly appear.

At school, I was taught to dive under my desk in the event of a thermonuclear attack, and all the fine trimmed lawns in the neighbourhood were being dug up to install fallout shelters. The nightly news was filled with pictures of coffins coming back from Vietnam and of Blacks being beaten up, water cannoned, and attacked by police dogs. The more socially aware youth were observing all this and thinking, "This just plain isn't right." Some joined political action groups, and some joined protest movements, but many Bahá'í youth began discovering answers in faith. What they found were dire warnings from the Writings of Bahá'u'lláh that these things were going to happen if humankind did not address the spiritual ills that were their ultimate cause. Suddenly, the Faith was not just a bunch of blue-haired old ladies sitting in endless meetings, but these youth were now seeing it as a tool that could be applied to heal many of these social ills.

When my dad and I joined the Bahá'í community in Casper, they were very involved with the local NAACP[38] group, and were working together toward greater equality in employment and housing. Casper had just opened its first 'indoor' shopping mall, and it was to be the 'new thing' in commercial merchandizing. However, on all the doors leading into the mall, there was a posted sign 'No Coloured Persons Allowed.' One of my classmates was a Black kid named Charles Mapp, and he was outraged that such a thing could still be happening in Casper, especially since the state Senate had passed the 1957 Wyoming Civil Rights Act, making it one of the leading states in this field. He convinced us to organize a protest against this violation of state law. We drew up placards, and were set to march that Saturday morning. However, someone must have pointed out that the signs on the doors of the mall were illegal, and the mall took them down before we got our chance to protest.

About this time, Jim Wonders and Reggie Newkirk, two young Bahá'ís in the United States Air force, were becoming very active. Jim worked in communications and Reggie was

---

38   National Association for the Advancement of Coloured People.

with the 451st Strategic Missile Wing (SAC) as an Air Policeman assigned to the Combat Defence Force, whose responsibility was to provide security for missile silos in Colorado. Both were on Lowry Air Force Base, which was between Denver and Aurora. They determined to get all the Bahá'í youth in the Rocky Mountain States activated. So they set themselves up as the 'Rocky Mountain Bahá'í Youth Committee,' appointed regional representatives (I was the Wyoming Rep.), and began organizing youth gatherings and teaching trips. All this was developing well until the National Spiritual Assembly heard about it—and, boy, were we in trouble!

The United States National Spiritual Assembly immediately sent Florence Mayberry out to shut down this renegade operation. We were told that no committees could be formed by individual initiative, and they could only function within their defined area of jurisdiction. If they were local, then a local Spiritual Assembly would be the responsible body; but, if they were regional or national, then the National Spiritual Assembly was the responsible body. As this committee had been formed to serve the whole Rocky Mountain area, we suggested that we could fall under the National Youth Committee, only to find out that there had not been a National Youth Committee for many years.

This seeming over-reaction has to be viewed in light of the dangers confronting the worldwide Bahá'í Community at this time. Charles Mason Remey had recently claimed to be the second Guardian,[39] which was an explicit contradiction of the covenant[40], and was expelled from the Faith by the Hands of the Cause.[41] (He was himself a Hand of the Cause at the time

---

39   See Shoghi Effendi in the Glossary
40   See Covenant in the Glossary
41   See Hands of the Cause in the Glossary

of his expulsion.) This had caused a crisis within the Faith, as some individuals and the French National Spiritual Assembly defected to follow Mr. Remey. The Hands of the Cause had quickly and courageously defended the Covenant and brought the worldwide Bahá'í community safely under the shelter of the Universal House of Justice. However, the followers of Mr. Remey were still very active, and brought an unsuccessful suit against the National Spiritual Assembly of the United States, claiming to be the true representatives of the Bahá'í Faith, and stating that all the assets of the Faith, including the House of Worship, belonged to them. The National Spiritual Assembly was, therefore, sensitive to any challenges to the Covenant or any deviation from the normal pattern of Bahá'í administration.

Betty Critez, unknown, Jim Wonders, Carol Manuelito, Marie Lee, and Reggie Newkirk at a 1963 teaching conference, Wind River Reservation, Wyoming

In the end, a solution was found, and the Rocky Mountain Youth Committee was put under the oversight of the Aurora Spiritual Assembly. The regional representatives were disbanded, but the committee could invite youth from throughout the Rocky Mountain area to attend gatherings. After this, the committee continued to function, but the original enthusiasm, energy and successes were just not there. The youth in the Rocky Mountain area were unhappy, and felt that a more effective system was needed to channel the energies of Bahá'í youth into the service of the Cause.

The National Convention[42] was coming up, and my dad and I were planning to attend, as usual. (The conventions were all 'open'[43] in those days.) Reggie phoned and asked if he and Jim could catch a ride down to Chicago with us. We agreed that we would all meet early Friday morning at Bob and Carol Manuelito's home in Laramie, Wyoming, and go from there. When we arrived, Reggie was already there, as he had come up the night before, but there was no sign of Jim. We called the Greyhound terminal to find out when the next bus from Denver was arriving, and, if Jim wasn't on it, we would have to leave without him. The bus arrived without Jim, so we headed off. As it happened, we had to drive through Cheyenne (which is on the bus route from Denver to Laramie) on our way. As we passed the Cheyenne bus station, we saw a bus just pulling out and my dad yelled, "Everybody wave goodbye to Jim."

In those days, it was customary to do home visits with isolated Bahá'ís whenever you travelled through their area, so

---

42   See Bahá'í Assemblies in the Glossary

43   When the Faith had only a few adherents, non-delegate Bahá'ís were welcomed as observers at the National Convention. Now the numbers are so great that this is no longer possible.

we decided to stop in for a few minutes at Orville and Jean Minnie's home. They were the only Bahá'ís in Cheyenne, and they invited us in to share a cup of coffee, so we relaxed and chatted for a short time, when the phone rang. It was a very agitated Jim Wonders, hoping against hope that we had decided to stop in to visit the Minnies. He had missed his earlier bus and was sure that this later bus would get him to Laramie too late to catch us. When his bus had stopped to pick up passengers in Cheyenne, Jim was sitting in the front passenger-side seat and was frantically saying the Fire Tablet, soliciting God's help that he not miss us. Then he looked up to see the whole carload of us waving goodbye as we drove past!

Now, with our full complement aboard, we headed East for Chicago. The National Convention was always exciting, and was a time to renew old friendships and make new ones. I wasn't aware of it initially, but it began to dawn on me that there were a lot more youth there that year than there had been in the past few years. The organizers noticed this also, so they hastily arranged for a hall and entertainers to provide a space for the youth to get to know one another. This seemed like a good idea, but no one could have foreseen what was about to happen. It seems that the Rocky Mountain youth were not the only ones who felt frustrated in their efforts to make the Bahá'í Faith an active force for positive change. Other youth, from across the country, also felt stifled and largely ignored by the administration. Or, as Howard Beale[44] would proclaim, "I'm as mad as hell, and I'm not going to take this anymore!"

The plan had been to start the event with greetings, and then have a professional dance troupe teach the youth some traditional folk dancing. However, some youth thought that the time would be better spent consulting on social action

44   Screwball character from the 1976 film 'Network.'

and the teaching work. One of the youth climbed up onto the stage, grabbed the microphone, and tried to get a straw poll from those present. But this broke out into raucous debate that lasted for about a half hour. Finally, the organizers put forward the suggestion that we follow the original program as planned, but all those interested in these other issues could meet, the next day, in the National Ḥaẓíratu'l-Quds,[45] formulate their issues, and select one of their number to present them before the convention.

The next day, the National Ḥaẓíratu'l-Quds was filled to the brim with those interested in these youth issues, and, after a lively consultation, we had drawn up our 'Manifesto'[46] and selected Steve Yamamoto to present it before the National Convention's assembled delegates. As a result, the delegates recommended that the National Spiritual Assembly appoint a new National Youth Committee and find ways to channel the energies of the youth into social action and teaching projects.

As we drove home, there was a strange energy in the car, as if we could feel that something really important had happened. Little did we know it then, but a rogue wave was forming that would utterly transform the character of the American Bahá'í Community and, beyond that, the face of the Faith throughout the world. The once-dormant Bahá'í youth arose, virtually en masse, to carry the Faith forward with a new vitality and vigour.

---

45   See Ḥaẓíratu'l-Quds in the Glossary

46   We don't have such things as 'manifestos' in the Bahá'í Faith. This nomenclature was common in the heady youth culture of the time.

20. Into Africa

In 1963, the Ten Year World Plan[47] had come to a successful conclusion. The Faith had grown significantly, and pioneers[48] had opened many new countries and territories to the Faith. The crowning glory of this plan was the election of the Universal House of Justice[49] (House).

After a year of assessment and planning, the House announced the Nine Year Plan. The primary focus of this plan was to consolidate the bridgehead made in so many new countries during the Ten Year World Plan. At the 1964 United States National Convention, this exciting new plan was announced, and the Hands of the Cause[50] attending the convention gave a stirring call for a wave of pioneers to rise up and rush forth to strengthen these nascent communities throughout the world. I was so excited, I started looking everywhere for my dad to see if we could go. Eventually, we saw each other in the throng. He came rushing up, and, before I could say anything, said, "Junior, I've been looking everywhere for you—let's go pioneering!"

Each country was given a list of goal areas that they should send pioneers to, and we eagerly waited for the list to appear in the U.S. Bahá'í News. The first country that we

---

47   See Tablets of the Divine Plan in the Glossary
48   See Pioneers in the Glossary
49   See Universal House of Justice in the Glossary
50   See Hands of the Cause in the Glossary

were attracted to was New Zealand, so we sent away for the appropriate immigration application forms. We eagerly filled them out and sent them back, but months went by and we heard nothing. Finally, we received notice that our application had been denied. We called the nearest New Zealand Consul office to ask for further clarification only to be told that current immigration was restricted to Caucasians only, and, as I was a half-breed, I did not qualify. Next, we contacted the National Spiritual Assembly of the Windward, Leeward, and Virgin Islands. This time, when filling out the forms for the various countries in this group, we were careful to neglect mentioning the fact that I was a half-breed. Still, a long time was going by, and we were not hearing anything.

Meantime, when attending the Geyserville Bahá'í summer school, we ran into some travel teachers just returned from Africa. They said that the National Spiritual Assembly of South Central Africa[51] was in urgent need of a couple of caretakers for the National Ḥaẓíratu'l-Quds.[52] Interestingly, we had seen a slide show presentation on some of the work going on in Southern Rhodesia when we had attended the Pine Springs Bahá'í Council Fire a couple of years before, and that had, at that time, aroused our interest about the possibilities of teaching in Africa. We immediately wrote to the South Central African National Spiritual Assembly, and they cordially invited us to come. Finally, the doors had opened for us! They recommended that we apply for a tourist visa, find

---

51   The regional National Spiritual Assembly of South Central Africa consisted of four countries: Nyasaland, Northern Rhodesia, Southern Rhodesia, and Bechuanaland. Today, these countries are known as Malawi, Zambia, Zimbabwe, and Botswana respectively, and each has their own National Spiritual Assembly.

52   See Ḥaẓíratu'l-Quds in the Glossary

work there, and then change it to a landed immigrant visa. So, in October of 1965, we were off to Africa!

I knew nothing about Africa and assumed it was a primitive place with grass huts and ferocious beasts. I had seen the movie *Swiss Family Robinson* a couple of years earlier and thought maybe we could build a large tree house in the jungle. Somehow, I thought I would continue my education through correspondence, working late into the night by lamplight, while lions roared in the distance. This was going to be such a cool adventure—or so I imagined.

We tidied up our affairs and bought our airline tickets. In those days, you could arrange as many stops as you liked between points, as long as they were along the way, so we set up our trip with stops in London, Paris, Rome, Athens, Cairo, Addis Ababa, Kampala, Nairobi, Lusaka, and, finally, Salisbury.[53] In London, we visited the Guardian's[54] grave and prayed for the success of our efforts in Africa. We then headed out for Paris, where we were able to meet with Madam Laura Clifford Barney, who had written *Some Answered Questions* from her table talks with 'Abdu'l-Bahá. This was such a charming visit, as it seems a special spirit surrounded those that had been in the presence of 'Abdu'l-Bahá, and He had favoured Madam Barney with so much of His time. We were unable to make contact with the Bahá'í community in Rome, so we visited several museums. One evening, my dad and I got separated, and I had to find my way back to the hotel on my own, all the while being pestered by the ladies of the night. Rome, after dark, was an anxious place for a sixteen-year-old kid from Casper.

---

53   This is now Harare, Zimbabwe
54   See Shoghi Effendi in the Glossary

*Junior and John Sr. in Athens on the way to
their pioneering post in Africa, 1965*

Next, we flew on to Athens. We were typical naïve
Americans who considered freedom of religion an internation-
ally recognized, inalienable right and boldly asked for information about the Bahá'í community. However, when we tried
to contact them, we were met with a very wary and tentative
reception. After they got to know us better, they told us that
Greece had been suffering various terrorist attacks, and, in
response, government hit squads were keeping an eye on all
suspicious groups, so the Bahá'í community was keeping a low

profile. Great caution was advised, not just for Greece, but other near East countries as well. In fact, when they found out we were going to Cairo next, they advised that we not attempt to contact the Bahá'í community there at all, and, in fact, it would really be better if we not even stop there. They arranged for us to meet Asfa Teasa, a Bahá'í who was a purser with Ethiopian Airlines, to change our tickets to go straight to Ethiopia. Asfa was so delighted to meet us that he invited us to stay with him in Addis Ababa until our scheduled flight to Kampala.

Addis Ababa was our first stop in Africa, and it was every bit as exotic and exciting as I hoped it would be. Asfa's house was in a middle-class suburb (by Ethiopian standards). It was a large brick and dagga[55] house with a strong timber frame supporting a beautiful thatch roof. It had no electricity or plumbing, and the servants would go, several times a day, to get water from the central fountain in the square. The house had deep overhanging eaves to shade the structure, and the monkeys would come in through these eaves and try to steal food from the kitchen. We slept under mosquito netting and were lullabied to sleep by happy revellers some distance away. The next morning, I was shocked to discover that my shoes were missing! I felt very vulnerable to think a thief had come right into my room while I was sleeping—only to trip over them, freshly polished, outside the bedroom door. Asfa's servant saw this, smiled, and said, "Good morning, master," in his best English. "Tea is ready."

Being a Bahá'í from North America, I found the whole idea of servants somewhat unsettling, and it took me a while to get used to it, especially the 'master' part, as we only have one Master and that's 'Abdu'l-Bahá! Eventually, we would get used to having servants once we had settled into our own

55   A plaster made from clay, straw, and cow dung.

home. Asfa had a couple of days off work, so he showed us around town and introduced us to many members of the Bahá'í community. There was an upper-class part of the city also, with electricity, plumbing, and paved streets, but I was so glad we were staying with him. To me, it was much more the Africa I had imagined.

After a couple of adventurous days, we caught our flight to Kampala, which is right on the equator. As we were coming in to land, an intense thunderstorm swept the airport at Entebbe. It dropped over three centimeters of rain in a matter of minutes. The aircraft hydroplaned down the runway for so long, that I thought we were going to take a swim in Lake Victoria. When the plane reached the terminal and the door was opened, it was just like a steaming sauna. As we were descending the air stairs, a humongous chartreuse grasshopper with blue and purple wings flew up and landed right on my neck. I batted the thing away and turned right around—that was enough Africa for me, thank you! Once I had regained my composure, I realized that I was just going to have to be courageous and get used to a whole new set of flora and fauna. In fact, I was later to discover that those grasshoppers didn't taste half bad once they had been roasted. To the Africans, they're a great finger food, enjoyed sort of like we eat popcorn.

We took a taxi up to the continental Bahá'í Temple for Africa and introduced ourselves to the caretakers. While my dad sat and visited, I asked if I could see the Temple. As there was no one around, it was locked, so the caretaker gave me the keys and I went up alone. The Temple looked solidly dignified in the bright African sun as I approached and unlocked the door. It had just recently been built, and, as I walked in, I noticed it still had that brand new smell. "Another victory of the Ten Year World Plan," I thought happily to myself, as I walked into the serene quiet of the temple's interior. I sat down in what I thought was the centre of the vacant auditorium and began to pray aloud that any difficulties that would interfere with our service in Africa be removed, and that our efforts would be helpful to this nascent community. I had no idea then, but would discover in the years ahead, how many times God would answer those prayers. The next day, we flew off to Kenya.

It was a bright sunny day when we landed in Nairobi. The city was clean and modern and was considered, along with Cape Town and Salisbury, to be one of the most beautiful in Africa. We stayed an extra day with Hand of the Cause Musa Banani. This was a very enlightening stop, as Dr. Banani had his finger on the pulse of the continent and was able to give us an objective update on the situation in South Central Africa. The political situation was very volatile, as Britain was in the process of granting independence to its former colonies, and many rival groups were competing to take power. In Southern Rhodesia, the whites were determined to hold on to power, and they had stopped the move toward 'majority rule' in that country. On the Bahá'í front, there were about twenty pioneers and 600-800 local Bahá'ís in the four countries. He said that things were going well, and that he was sure that our services would be greatly appreciated. We were now a day behind schedule, so we skipped our stop in Lusaka and flew straight on to Salisbury.

We arrived in Salisbury on a sunny Saturday afternoon and deplaned down a long flight of airstairs to the apron. As we did, we heard a mighty cheer go up from the balcony above the arrivals lounge. We looked up to see that we were being greeted by a crowd of smiling faces and a chorus of Alláh-u-Abhás.[56] We waved vigorously and shouted back our greetings. We had our visitor's visas in order, but, as we had no airline tickets home, it took us some time to clear customs and immigration

---

56   See Alláh-u-Abhá in the Glossary

before we could join the excited throng waiting outside. Most of the friends were pioneers from the Salisbury area, but some had come in from the more outlying areas, including Hand of the Cause John Robarts and his wife Audrey from Bulawayo. We would be staying with Shidan Fatheazam and his family for the first little while, until we had what we needed to set up housekeeping in the National Ḥaẓíratu'l-Quds.

Everyone was invited back to Shidan's house for tea and goodies. As we drove through the clean and beautiful city of Salisbury, past modern schools and the university, any pre-conceptions I had about life in Africa were quickly dispelled. There would be no tree houses or lions roaring in the night here. This very welcoming greeting on the part of the friends in South Central Africa was greatly reassuring to us, and we were eagerly looking forward to our new life in Africa.

Downtown Salisbury, Rhodesia, 1965

21. Starting Over

When we arrived in Africa, we had nothing but our clothes in our suitcases. We had no job, no school plans, and no knowledge of the language, customs, and taboos of the local people. We were virtually starting over from scratch. We had come, at the invitation of the National Spiritual Assembly of South Central Africa, to be caretakers of the National Ḥazíratu'l-Quds (National Centre). Though the National Centre was furnished, we had to get all our own personal effects, such as bedding, dinnerware, cookware, and whatever else we needed to make the place livable. The Fatheazams insisted we stay with them until everything was in order, but we were anxious to settle in, so we quickly got the essentials and moved into our new home. One essential was a vehicle, so my dad went out and bought a used Vauxhall Viva as a temporary measure. However, the car turned out to be a real trooper, and we kept it for many years. The friends also advised us to get servants and a dog right away. We were not quite ready to take those steps yet, but it was soon to become apparent why both of those were necessary.

The National Centre had not been lived in for about a year by the time we got there, and, while the buildings were in good structural shape, there was a lot of work that needed to be done. The NSA had hired a security guard who had lived in the servant's quarters while the main house was empty, but his contract ran out a week before we came. Security was the big issue, and we were again advised to hire servants. We learned that if the house is left unattended, even for a couple of hours, everything will be taken—and I do mean everything! We were robbed twice while we lived there and they did an amazing job. In North America, the only things with real resale value are electronics, jewelry, silver, and gold. But in Africa, things like clothes, bedding, dishes, and cutlery are the things that have value to the local population. So the thieves move quickly, pull the bedding out from under the mattress, dump all the clothes from the closet and the contents of all the drawers from the dressers onto the bed, bundle it up in seconds, and take it out to the waiting pickup truck. Additional bedding is spread on the dining room table, all the dishes and cookware are tossed on top, and this is also bundled up. In less than ten minutes, everything is gone. So, like it or not, hiring a servant was added to our 'to do' list.

The next goal was to get me into school. The nearest high school was Lord Malvern in Waterfalls, so I went there to enroll. The Rhodesian school system was based upon the British model, and, in fact, the exams are set and marked in England. The students of my age were in Form Four and they would sit their (Ordinary) 'O' Level exams at the end of the year. Passes in seven subjects were required to obtain the 'O' Level. Based upon the results of these exams, the students would be streamed into: Form Five for those who did not receive seven 'O' Level passes but wanted to try again, Form Six 'M' (Matriculation) Level for those who passed the 'O' Level and wanted to go on to university and Form Six 'A' (Advanced) Level for those who wanted to go to Oxford or Cambridge University. This was going to be a challenge for me, as the other students had studied for four years for the 'O' Level exams, and I had less than one year to catch up.

Next, I needed to get a school uniform. The Lord Malvern uniform consisted of a royal blue blazer with red and white pin striping, matching tie with the school crest on it, grey pants, white shirt, and a straw boater with a matching hat band. Most of the kids said they hated it, but I thought it was a rather natty getup, especially the cool straw boater, which made me feel like I was in the FBI.

1967 National Convention of the Bahá'ís of South Central Africa, held in the National Ḥaẓíratu'l-Quds, Salisbury, Rhodesia

Meanwhile, my dad prepared his résumé and had professional typists make several copies of it for him. Now he was ready for job searching in earnest. He had no idea what to expect, as there were a limited number of companies that utilized professionals in his field. We said some heavy-duty prayers before he set out. Rather than call and set up an appointment, he thought it would be better to go down in person. Perchance he could meet the head of human resources face-to-face. His first stop was Anglo American Mining Corporation, one of the largest and most profitable mining companies in the world. He walked into their gleaming office tower, downtown, and asked to see their head of human resources. The receptionist looked at him blankly and asked, "Who?" My father elaborated, "You know—personnel, recruitment, hiring?" Still no light was dawning, so he said, in exasperation, "I'm looking for employment. Could you please give my résumé to whoever does your hiring?" She tentatively took the envelope, and my dad left feeling completely dejected.

I had just come home from school and was changing out of my uniform, when the phone rang. I picked it up, and a voice asked, "Is Mr. Sargent there?" "No," I said, "He's out at the moment. Can I take a message?" "This is Mr. Peterson, Regional General Manager of Anglo American. Can you have him call me as soon as he gets in? I'll give you my office number and my home number. Please have him call me whenever he gets in, even if it's late." I interrupted Mr. Peterson and said, "Hold on a second, I just heard him come in." I handed the phone to my dad and he talked for a few minutes, then hung up. He looked at me and smiled broadly, "I have a job interview right now." And he turned right around and headed back downtown.

Southern Rhodesia had a real shortage of professional people, and all the main corporations and the government recruited overseas in Europe and America and paid large sums of money to relocate these professionals and their families down to Southern Rhodesia. They never have professionals with my dad's qualifications just walk in off the street and drop off their résumé! Anglo American didn't even have a recruiting department in Salisbury. All their recruitment took place out of their main office in Johannesburg,

South Africa. Here comes my dad with a master's degree in Geo-chemistry and experience as an analyst with the United States Bureau of Mines, and all they have to do is say, "You're hired!" Apparently, Mr. Peterson was afraid that, if he didn't act quickly, some other mining corporation would surely snap him up. They were so glad to have him that they prepared all the immigration papers, and we were landed immigrants within a few weeks. So it was that, on the first day of job-hunting, my dad landed a position as a senior geologist with Anglo American.

Next, we needed to hire a servant, so we let it be known around the block that we were looking, and, the next day, several people turned up for the job. We quickly realized that having servants was an important part of the economy for the local people and was considered a good job to have. We were able to find a good man who came with an excellent reference from his previous employer, so we hired him. One of those who came gave my dad a long story of how he spent his last penny to come for the interview, so my dad gave him a ten bob note[57] to get home. The next day, when my dad came home from work, there were two individuals there with stories about needing this or that, and any spare change would help. Again, my dad gave them each ten bob and sent them on their way. The next day, the line-up of people in need was around the house and out into the street. My father realized that this just wasn't going to work, as he didn't have the ten million dollars required to give a couple of bucks to everyone who needed it. Another lesson learned—helping the poor in a country where nearly everyone is poor is a real tricky proposition.

Our new servant's name was Raphael. He quickly got the kitchen set up to his liking, shooed my dad out from helping,

---

57   Ten Rhodesian Shillings – about $2.60 US in those days.

and said he would prefer to do things himself. He, rightly, figured out that we were new to having servants, so he got us all straightened out as to how the household would run. One thing we did insist on, however, was that he never call us 'master.' So he started calling my dad 'bwana John' and me 'little boss.' Another thing we wouldn't do was call him 'boy' but always referred to him by his proper first name. Once we got all those things sorted out, we all got along fine, and the household ran smoothly.

Now came the question of a dog. Most whites had at least two dogs: a little, yappy 'alarm' dog and a big, mean 'guard' dog, usually a Shepherd or a Doberman. They had fenced yards and kept the big dogs leashed during the day but free to roam the property at night. But, as we were caretaking the National Ḥazíratu'l-Quds, we wanted to keep it welcoming to the friends at all times, so locked gates holding back vicious dogs was just not on the menu. In the end, my dad brought home a beautiful, young Rhodesian ridgeback bitch named Sheba. She would grow into quite a large dog, as they were bred to hold lions at bay. However, they are extremely friendly and loyal to their owners, but tend to be shy of strangers. This worked out well for us as her size would discourage prowlers, but if one of the friends approached her, she just ran away.

The confirmations were flowing freely. All these seemingly problematic issues quickly fell into place. In no time at all, we were all set up in our new home.

22. Creepy Crawlies and Ambush Bushes

When we arrived, the National Centre had sat empty for over a year. This was enough time for all sorts of beasties to take up residence and for the one-acre lot to go wild. Africa seems to be owned by the ants and termites; to me there looked to be at least three ants per square meter of the continent. The ants around our house were the tiny sugar ants, so they didn't bite, but they were a constant nuisance. A lot of people put the legs of their dining room table in saucers of water so they could eat their meals without competing with the ants. The termites were a constant threat to wooden structures of every kind. Once, one of the friends asked me to get his ladder, which he had set on its side behind his garage. I came back with what looked like a giant comb, as the termites had completely eaten the rail that was in contact with the ground. All the telephone poles, railway ties, and fences in the country were made of steel; otherwise, they would be gone in no time.

The local kids, on the other hand, found live termites to be a great snack. They would poke a thin branch down the nest so the soldier termites would attack it, then they could pull them out and eat them. Eventually, I got brave enough to eat cooked insects, but eating live insects was always going too far for me. Once a year, at the beginning of the rainy season, the termites grew wings and the queens and males took to the air. This was an incredible spectacle, as the evening sky was filled with billions and billions of insects. Driving became virtually impossible, as the windshield wipers would get completely gummed up with the squashed insects.

Spiders were also a problem. On the second day at our new home, I got up and put my pants on. As I pushed my foot through the pant leg, I heard a dull thump on the floor. As I looked down, to my horror, I saw a gigantic reddish-brown baboon spider scurrying away. I ironed my pants every day for a month after that, before putting them on. One day, I heard a commotion in our front hedge. A bird had been caught in the web of a red-legged golden orb spider. I don't know if these spiders actually eat birds or if the birds were just a nuisance messing up their web. These were pretty formidable spiders nonetheless, and I dreaded walking through the bush and ending up wearing one on my face. The house was also full of wall spiders, and I carefully went around killing as many of them as I could find—until one of the friends suggested I leave them, as they were good at keeping the ant population down.

African King Baboon Spider

On the whole, though, Southern Rhodesia was not a very spidery place. What Southern Rhodesia did have in abundance was snakes. There were over thirty different species of snake there, and many of them are among the most poisonous known to man. Everyone kept a snake-bite kit with appropriate anti-venoms in their fridge, and these had to be changed every few years. While cleaning up the property, we encountered several harmless grass snakes but also came across two Egyptian cobras. One time, I put my hand over the back gate to unhook the latch, when I felt something soft and moving. I pulled my hand away quickly and investigated. A beautiful, but deadly, green mamba was moving along the top rail of the fence. Among the most dangerous snakes there were: black mambas, Gaboon vipers, boomslangs, puff adders, black adders, and spitting cobras. These last snakes were the ones I feared most, as they could blind you with their venom from up to two meters away. A few days after we arrived, one of the pioneers, Larry Hautz, who ran a snake park, called to say that a lady had phoned the Park to complain about a python in her chicken coop. He asked us if we wanted to come along to help catch it. Pythons are protected game in Rhodesia, so you can't kill them, but Larry's Snake Park provided a removal service. So my dad and I, along with Larry and a worker from the park, went after this snake to relocate it far from the city. This monster was about four and a half meters long and weighed over 70 kg. It took all four of us to get it into the truck. Lugging this thing along was the first time I really realized that a snake is an animal, not just some slimy underworld creature.

One school break, a friend of mine asked if I wanted to go camping with him and his father in the Nyanga Mountains on the eastern border of the country. They owned a plot of land and had built a small cabin on it. It was safer to stay in a cabin than a tent, as the area had large populations of warthogs and baboons as well as a fair number of leopards, any one of which could easily enter a tent if they smelled food. My friend and his father slept on army cots, while I slept on the floor between them in my sleeping bag. In the middle of the night, I heard an animal or animals rooting around outside the cabin. I was hoping it was warthogs, because baboons have little hands with opposable thumbs that can open doors and latches as well as a human can. Suddenly, I heard the door to the cabin jiggle, and I thought, "Oh no! The baboons are trying to get in." So I pulled the sleeping bag tightly over my head and lay there motionless. My friend was also awakened by the muffled sounds and thought it might be me going out for a pee. He looked down at the sleeping bag in the pale moonlight coming through the window. Because I had it over my head, he couldn't see me, so he put his hand down to check if I was still there. Meanwhile, I felt a hand patting over my face through the sleeping bag and thought, "Oh my God! A baboon is trying to get into my sleeping bag!" I quickly thought of a plan. I forcibly threw off the sleeping bag and yelled as ferociously as I could, hoping to scare any baboons completely away from our campsite. When I looked around, all I saw was my friend and his father, backs up against the sides of the cabin, eyes wide as saucers. After a moment, my friend said, "It's okay. It was only me checking to see if you were still there." Nothing was said in the morning, but I noticed that my friend's father seemed a little suspicious of me after that.

Generally, Rhodesia was not as friendly a camping country as North America. There were just too many things to be careful of. And I'm not just talking about lions, elephants, and rhinos; little things like flies, mosquitoes, and snails can be deadly too. My dad's job kept him pretty much in the bush, and it wasn't long before he had contracted malaria. Another fear was contracting trypanosomiasis (sleeping sickness) from the tsetse flies or schistosomiasis from infected freshwater snails. Once, on a teaching trip to Zambia's Zambezi Valley, I stupidly drank some water that had not been boiled first and came down with amoebic dysentery. Fluids came pouring out of both ends, and I was in danger of severe dehydration. My doctor gave me the appropriate medication and told me to drink plenty of Coke. "It tastes as good coming up as it does going down," he enthused.

And it was not just the fauna that was problematic. I found that I was allergic to several of the trees and bushes there. It seemed that the doctor was continually prescribing one type of salve or another for the rashes on my hands or feet.

I don't know if you saw the movie 'The Gods Must be Crazy.' If you did, you'll remember when Dr. Steyn flushed the terrorist out from his hiding place by shooting the rubber tree plant over his head. Its caustic latex can cause severe burns to the skin and eyes. We had a rather old and unsightly rubber tree in our garden at the National Centre, and I thought it should come down. I tried cutting off one of the lower branches with an axe, but found it bounced too much to cut cleanly. After examining the problem more closely, I surmised that one hard, swift chop, just at the junction of the main trunk, should snap it off cleanly in one blow. About shoulder height there were two other branches of about the same diameter on either side of the tree, so I mischievously called Lazarus, our gardener, over to help. I bet him I could cut off the one branch with fewer strokes than he could the other and suggested he go first. Just as I had done earlier, he started chopping about 30 cm out from the trunk, and, with all the bouncing around, it took him ten or eleven chops to cut it off. Now it was my turn. I got a good grip on the axe, lifted it high above my head, and, with as much speed and power as I could, brought it down. This plan might have worked—however, I forgot to check my overhead clearance. The axe grazed an overhanging tree and, instead of cutting the branch off cleanly at the trunk, landed on its side ten to twelve centimeters out and sprayed white, sticky, caustic latex right into my face and eyes. For about two days, I had a big, fat, red face with my eyes swollen shut. Probably just as well, as I didn't have to see Lazarus's smirk every time he looked at me.

I wasn't the only one who had trouble with the flora. My dad came home one day with his face all scratched up. "What happened to you?" I exclaimed. Apparently, he was driving his Land Rover over a muddy track, and his windscreen got covered with mud. He had a windscreen wiper but no washer. He had stopped several times to wash the mud off but finally decided to drive with his head out the window. Unfortunately, he drove by a wataba tree and it swiped right across his face. Wataba trees are notorious thorn bushes covered with 8-10 cm, super-sharp thorns. "Confucius say," he replied, "man who drive with head out window—lose face."

23. What am I doing in the 'In-Crowd'?

My entire school career I was always the chubby, little half-breed, who was bullied by just about everyone. By the time I was in high school, in Casper, I had developed a haughty disdain for cliques and felt self-righteously proud to be an individual and not some striving sycophant. I would watch the group dynamics with a detached interest: the charismatic leader, some of whom loved the attention, while others appeared vaguely annoyed by those clinging to them; the sidekick(s), who loved the leader and desperately wanted to be like them; a larger group of individuals that wanted to be where the action was; and a group of more loosely attached kids who moved from group to group. I did have some good friends at school, but we were definitely not part of the in-crowd. My last six months in Casper were the worst, as we had moved down to the Sandbar. This was the part of town where the Blacks and Hispanics lived. The local Hispanic clique took a dislike to me or rather, I should say, took a liking for harassing me, so I had to take a different route home from school each night to make my movements unpredictable.

I was not sure what to expect in a racially segregated society like Southern Rhodesia. I kept the fact that I was a half-breed quiet and passed for White. All of the public schools were segregated into Black, White, and Coloured. The Catholic Schools were integrated, but, as many of the White Catholic parents preferred segregation, they sent their kids to the public schools. The Coloured schools were mostly for the East Indian children, but biracial Black/White kids went there too.

*Junior on the cricket pitch. "How do you play this game?
And why is it named after a noisy insect?"*

As the climate in Southern Rhodesia was almost perfect all year round, sports was the number one social activity, with soccer, rugby, cricket, and water polo the main events. In the evenings, after the games, it seemed that everyone gravitated to the numerous beer gardens to drink the night away. This proclivity for sports was evident in the schools also, and most of the cliques developed around the school's sports heroes. In other words, my new school was a very jock-oriented culture.

I was obviously not going to fit in with that, as I was never very interested in sports in general and knew nothing at all about soccer, rugby, cricket, or water polo. It seemed clear that I was going to be in the out-crowd again in this new school.

I arrived at school about a quarter of the way through the year and, at first, everyone seemed excited to find out about the 'Yank;' however, after the initial interest, things cooled off quickly. Now remember, this is 1965, and the youth counter-culture revolution is sweeping America and Europe but is many years away from Southern Africa. Even so, a number of young people at my school were aware something was happening. Two days after I arrived, a new kid from Liverpool, United Kingdom, also started at the school, and, even though we could hardly understand each other's English, we immediately became friends. His name was Allen O'Shea and he was from the hometown of the Beatles, which, in those days, was absolutely the coolest place in the world to be from! Although most of the recent albums for the popular music groups were also popular in Rhodesia, there was about a two-month delay before they reached the record shops in Salisbury. So Allen and I hatched a plan: we pooled our money and sent it to a friend of Allen's in Liverpool, who would buy a copy, on the very day it was released in England, of the latest Beatles' album and airmail it down to us. We had their latest album almost two months before anyone else, and we would host special listening parties for a group of interested friends. This became a hot ticket item, and a number of kids wanted to be included. So that I also had a copy of our new album, I bought a HiFi reel-to-reel tape recorder. Knowing this, some of the students asked me to record some music for one of the school dances —so I got a bunch of friends together and asked them to bring all their records over. We made a four-hour tape of our favourite music mix that we took to the dance. This went over so well that the tape was used for several more dances. While making these music mixes, my friends and I would talk about issues like the anti-war movement, banning nuclear weapons, social justice, and de-colonization. Soon we had developed a little counter-culture group all our own.

Toward the end of the school year we had a school play competition. The play put on by our house[58] won the best play award and I won the best actor prize. It wasn't fair, though, as I played an American tourist in England, and I seemed to have the accent down perfectly. The local repertory group was asking me to join, but I didn't have enough time. It seemed that I was becoming interesting; I even belonged to some weird oriental cult—how cool was that! Before long, a group of the school's intellectuals and artists had gathered around me. They had always been at the school, but, until now, they had never had a collective centre to bring them together. To my chagrin, I discovered I was not only the centre of a clique—we were the new in-crowd!

The school year was coming to an end, and the 'O' Level exams were fast approaching. However, graduating from high school in Rhodesia was kind of an anti-climactic affair. The last day of school came like any other day, and we went home. There was an exam schedule posted on the bulletin board, and we showed up in the school auditorium to take the exams at the appointed time. Some of the exams were three to three-and-a-half hours long and were quite difficult. Afterward, our group would head out to the 'cave' for chips (French fries) and Coke. (We called it the 'cave' because the é on the neon sign for café wasn't working, and we started calling it the 'caf,' which soon morphed into the 'cave.') Somehow, it felt like we

---

58   The students at the school were divided into four houses for intramural competitions.

were French intellectuals at the turn of the twentieth century discussing the latest events in politics and the arts in the cafés of Paris. When the exams were finished, they were sent to Britain for marking and we would receive our marks by mail a month or so later.

I passed the required seven 'O' Level subjects, so I moved on to Form Six-M. I needed four 'M' Level subjects to matriculate into university, so I selected only five subjects for the year. This meant that I went to school four days a week and, most days, had one two-hour class. We had a Sixth Form common room that was quite comfortably set out with sofas, plush chairs, and a work table in the middle. I did all my homework in the common room, which left my evenings free. The windows of the common room faced west, and, one sunny afternoon, a group of us were sitting looking out at the clear blue sky with the sun brightly shining in, and I was going on about the process of progressive revelation. What we couldn't see and didn't know was that a huge thunderhead was moving in from the east. One of my fellow students had heard enough and stood up, boldly proclaiming, "I don't believe in God!" Just then, a bright lightning bolt arched across the clear blue sky and hit a lampstand right outside the common room window with an almighty crack and a boom that shook the whole building. We all jumped in surprise! I jokingly turned my eyes heavenward and said, "Okay, okay, no need to make all that fuss about it." [59] We all laughed—except the chap who had made the comment. He looked genuinely shaken by the event.

As our former clique was now scattered between different Forms with different subjects, it was not as tight a unit as it had been the previous year. However, we would meet from

---

59   Quoting Clarence the angel from *It's a Wonderful Life*.

time to time at 'our' table in the 'cave' and continue our enjoyable discussions. At the end of the year, I passed my 'M' Level exams, and our little band of counter-culture revolutionaries went our separate ways. For a while after I graduated, I would often meet with these friends in the various beer gardens around town, but, as I did not drink, I soon tired of this and gradually became a recluse. Still, I often think with fondness of the friends I made during my short stay at Lord Malvern High School.

24. Lunch with Lafayette

"Junior, you wanna go swimming at Larry's?" I had heard the phone ring and my dad answer it, so I set down my new Scientific American and yelled, "Sure."

Larry Hautz was an elderly pioneer to Southern Rhodesia who Rúḥíyyih Khánum[60] once called 'one thousand percent American'. He had been a successful businessman in Milwaukee and was a 32nd Mason and a charter member of the Izaak Walton League of America. Anything that he wanted to do had to be done right now and obstacles fell in front of him like a house of cards. When he became a Bahá'í, in the late '40s, he left the Masons and soon applied for pilgrimage.[61] The first day in Haifa he went to put a sandwich in the fridge at the western pilgrim house only to discover there wasn't one; he went straight to the appliance store and ordered four of them. When the delivery truck arrived, an amused Shoghi Effendi graciously accepted one for the western pilgrim house and one for the house of 'Abdu'l-Bahá and sent the other two back.

Shoghi Effendi knew talent when he saw it and asked Larry to stay on after pilgrimage and assist him with some stalled property transactions with the City of Haifa. Within a couple of months Larry was able to bring these transactions to a successful conclusion. I understand that, for some time afterward, personnel at the planning department would break out

---

60   See Amatu'l-Bahá Rúḥíyyih Khánum in the Glossary
61   See Pilgrimage in the Glossary

in a cold sweat just at the mention of his name. One day when Larry flushed the toilet at the western pilgrim house it backed up. No one knew where he got the overalls and shovel from but soon he was out in the yard digging up the septic system. While he was working, Shoghi Effendi and Rúḥíyyih <u>Khá</u>num came by the pilgrim house and were surprised to see Larry in the ditch. The Guardian smiled and nodded and went into the pilgrim house, but <u>Khá</u>num looked back and gave Larry a 'What the heck!' look. They had barely entered when <u>Khá</u>num came flying back out and ordered Larry out of the ditch. "We can't have Shoghi Effendi's personal representative to the city digging sewers—get cleaned up, the Guardian needs to discuss something with you."

When Larry had completed the work with the City of Haifa, he asked the Guardian if there was anything else he wanted him to do. Shoghi Effendi said, "Yes, I'd like you to pioneer to Africa." So Larry went home, tidied up his affairs, and, with his wife Carol, headed out for Southern Rhodesia.

It was a warm, sunny morning as my dad and I drove the twenty-odd kilometres out from Salisbury to Larry's farm. Larry had a large market garden supplying fresh vegetables to the Salisbury wholesalers. In addition, he had a motel and a snake park. The snake park was a roadside tourist trap with an incredible array of snakes, baboons, crocodiles, and a cheetah, but that was only a front for the park's real function as a supplier of anti-venom for snake bite kits. Behind these buildings he had a beautiful house on a hill overlooking a fairly large man-made lake, with the African savannah stretching out as far as the eye could see.

Carol greeted us at the door and ushered us through to the covered patio out back. Larry was out there and he introduced us to his guest—L. Ron Hubbard. After a cursory introduction, I went and got my swim trunks on and did a few laps of the pool, while the men sipped lemonade and talked on the patio. The pool deck was three steps down from the patio and was separated by a low wall topped by a flowerbed. I lay down on a deck chair just below the guys and resumed reading my magazine.

Larry Hautz at his snake park in Rhodesia. 1000% American!

At first I was not interested in the conversation going on just above me, but then I heard Larry say, "Tell John how you got involved in all this scientology stuff." Mr. Hubbard cleared his throat and said[62], "Yes, it's quite an interesting story, actually. As I mentioned, I was a science fiction writer before the war. When the war broke out, I was made a commissioned officer in the Navy because of my extensive sailing experience. But we got into some heavy combat in the Dutch East Indies and I was wounded and almost blinded and ended up in the VA hospital stateside. After the war, I found that I just couldn't write anymore, and, although I tried many things, my life seemed to spiral downhill. I fell into a deep depression and thoughts of suicide kept creeping into my mind."

Larry's servants interrupted the conversation to bring out a nice summer lunch of sandwiches, salad, and fruit. I moved up onto the patio with the adults. Carol joined us and we served ourselves as Ron continued.

"So my life was going to hell, and I began to try to analyze what was happening to me. One night, after a dream, I had a revelation—all these things that were blocking me were just obstacles in my mind. They were the remnants of negative things that had happened to me in my earlier life, and, if I could devise a way to root them out, I would be clear to move forward. So I developed, through trial and error, a system of techniques that would allow me to do this. I called this process 'Dianetics.' I found that, by utilising these techniques, I had cured myself, and I was happy and productive once more. So much so that my friends noticed the change and asked me what I had done. Once I had finished explaining it, one of my friends said, 'You know, I've come to a dead end at my work. Maybe your process could help me.' So I worked with him and he quickly regained his interest in his work. Then my friend said to me, 'This is really great! You could develop

---

62   Although this story is placed in quotation marks, these are not direct quotes but only my memories of his story.

seminars and sell this technique.' On reflection, I felt that this could really be useful to the many thousands of people who had hit dead ends in their lives, so I agreed."

"I wrote the book 'Dianetics' and began giving seminars and, to my delight, it was an overnight success. It became obvious to me that the best way to disseminate these ideas was to franchise it. But there were so many people needing help, I thought I should show this technique to the American Medical Association. But the College of Psychiatrists saw this, not as an opportunity, but as competition, and tried to charge me with practicing medicine without a licence. When that didn't work, they got the IRS on to me about where all the money was going and who was going to pay all the taxes. I was hounded from every corner until a friend said, 'This is ridiculous. People take their problems to their ministers all the time, and the church is never hassled. In fact, they get away tax free.' 'What did you say?' I asked. 'The church is never hassled,' he repeated. Suddenly, the light dawned—I'll start my own church!"

The servants cleared the table and brought out some more lemonade and pastries.

"'You're going to need a bible,' my friend said. Well, I always thought the Bible was a rather poor bit of pulp fiction, and I'm a fantasy writer—producing a better bible should be no problem. In no time at all, The Church of Scientology was born and the AMA and the IRS were just going to have to lump it. In the meantime, tens of thousands of people have reached 'Clear' with the help of the 'Dianetics' program."

The afternoon was wearing on, so I went and got dressed, and, when I came back, everyone was saying their goodbyes. The sun was getting low to the horizon as we drove silently back to Salisbury. "Dad, why did the AMA oppose Mr. Hubbard's helpful program?" I asked. My dad was silent for a minute, then said, "Junior, you have to thoroughly investigate ideas before buying into them. In reality, things are seldom as they seem on the surface."

I thought about that for a moment, then went back to reading my magazine.

25. The Dynamite Express

During the Nine Year Plan, the principle objective was to open new localities to the Faith and to work with these localities to help them form local Spiritual Assemblies. The pioneers would work with the African township communities in the evenings, during the week, and go out to the more remote areas of the country on the weekends. A group of active Rhodesian Bahá'í youth got together and decided that we could help by planning a teaching trip to a remote area and trying to establish a new locality there.

We set up a planning group and met in Shidan Fatheazam's study/guestroom to work out the details. This planning meeting stood out in my mind, as it was an occasion for one of those infrequent 'hyper-reality' moments that I've had during my life. We were moving along fairly easily with our consultation at first, but soon Denny Fatheazam and I started butting heads over some issue or other, and we bogged down. We were getting nowhere fast, so finally, Don Fouché said, "Okay, stop. Let's say a prayer and regroup before we continue." I was not in the mood for praying, but I tried to sit there reverently as someone started saying the prayer. I could not see what Denny was talking about, for it was obvious: I was right. Why was he insisting on doing it his way? While I was mulling this over in my mind, I suddenly saw what he was saying, and it was brilliant! At the same time, Denny was also thinking about the issue and suddenly saw what I was saying, and realized that the two ideas were not incompatible.

At that moment, something inexplicable happened. Normally we live our lives alone. That is, everyone's consciousness is mutually exclusive and closed to others, even those we love and empathize with. Suddenly, Denny's consciousness and mine became one. For the first time in my life, I had the experience of feeling like we were one soul in two bodies. It's very hard to explain. It was not as though I was in his mind and he was in mine. It was more like our minds were free and connected through some higher consciousness, and a feeling of great joy and wonder pervaded us both.

We looked at each other and knew instantly that we were both experiencing the same thing. The joy was so overpowering that, right in the middle of the prayer, I leaned back and started exclaiming, "Wow! Wow! Wow!" over and over. Denny got up on the bed and began jumping up and down. All the other youth stopped and just stared, startled, and confused. Don was the first to say something and he began, "Oh, I've seen this before, it's blah, blah blah. . ." Both Denny and I spontaneously laughed, because, in our shared reality, we knew that he had no idea what we were experiencing. This shared consciousness lasted only a minute or so and slowly began to fade back into normal reality.

I left the meeting, went out into the warm night, and lay on the grass wondering what had just happened and why. Over the years, I have often thought of that experience, but I can't decide if it was just a gift given by God to Denny and me because we were able, in consultation, to look beyond our own point of view to objectively see the other person's perspective and thus win for ourselves His good pleasure, or if this was a more important glimpse into the future of human consciousness. 'Abdu'l-Bahá tells us, *"Wherefore must the friends of God, with utter sanctity, with one accord, rise up in the spirit, in unity with one another, to such a degree that they will become even as one being and one soul. On such a plane as this, physical bodies play no part, rather doth the spirit take over and rule; and when its power encompasseth all then is spiritual union achieved. Strive ye by day and night to cultivate your unity to the fullest degree.*"[63] If Denny's and my experience that night is the future of human consciousness, then the coming civilization will be incredible beyond belief! It will truly be the Kingdom of God!

Soon we were able to get our act together again and we finalized our planning. We chose a village near a nickel mine, in the remote highlands area of the country. However, this area was only accessible by rail. Originally, there was a small tribal village in the area, but, as the mine grew, dormitories were constructed for migrant mine workers and a number of shops set up business to serve the growing number of wage earners there. As the new mining town was likely rough and transient, we would concentrate our efforts on the nearby traditional tribal village.

Some of us worked and some of us were still in school, so we decided we could take the mining train up on Saturday morning and take it back home on Sunday afternoon, as the train took only one trip up and back per day. We would be staying overnight, so we got our camping gear together, selected some teaching materials in the local language, and bought some candy and hostess gifts for the homes we would visit. Two in our group spoke the local language so we wouldn't need to find a local translator. All seemed well prepared, and we were very excited about the whole enterprise.

We gathered together early Saturday morning, said prayers for the success of our trip and headed off for the train station. Then we hit our first snag. "Sorry," the agent said, "we take

---

63   Abdu'l-Baha, *Selections from the Writings of Abdu'l-Baha*, p. 203

no passengers up to the mine on Saturday morning, because that's the explosives train." What? That would ruin our whole Plan! "We need to take the Saturday morning train. We have no other time available," we explained to the agent. "Are there no coaches on this train?" The agent said there was one third-class coach, but we would need to talk to the supervisor before he could issue us tickets. The supervisor didn't arrive until almost time for the train to depart, but he was sympathetic to our plight and agreed we could go as long as the leader of the group signed a waiver indicating all understood the danger and freeing the railroad of all liability. We hurriedly boarded the third-class coach and settled in for our great adventure.

A third-class coach had wooden bench-type seats and there was no glass in the windows, so the smoke and grit from the engine and track swirled around us as we sped along. It was a perfectly beautiful day with the warm sun streaming in, so being in the open air was actually quite nice. Behind the coach were two boxcars and a caboose. We assumed that the explosives were in the boxcars, but after a few minutes we forgot about them and enjoyed the beautiful African savannah as it swept past.

We arrived at the mine about noon and asked directions to the local tribal village. The village was about a kilometre down a narrow footpath, and we passed through orchards of mango, guava, and papaya as we got nearer to the compound. I noticed that the wataba hedge went all the way around the village, not just the livestock enclosure, which was unusual, compared to most villages I had seen. We met with the kraal head and gave some tea and condensed milk to his wife. We told him we were there to tell the people about the new Mondiwa (spiritual teacher) who had come from Mungu (the Creator) to bring peace to the world, and we would like his permission to home-visit with the families in the village.

We also asked permission to camp for the night outside the compound.

Don Fouché (on overturned grain mortar)
explaining the Faith in a remote village

The kraal head was very welcoming and told us to feel free to tell the people our message, but he said camping outside the enclosure was not safe and that we could use his guest-house for the night. I asked if there were a lot of wild animals around the village and he said, "Yes, but it is drunken miners that pose the real danger these days." We thanked the kraal head very much and headed out of his house. The afternoon was a good time to teach because the morning chores had been done, and it was usual for the people to rest in the heat of the day. Outside, a group of kids had gathered to see the strangers, and Don had a bag of candy which he began handing out. Soon, Don had a huge gang of excited kids surrounding him as we walked through the village.

We met one of the villagers and asked if we could share our message with him. He agreed and suggested we sit under a nearby mango tree as it would be cooler there. Other villagers came, and soon we had a whole circle of men eager to hear why we had come. (Women did not usually take part in such meetings.) We talked and joked with them most of the afternoon and there was a general atmosphere of good fellowship. Several times we asked if any of the villagers would like to be part of our Faith, and, by late afternoon, about a dozen had indicated that they would like to join. As the sun began to set, we thought we must let them go to supper, and we could settle into the guesthouse and eat the sandwiches we had brought for our supper. But, while we were meeting, other arrangements had been made, and soon bowls of sadza (the traditional cornmeal staple in Southern Africa) and relish[64] began to appear. We got out our tea and condensed milk that we had intended as hostess gifts and gave it to some of the

---

64   A thick stew made of chopped meat and vegetables. A small amount of sadza was shaped into a shell-like configuration and dipped into the relish and eaten that way—mmm mmm good!

women to prepare for the group. So it was that we spontaneously shared the evening meal with the whole village.

Some men had gathered firewood, others had brought out bowls of corn bia (a locally brewed alcoholic beverage), and several of the women began to sing softly in the background. Before long, the bia was working its spell and the drumming and beautiful four-part harmony of the singing became louder and more exuberant. In this little village, in the middle of nowhere, this impromptu concert was one of the most powerful I have ever attended.

For me, the day had been long and emotionally draining, so I thanked the kraal head and headed up to the guesthouse for the night. As it was still quite warm, I just slathered my exposed skin with mosquito repellent and lay down on top of my sleeping bag. The singing was a pleasant lullaby as I drifted off to sleep. I don't know how long the singing went on or when the other youth came in, but soon I was aware that it was morning. However, I also became aware that I was not alone on my sleeping bag! I startled fully awake and sat up. This sudden movement also awakened my bed companion— a scrawny, flea-bitten, Rhodesian ridgeback dog—who got up sleepily and wandered out of the guesthouse.

Most of the villagers were up and about their chores as we packed up and prepared to head back to Salisbury. We gathered together for a few minutes with all the villagers that had indicated they wanted to join the Faith, left them literature, and said prayers with them before heading off to a happy chorus of goodbyes. We felt that this teaching trip had been a real success, and we had made many good, new friends with these people, who we looked forward to visiting again.

We arrived back at the mine in plenty of time for the train and bought some sugar cane, from some young venders, to munch on during the trip home. This time, we rode in a second-class coach with padded seats and windows, but I wasn't really comfortable as I kept squirming and scratching all the way home, chasing real or imagined fleas from my erstwhile bunkmate.

26. The Bored Computer

Ever since I was old enough to know what an occupation was, I wanted to be an architect. As soon as I left high school, I began to wonder what I was going to do next. The University of Rhodesia and Nyasaland, which was located in Salisbury, did not offer Architecture or Civil Engineering. Therefore, I would have to leave my pioneer post to become an architect, and this was something I just wasn't prepared to do. So I prayed for guidance, and Bahá'u'lláh provided the following advice: *"Concerning the means of livelihood, thou shouldst, while placing thy whole trust in God, engage in some occupation. He will assuredly send down upon thee from the heaven of His favour that which is destined for thee. He is in truth the God of might and power."*[65] So I needed to look for some job while I waited for God to provide what was destined for me.

Rhodesia, in those days, was very much a colonial country, with a very stratified society. All of the menial jobs were done by the blacks; almost all the mercantile jobs were done by the East Indians; and the technical, administrative, and clerical jobs were done by the whites. So that left me to find some sort of clerical position. After several weeks of frustrating, fruitless search I noticed an interesting newspaper ad for a computer in the Department of the Surveyor General.

We know computers today as those little black boxes and display screens, but back in the '60s computers were people

---

65   *Tablets of Bahá'u'lláh* p.268

who—well—computed. I went down for an interview with Mr. White, who was head of the department, and I was hired. While I was happy to have gotten any job, I must say I was surprised to get this particular one, as the work was basically doing trigonometry all day, and it was ironic that my lowest 'O' Level pass was in trigonometry.

All the cadastral surveys[66] done in the country had to be submitted to the Surveyor General for review and approval prior to their being registered. The computers had to take all the survey documentation and field books and redo the surveys at their desks, looking for errors. The front desk clerk placed each survey in a file folder with a review sheet, numbered them in the log book, and placed them in the 'For Review' box in numerical order. When a computer was ready to check the next survey, he went to the log book, dated and signed out the next one, and took it back to his office. We were not allowed to pick and choose; we had to take the next survey in order from the list. The job was to take the review sheet and sign it and then begin to tick off each review step as we completed it. If the survey was a basic subdivision of a property by a straight line, the whole review process could take only an hour or two. However, if the survey was for twenty-seven kilometres of railroad right-of-way winding through the Nyanga Mountains, it could take months to review! Having completed the review, we placed the survey in the 'Approved for Registration' box and signed out the next one.

There were eight of us computers and we were assigned two to an office. Ken was my partner, a thirty-something young man hugely into motorcycles and motocross. He had been a computer for about eight years and was very helpful

---

66   Cadastral Surveying refers to the cadastre, or collective record of lands that many nations have established.

in getting me up to speed with the work. At first, it was interesting and challenging, but, as the months went by, I began to wane in my enthusiasm for it. For one thing, it was I who happened to go to the 'For Review' box at the wrong time and ended up with that survey for twenty-seven kilometres of railroad right-of-way! For another, once you got the hang of the process, that was pretty much the end of the stimulating aspect of the job. After several months of this, I had to admit I was getting kind of bored with the work.

On the weekends the pioneers would go
out to the remote areas of the country.
Counsellor Shidan Fatheazam at top left

One morning, as I was working on a survey, the door to our office unexpectedly opened. I heard a sudden commotion behind me, as Mr. White, our department head, surprised Ken sitting with his feet up on his desk, reading the morning paper. After things had settled down, he said, "Morning gentlemen," and left, closing the door behind himself. I looked at Ken, who was red as a beet, and said, "What was that all about?" Half an hour later, Mr. White's executive assistant (EA) stuck her head into our office and said that Mr. White wanted to talk to each of the computers, one at a time, and Ken was next. Apparently the 'In-box' was full and it looked to Mr. White like the productivity of his computer unit was falling behind. He decided that it was time to give us the ol' pep talk: telling us how important our work was to the progress of the country; how property owners depended upon us to turn these surveys around quickly and efficiently; how substantial amounts of money were hanging in the balance on these property transactions, etc., etc.

Soon Ken came back. "You're next," was all he said and pointed out the door. I made sure my jacket and tie were neat and straight and that my longish hair was as under control as it would allow itself to be, then headed off to Mr. White's office. As I entered, Mr. White smiled and offered me a cigarette. He was a genial man in his late fifties or early sixties, balding, and with a grey mustache. I waved away the offer of a cigarette as he bade me be seated in a chair opposite him. As I sat down, I noticed that he had all the computers' names listed on a yellow pad with numbers written to the right of each name. As I was the newest member of the crew, I was last on the list. The number 14 was written after my name and it was double underlined. I suspected that this was the number of surveys done by each of his computers so far that month and my number was higher than anyone else's on the list.

This was, by no means, a fair measure of productivity. As it happened, every time I had gone to the 'For Review' box that month, it had been a rather simple survey. If this morale booster had taken place two months earlier, he would have written a big fat '0' next to my name, as I was still working on that blasted railroad! It was obvious from his manner that he felt he was interviewing the new rising star of his department. "Well tell me, Mr. Sargent, you've been with us what—five months? How are you liking the work?"

Now I was caught between honesty and not wanting to hurt Mr. White's feelings or his high expectations of me, because, in truth, I really didn't like the work that much. I shifted uneasily in my chair and fumbled for the right words to say. Finally, I said something like, "This is not the type of work I saw myself doing for very long." I could see the surprise and disappointment in his eyes, but there was nothing I could do to take the words back. He then asked, "What type of work is it you see yourself doing?" Without hesitation, I said I wanted to be doing architecture. "Architecture!" he said, "Well, that's very interesting." He had a good friend who was an architect with the Department of Public Works (DPW), and, just the day before, had had lunch with him. His friend, Mr. Capon, had recently been put in charge of a new co-op program to train architectural technologists. Mr. White suggested that, if I liked, he could call and see if there were any vacancies in the program. I smiled, shook his hand, and said, "I would like that very much indeed!" and headed back to my office.

As I have mentioned earlier, Rhodesia had very few highly trained technical people. As a result, both industry and government had to advertise in Europe and America and pay the cost of relocating them and their families. Therefore, the government, in cooperation with the Salisbury Polytechnic College, had embarked on a series of co-op work/education programs to fill the need for technicians in several areas. One of the first of these was the architectural technology course which consisted of a three-year diploma program where the students worked four days a week and attended classes at the technical college one day and two nights a week. All while being paid.

The next day, Mr. White called me into his office and said he had wonderful news. The program was for six trainee technologists and had started the week before, but one of the trainees had suddenly dropped out. Mr. Capon was anxious to re-fill that position and would be most interested in interviewing me that afternoon. Also, as this was going to be an interdepartmental transfer, I would retain my grade and pay rate even though the trainee rate was lower.

The interview with Mr. Capon went very well, and first thing Monday morning I was to report to the Department of Public Works to start training as an architectural technologist. In the Quran it says, "Man plans, and God plans and surely God is the best of planners."[67] I couldn't see how it would be possible for me to study architecture and remain at my pioneer post, but apparently, God had destined it for me. I was amazed how answering an ad for a dead-end clerical job could lead me straight to where I needed to go!

---

67   *Qu`rán,* Surah 8 v.30. I have used a bit of poetic license here, as the
      quote refers to those evil ones who plot against God and are defeated.
      I've used it to indicate how the plans of the ignorant (me) can still be
      guided aright by God.

27. A Case of Mistaken Identity

Now I had been accepted into the Architectural Technology co-op program of the Department of Public Works, and I was all excited to get started. The program had started a week and a half earlier and I was a late arrival. I walked into the Public Works complex, which had been the old British South African police barracks and stables. It was a two-square-block labyrinth of single-story buildings that would take me a couple of months to fully be able to find my way around. I walked in the main entrance and up to the reception desk, announced that I was the new architectural technologist, and waited expectantly. The receptionist just stared back blankly. "And?" . . . "And I haven't got a clue where I'm supposed to go," I said. "Who are you here to see?" she asked. The only person I had seen previously was Mr. Capon, who was head of the program, so I suggested maybe I should be talking to him. "No . . . it says here he's out of the office today," she mumbled, half to herself. "Wait, here it is. New architectural technologist to see Mr. Fielding," she said triumphantly. "Just a moment and I'll try his number."

Shortly, a nervous little man came squeaking along to the reception area and eyed me up and down in a suspicious manner. "You're the new architectural technologist?" he asked. "Yes," I responded uncertainly, as I eyed him up and down suspiciously. "Good, good, good. Follow me. My office is just here," he said as he squeaked off down the corridor at full speed. All the floors in the building were covered in a dung-coloured ship's linoleum, and, as I was to observe, the only shoes that Mr. Fielding wore were Hush Puppies. Of course the crepe soles squeaked loudly on the linoleum with every step he took.

Mr. Fielding had been an architect in Edmonton, Alberta, but his practice had failed there, so he had responded to an ad for an architect for the Department of Public Works in Rhodesia. He had a quick and nervous manner and reminded me of an absent-minded professor who knew exactly what he wanted and concentrated intently on it to the exclusion of reality going on all around him. Mr. Fielding would become my great friend and an important mentor in my life.

We chatted for about half an hour, and he was particularly interested in the fact that I had grown up on Six Nations Reserve in Ontario. Then he showed me my first assignment. These days, if anyone wants a desk, they go to Staples or another office furniture store and select the one they want. In those days, in Rhodesia, there were no office supply stores. You designed what you wanted and a carpenter built it for you. Mr. Christopher, the Comptroller of Public Works, was the head honcho for the department and he wanted a new desk. He had called Mr. Fielding into his office and drew on a piece of paper what he wanted. Mr. Fielding handed me the diagram and said, "Just draw it up, giving all appropriate dimensional data, but do not bother with the joinery as the master carpenter will decide that." With that he showed me to my cubicle, introduced me to the other three technologists in the office, and left.

I must admit I felt a little apprehensive. A bit like being thrown into the deep end of the pool and watching as the swimming instructor just walked off. I wasn't sure where to begin, and, as I sat there on my stool, I happened to look up at the ceiling. Just above me I saw a slim government manual stuck to the ceiling with a drafting pin—*Government of Southern Rhodesia, Department of Public Works, Manual DPW 167-64, Drawing Office Procedure.* I climbed up on my stool and pulled the manual down. In it was all the basic drawing office procedure, right down to how to sharpen a pencil; which pencil to use—7H for basic layout, 5H for construction lines, etc.; how to lay out a drawing; and what size paper to use. Interestingly, the example they used to illustrate these concepts was—a desk! I found out from the other technologists that there was a stack of appropriately sized blank sheets with proper borders and title block already pre-printed on them. So I placed the sheet on my drawing board and set to work. I had taken a drafting course in high school, back in the States, so I wasn't a complete newbie at it, and it wasn't long before I had the desk drawn. The desk in the illustration was not identical to what the comptroller wanted and also had what I thought was an old-fashioned style, so I made the appropriate modifications to the design.

A teaching trip to a remote village. Pioneer Eniyat Sohaili in the upper left

I was just starting to dimension the drawing when I heard, somewhere in the background: blam, squeak, squeak, squeak, vrumph, squeak, squeak, squeak, CRASH! I jumped as Mr. Fielding burst into the room. Advancing menacingly towards me, he said, "You're not the new technologist!" But, as he approached closer, he saw the work I had accomplished so far and stopped with a perplexed look on his face. Seeming to have forgotten why he came in, he carefully surveyed the design and muttered to himself, "Good, good, good, yes, well . . ." Then, more particularly to me, he said, "Good, Mr. Sargent. Yes. Well. You just carry on and I'll have a talk with you a little later." And he squeaked off rapidly down the hall.

The Trainee Architectural Technology program was overseen by Alexander (Sandy) Jacks and all the students were in a common drawing office under his direction. Mr. Jacks was a technologist himself, but his real talent was in architectural rendering. He rendered projects for all the architects in the department, and just about every office had at least one framed copy of his beautiful renderings. I don't know whether he was happy babysitting (as he would say) the trainee technicians or not, but he kept a tight rein on them. The trainees were given basic drafting exercises, their efforts were adjudicated by Mr. Jacks, and their progress was carefully monitored.

When I had first walked into the department, I should have said I was the new TRAINEE technologist, and I would have been sent directly to Mr. Jacks' office. As it happened, Mr. Fielding was expecting a new trained architectural technologist that very day, and I had been mixed up with him. After our chat, and after he had set me to work, the real technologist had turned up. He was an Armenian refugee from Turkey, and although, he had a Certificate in Drafting Technology, he could hardly speak any English. After a frustrating hour of attempting to communicate with him, Mr. Fielding asked him to wait while he tried to sort all this out. It was at that point that he had stormed into my office, noticed what progress I had made, and set off to discuss the situation with the comptroller.

Mr. Fielding was so frustrated trying to communicate with the real architectural technologist that he was adamant that he could not use him. The government had brought the Armenian and his family all the way from Britain and felt obliged to find a position for him. In the end, they came up with a strange plan. The Armenian would take my place in Mr. Jacks' drawing office and take a course in English as a second language. I would work for Mr. Fielding as his technologist but would attend the Polytechnic courses with the other trainees.

Mr. Jacks apparently did not like the arrangement arrived at by the comptroller and Mr. Fielding, and I quickly came to see that Mr. Jacks and Mr. Fielding had conflicting personalities. Now, Mr. Jacks was just as puzzled as everyone else about what to do with the Armenian and didn't like the fact that I was not under his direction like the other trainees. He made his dislike of me clear, even though I was always pleasant with him and was effusive in my praise of his rendering work. "You have to learn to walk before you can run, Mr. Sargent," he would say at every opportunity. He was referring to the slow and deliberate curriculum that had been developed for the trainee program, but I had skipped ahead and was working on actual projects. Meanwhile, Mr. Fielding just assumed I was a trained technologist and used me as such. I enjoyed the challenge, came up to speed quickly and developed a good working relationship with him. Another factor that made our relationship click was that I had recently come from North America and my design sensibility was very much in accord with his. We enjoyed talking about architectural style during tea time. These were some of the very happy days of my early career. At the time, I didn't know or appreciate the significance of this mix-up, but it proved crucial to my development as an architectural technologist. In the end, it was another sign of the Creator's invisible hand always at work in the background.

28. There but for the Grace of God

I was in the Education section of the Department of Public Works. We had four architects and four technologists. Although there were no hard and fast boundaries, each technologist was loosely assigned to one of the architects. I was Mr. Fielding's technologist. The other young technologist, Ray (about four years older than me), was assigned to Mr. Cunningham. Ray was a handsome, young, energetic go-getter with a red Alfa Romeo and a model for a girlfriend. He was gregarious and inclusive, trying to get everybody involved in whatever he had going. (It was he who had pinned the drawing office procedure manual to the ceiling because he thought it was 'stupid simple.') Mr. Cunningham was a middle-aged Scotsman, and, in my opinion, the most capable architect in the department. His work was beautiful, not only in the design but particularly in his drafting. Both Ray and I copied many of his techniques and were far better draftsmen for it.

Another of our technologists was Steven. He was thirty-something and married, with one child. He was building his own home and went on endlessly about the ups and downs of the process. He was the technologist for Mr. Martinis, a flamboyant English/Italian who was always punning and joking around. In many ways, I felt that he was not a serious architect, and, fortunately, Steve was able to carry him quite well.

Mr. Stanley Smyth was the fourth technologist on our team. He was an older, quiet English gentleman who had been a draftsman most of his life. His freehand lettering was perfect and it looked like it was stencilled on the drawing. It was a peculiar font that I really liked, and I tried to copy it, eventually with some success. He never took part in the general discussions at tea time, and I never knew much about him or if he was really aware of the rest of us in the drawing office—except one day when I had a tune stuck in my head and must have been whistling it incessantly, because suddenly, from the far corner of the drawing office, Stan slammed his pencil down and shouted, "Mr. Sargent! If you whistle that tune one more time I'm going to break your arm!" Stan was the technologist for Major Fenshaw,[68] an ex-British Army Corps of Engineers architect who ordered everyone around like he was still in the service. He was particularly annoyed by Mr. Martinis' joking around and we could frequently hear him shout, "Come to your senses man!" Quiet snickering would break out in the office, because I think all of us were secretly pleased that Mr. Martinis was a constant thorn in Major Fenshaw's side.

The Major was somewhat of a cartoon of himself and always walked quickly and proudly, with an erect posture and his umbrella folded up under his arm like a swagger stick. The one story of Major Fenshaw that everyone in the department liked to tell and retell was the time that a new school building was under construction in Highlands (an upper-class suburb of Salisbury). The foundations and drainage line trenches had just been dug when a huge cloudburst had flooded the whole site. The site superintendent had phoned in a panic, saying that everything was ruined! So Mr. Fielding and Major Fenshaw went out to take a look. Fortunately, it looked as if no real damage was done, and Major Fenshaw told the superintendent to send everyone home and that, when the

---

68   I believe his name was spelled Featherstonehaugh, but it was pronounced Fenshaw

water subsided and the site had dried, he was sure everything would be okay. The site was made of thick, red volcanic clay, and, as he and Mr. Fielding got back to their car, they both had big globs of thick, red mud on their boots. Mr. Fielding pulled up a nearby survey stake and began poking at the mud. Major Fenshaw watched this process for a few moments and then impatiently said, "Not like that, man—like this," and waded into a nearby puddle. It turned out that the puddle was a two-metre-deep drainage trench that had just been excavated, and Major Fenshaw went down over his head in the muddy water. With the area covered in slippery mud, it was all Mr. Fielding and two nearby labourers could do to drag the Major out of the trench.

Mr. Fielding was a hardworking, diligent, and creative architect who knew what he wanted and insisted on getting it. However, he was also a man of nervous disposition and could become overwhelmed by the complexities of ordinary life. When he had his own practice in Edmonton, his office was on the second floor of a three-story walk-up. After an initial blush of success, his practice had floundered; he was in severe financial distress and his wife had left him. One day, his mind on other things and not paying attention to where he was going, he walked up to the third floor by mistake and found himself confronted with a recently vacated office space. Thinking the bailiffs had repossessed everything, he just sat on the floor and went to pieces. When he came out of the mental hospital, he cleaned up all his affairs and headed off to a new life in Africa.

One day, I came into his office to find him trying to put together ten copies of a progress report on a project we were working on. Unlike today, when it would all be done on computer, he had had the typing pool type up ten copies of the report, leaving spaces to paste in the photos he had taken. He had partial reports and stacks of photos all over the place, and was trying to find the right photo for the right page, in the—which copy? It was a disaster! I suggested that this was a job for a technician, and that I should take it to the drawing office where there was room to spread out. This was a pet project of his and he was reluctant to lose control of it, but, in the end, he let me finish assembling the report for him.

Birthday of the Báb Holy Day celebration in Highfields African Township

Another episode showing the kind of Mr. Magoo world Mr. Fielding lived in was during a meeting with the Minister of Education. We were presenting a proposal to the Minister about a new project, and Mr. Fielding was talking on at great length about its many features. When he wanted to read something from the report, he would reach into his breast pocket, take out his glasses, and then replace them when he was finished reading. He had done this many times up to this point in the presentation. The Minister, who was seated immediately to his right, was growing weary and took off his glasses, set them on the table, and began rubbing his eyes. At that moment, Mr. Fielding said, "It says right here on page 24 of the report. . ." Reaching down, he picked up the Minister's glasses. My heart skipped a beat, because I wasn't sure Mr. Fielding's nervous system could withstand what was about to happen next. Suddenly, and inexplicably, Mr. Fielding found himself in an alternate universe. He stared at us for some time uncomprehendingly, blinking his eyes in complete bewilderment. Everyone at the table choked back laughter as the Minister said, "I believe those are my glasses Mr. Fielding."

As I mentioned before, Mr. Fielding was partial to Hush Puppies shoes, which were not available in Rhodesia, so he had them sent to him by a relative in Canada. Because of the loud squeak they made on the linoleum, everyone in the department knew when he was coming. Our drawing office was next door to his office along the long central corridor. However, his office had two doors into it, the second of which was blocked off. In the three years I worked in the department, Mr. Fielding never once failed to try to enter our office through that second blocked-off door. We could all hear him coming—blam squeak, squeak, squeak, vrumph (against the blocked-off door), squeak, squeak, squeak, and then our door would open! Often we could hear him charge out of his office and seem to forget where he was going. Blam, squeak, squeak, squeak, squeak (long pause) squeak, squeak, squeak, blam! Back into his office.

Tea time at the department was at 10 a.m. and 3 p.m. A servant would bring the tea trolley to the drawing office, and we would all gather round to gab. The tea consisted of hot tea and sweet warm milk expertly poured by the servant into each cup. Eventually, both Mr. Fielding and I preferred coffee, so the department supplied us with a bottle of 'Camp Coffee.'

This was a bottle of coffee syrup about the size and appearance of HP Sauce. Two teaspoons of this syrup and warm milk made a not bad cup of coffee. Often, Mr. Fielding and I would leave the others and go to his office to discuss progress on our latest project. These discussions would sometimes lead off into long, casual conversations about architecture in general. I gathered much useful insight into the profession from these talks and was grateful for the time he would spend with me.

I had a strange relationship with the five other trainee technologists who worked together in Mr. Jack's drawing office. Although I went to school with them, they had developed an esprit de corps among themselves, and I was a bit of an outsider. I don't think they were jealous of me per se, but I was working on completely different projects and never interacted with them at the office. Initially, the only one I got to know well was Dean. Dean lived out my way, and so, after school, he used to give me a ride home on his motorcycle. This was particularly helpful for the night classes as the buses ran more infrequently after six o'clock in the evening. The night classes were Wednesday and Friday nights from seven until nine. Dean and I would meet in the Polytechnic cafeteria for supper, attend the classes, and ride home together.

One Monday morning at tea time, Paul, one of the other trainees, came running up to me and asked me if I heard what had happened. "No. What happened?" I asked, seeing the concern on his face. "Dean was killed riding home from school on his motorcycle Friday night."

I was shocked and appalled to hear this sad news, both because Dean was such a good and talented kid that it seemed like such an incredible waste, and because the accident must have happened just after he had dropped me off at home. That second thought hit just a little too close for comfort and shook me up—thinking, "There but for the grace of God go I."

29. The Nuffield Czar[69] of the DPW[70]

It was my opinion that pioneering was a source of Divine blessings and that the mighty wind of God was at my back. I progressed rapidly in my training as an architectural technologist, both at school, which I enjoyed and for the first time in my life excelled at, and at work where Mr. Fielding provided me with a constant stream of challenging projects. One particularly challenging and interesting project, which was to affect my career throughout my stay in Rhodesia, was the Nuffield science lab conversion.

When I went to school in Rhodesia, science was taught in the traditional English way. The teacher worked at a demonstration bench at the front of the lecture hall, while the students sat in rows of tiered seating, watched the demonstrations and took notes. But all of this was about to change. A revolution in teaching the sciences was taking place in Britain. Based more on the American pedagogy, the Nuffield Science Foundation developed a new curriculum, where the students performed the experiments themselves and the teacher roamed the lab providing instruction and advice. The Ministry of Education decided that Rhodesia had to transition to this new approach also, and Mr. Fielding was to head up the conversion of the lecture halls to the Nuffield style labs.

---

69   A person appointed by government to advise on and coordinate policy in a particular area
70   Department of Public Works

Poring over all the data for the Nuffield curriculum (three full 3" ring binders), it soon became obvious that such a conversion was impossible. What was really needed were all new specifically designed lab units. The Ministry of Education agreed and asked us to prepare a standardized lab module to be built at every high school across the country. The first step was to study the curriculum to determine every piece of apparatus and equipment needed, all safety requirements, all consumables and their safe storage and disposal needs. Based on this data, we came up with a design utilizing two lab classrooms with a teacher's preparation and storage area between them. Once the concept for the standardized module had been agreed upon, it was time to get down to the detailed design.

As I mentioned before, in those days in Rhodesia, you couldn't go to a lab equipment catalogue and order what you needed. You had to design every lab bench, stool, cabinet, cupboard, and drying rack and have them specially made. So I had my work cut out for me and I energetically began this rather enjoyable task. However, change was afoot at the Department of Public Works (DPW).

This was the late '60s and the face of international travel was rapidly changing. Air travel was becoming cheaper and within the reach of the average citizen, and airplanes were changing to the larger commercial jetliners. All these things made the current Salisbury International Airport woefully out of date and inadequate. The Minister of Transportation decided that a new international terminal building was required, and Mr. Christopher, the Comptroller of the DPW, decided that Mr. Fielding was just the man to head up the project. I must admit I was apprehensive to see my mentor leave and was wondering what his replacement would be like.

Time was going by and I continued to work on the standardized lab module, but no new architect was forthcoming to replace Mr. Fielding. Also, interestingly, none of the other architects showed any interest in what I was doing or asked how things were coming. By that time, I had completed all the detail work and was working on the site plans and elevations for the three modules that were planned for the first year of the conversion project.

Pioneer Dale Allen (upper left) with the Musarura family in Highfields African Township

Then one day the Minister of Education was talking to Mr. Christopher and asked, "Oh, by the way, how is the Nuffield lab conversion project coming along? We only have five months before the first three conversions need to be completed." Mr. Christopher said he would check and get back to him, hung up the telephone and hit the panic button! He called Mr. Capon, the chief architect, and asked who had replaced Mr. Fielding on the Nuffield project. Now Mr. Capon hit the panic button and called all the education architects and technologists to a meeting in the boardroom—RIGHT NOW! Mr. Martinis stuck his head into our drawing office and said, "Emergency meeting in the boardroom chaps. Let's go." We technologists looked curiously at one another, put on our jackets and headed out. When we arrived, Mr. Cunningham and Mr. Martinis were there, but Major Fenshaw and Stan were away in Bulawayo inspecting a project. Mr. Cunningham asked no one in particular, "Anyone know what's up?" Mr. Martinis suggested someone must have eaten the strawberries,[71] but we were all too nervous to laugh. Then Mr. Capon and Mr. Christopher came in together and our anxiety level went into high gear.

Mr. Capon asked, "Who's working on the Nuffield project?" Instantly, all eyes in the room turned and looked straight at me! Suddenly, I felt guilty of something terrible, but I wasn't sure what. I said, "I am, sir," in a weak voice. "What stage are we at?" he asked anxiously. "Well . . . well I, ah . . . in my opinion . . . we should be able . . . that is, once my work has been checked . . . to go to tender in a week . . . or so?" There was a long silence like everyone was not sure if they could feel relieved yet or not. "Can we see what you've done so far?" Mr. Capon asked. I brought in the drawings and spread them

---

71   To make a big fuss about nothing – This is a reference from *The Cane Mutiny* with Humphrey Bogart (1954)

on the table, and everyone began going over them diligently, but with no particular purpose in mind. Mr. Christopher, who looked almost giddy, stood up and quietly said to Mr. Capon, "I'll go tell the Minister we're going to tender in a week or so," and left the meeting.

The three lab projects were constructed and were a big hit. But, because of the complexity of the program, nobody else wanted to touch it. I continued on with the conversion projects—even after I transferred from the Education Unit to the Transportation Unit, and even after I left government altogether and worked in the private sector. All the Nuffield lab conversions followed me wherever I went.

30. When Jacks Become Jokers

The trainee technologists were in the break between second and third year when Mr. Christopher stuck his head into my drawing office, curtly said, "Mr. Sargent, I want to see you in my office in five minutes," and disappeared. "What the heck . . . what have I done now?" I thought to myself. I had let my hair grow quite long and had stopped wearing my tie around the office—maybe he's calling me up on my personal appearance. Where is my tie anyway? I got my tie and blazer on, slicked down my hair the best I could, and set off. When I got to Administration, Mr. Christopher's executive assistant smiled welcomingly and said, "He's expecting you," and nodded toward his door.

"I see, Mr. Sargent, that you've done very well in the first two years of our program," Mr. Christopher began, without looking up from the papers he was studying. Now looking right at me, he continued, "Mr. Capon, Mr. Fielding and I have decided that you will not continue on to the third year with the others." I just stood there motionless; this was not making any sense. "We feel you are a competent technologist now," he continued, "and therefore I am promoting you to Architectural Technologist level 1 grade and rate as of the end of the current pay period. Furthermore, I am transferring you, at Mr. Fielding's request, to the lead technologist on the new International Airport Terminal Project."

I was stunned, yet delighted, with this turn of events, but I was completely unaware of the hardships ahead. Even though

I was in the middle of another set of Nuffield lab conversions, they moved me out of my cubicle in the education drawing office into a two-board drawing office in the Transportation Unit. I shared this office with Mr. Ted Savage. As lead technologist, I worked directly with Mr. Fielding and controlled the work flow for the other team members. Besides Mr. Fielding and me, our team consisted of Ted Savage, Paul Robbins, and Amir (the Armenian with much improved English).

Although Mr. Savage was a technologist, next to Mr. Cunningham I considered Ted the best architect in the department. His bold use of structure to define his design ideas for a building and his innovative use of materials set his designs apart from the more pedestrian work of his contemporaries. It was, I thought, unfair, both to him and to me, that he was not the lead technologist on this project. On the other hand, I could see the office dynamics that made this set-up necessary. Ted found it hard to work as a team player, and, to a certain extent, so did Mr. Fielding. It seemed to me that I was placed in this position as a sort of buffer. Unfortunately, an additional problem was that Ted was a good friend of Mr. Jacks, who persisted in his disapproval of me and began playing the role of mischief-maker behind the scenes.

While I was happy for the promotion, I felt very uncomfortable to be put in that position. Mr. Jacks' constant disparaging comments made me want to avoid him, but both Paul and Amir were in his drawing office, so that was impossible. To make matters worse, Mr. Jacks began undermining me in the eyes of all three of the project's technologists. No direction I gave or help I offered seemed to escape his criticism. I thought, "'Abdu'l-Bahá was often put in this position by his brothers. What did he do?" He did not attack back. Rather, he prayed for them and put his trust in God—so I would try to do the same. I prayed and was patient, while working hard to build trust with each of the technologists.

Pioneer Marty Dean (second from right) teaching in a remote village

The first phase of the project had two parts: to build a new fire station to bring the airport up to the new International Air Transport Association (IATA) standards; and to transform a hangar into a new temporary domestic terminal. After some preliminary concept discussions for the fire station, the team agreed upon a design utilizing a precast, pre-stressed, concrete 'U' channel roof system that had been proposed by Mr. Savage. This appeared to be the best solution from both an aesthetic and budgetary point of view. I set Ted to work on that project and told him that he should let me know if he needed any drafting assistance, and I would get Paul or Amir on it right away. But I knew he wanted to handle every single detail himself. This had two benefits from my perspective. First, it would give us a first class building, and second, it would keep Ted happy, busy, and off my back. I tackled the hangar conversion myself. All of this work was done under the direction of Mr. Fielding, who had final say on all aspects of the projects.

While designing the lounge for the temporary terminal, I decided to do something more daring, so I came up with a more Miesian[72] design, utilizing aluminum, chrome, glass, mirrors, and neon, which I thought was a younger, fresher approach. Mr. Fielding was not impressed. He felt people expected a more traditional English pub atmosphere, with subdued lighting, dark, rich colours, and dark-stained, heavy, oak millwork. I insisted that we should give it a try. After all, it was a temporary terminal, and, if people didn't like it, we could always go back to the traditional style in the new, permanent terminal building. But Mr. Fielding wasn't buying it. "You know, Mr. Sargent, I have given you lots of room to incorporate your design ideas in the work we have done together, but in this case I'm going to have to insist that you do it in the manner I have suggested." "No problem," I said and headed back to the drawing board.

With that clear direction, I was able to quickly rework the design into the more traditional English pub style and came up with what I thought were some nice classic millwork details. When I had completed a sheet of these new details, I sent for a copy to be printed, so I could go over them with Mr. Fielding, and headed out for lunch. When I returned, Mr. Fielding called me into his office. He did not look happy; in fact he looked almost ill. "I thought, Mr. Sargent, that we were friends, that you were very mature for your age and that you were able to handle responsibilities in a trustworthy manner,"

---

72   Referring to Ludwig Mies Van Der Rohe – Master of the international style of architectural design – "Less is More"

he began almost through his teeth. "What on earth. . . ?" I thought. "Now I see that when I ask you for one simple request," he continued, "how childishly you have responded. I can't express my disappointment in you." I had no idea what he could possibly be talking about. Then he unrolled the print I had asked for just before lunch. Marked all over it in red pencil were derogatory remarks, calling the design weak, inept and juvenile, and with a big red 'F' circled in the bottom right corner. I looked at the print in amazement and said, "I didn't do that. That's not my handwriting. That looks like . . ." We both said, in unison, "Alexander Jacks' handwriting!" "That's okay, Mr. Sargent," he said. "I'll handle this." I returned to my office still shaken by the incident.

I heard through the grapevine that Mr. Fielding had gone straight to Mr. Christopher and complained about Mr. Jacks interfering in his project. They had called Mr. Jacks in and there was an almighty row. I don't know what was said, but it appeared that Mr. Jacks was "hoist with his own petard"[73] and there was no further interference with me or the other technologists after that.

---

73   Shakespeare, Hamlet. To be hurt by a trap you have set for someone else.

31. The MG from God

The transfer to the Transportation Unit turned out to be a blessing and a curse, and I wondered what the point of it all was. Soon I was to discover what I ultimately came to regard as the real reason behind those changes. Not long after I had transferred to the new unit, Mr. Fielding asked me to do the preliminary flow charts for all the airport operations. One day, as I was drawing these charts, Paul Robins came in, sat on the plan table behind me and watched me work. Paul was one of the trainees who had started the program with me a couple of years before. As he didn't say anything, I just assumed he was lost in amazement watching me quickly set out all the complex interactions that a modern international airport involved, and I began working more rapidly and with added flourish, when . . . "Do you believe in God?" came Paul's perplexed voice from behind me. I stopped in my tracks. "Yes, of course," I said as I turned around to face him. He looked at me in a pleading way and said, "How?"

I could see before me a true seeker, desiring to know the truth and not knowing where to go to find it. "The universe was created out of love," I began. "God desired that there be minds that know and hearts that love." Communication between individuals can sometimes be difficult, even impossible, but as I spoke, I felt the bounds between us dissolve and an ideal communication being established. It was as if I was drawing back a curtain and revealing a panorama of true understanding. I was as amazed as he was! He suddenly grabbed my arm and said,

"God has sent you to me!" That forceful exclamation broke the spirit of the moment, and I jumped back in alarm. "No, no," he said, "Not like that . . . Let me explain."

Paul had grown up in a strict Dutch Reform family and faithfully went to church every Sunday. As he became a teenager in high school, he began to be influenced by his peers. He stopped going to church, and, although he still maintained a strong internal moral code, his belief in the Dutch Reform Church was weakening. Not long before our conversation, he and his girlfriend had parked along lovers' lane, and soon things were getting out of hand. He was caught between desire and what he thought was a mortal sin. He prayed to God to show him a sign. Just then the driver's side window was smashed and someone reached in and stole his shirt off the dash. To his girlfriend this was a traumatic event and she demanded to be taken home immediately. But to Paul—IT WAS A MIRACLE!

He determined to re-establish a close connection with God and started to go to church regularly again. But, he said, after a couple of weeks, he felt that he had been closer to God that night on lovers' lane than he was in church, and he began to wonder if he was going to the right church. Maybe God was in the Baptist or Methodist or even the Catholic Church. Paul didn't know where or how to start his search, so he prayed earnestly to God, "Please lead me to the church that You want me to belong to." The next day, when he went into work, he was told that the trainees were being assigned to various design units within the department, and that he was being assigned to the Transportation Unit and would be working with Mr. Sargent.

I smiled, because that seemed to explain this strange reshuffling of my work assignment. There were very few Bahá'ís in Rhodesia at the time, but it would have been easy for God to shuffle personnel within the government to connect a true seeker to the object of his quest. Now, however, was not the appropriate time to discuss this. I told him that I had a friend who had a Bahá'í discussion group on Thursday nights, and I invited him to come along with me to his place so we could discuss these things further.

Don Fouché was a flamboyant, young Afrikaner Bahá'í from South Africa and a very enthusiastic teacher. When Paul and I arrived at Don's apartment, Jeff Gruber, another young Bahá'í pioneer, was also there. We had a wonderful evening, and Paul said he was very attracted to the Faith. Don invited him to enroll and was becoming what I thought was a little too aggressive in his approach, but I didn't say anything. Paul was hesitant, so Don said, "Do you want a sign? Just ask God for a sign and he'll give it to you!" At that point I became alarmed and said, "Okay, hold on there Don, let's not get carried away." That only seemed to encourage him and he said, "No, ask for whatever you want. If you want a new car—just ask for it, and God will give it to you." At that point I said, "My, look at the time. I've got to catch the bus out to Waterfalls, so I think we'll be going. Thanks again for the lovely evening." With that I shuffled Paul out before things got any weirder. I only hoped Paul had not been offended by being put on the spot like that.

I was having a quiet Saturday afternoon, reading in my living room, when I heard a car speed down my driveway. I got up and headed toward the rear entry, when I heard a loud, vigorous pounding on the door. As I approached, I saw Paul standing there. He burst in before I could even offer a greeting. "I got it! I got it! I got the car!" he said excitedly. "What car?" I asked, perplexed at this announcement. "You know—Don said I could ask for a new car and God would give it to me— well He did! Come on—look at this!" I followed him outside and there was this incredible, brand new, Inca-yellow MGB GT convertible. "What do you mean God gave it to you?" I asked as we walked around it.

Apparently, a couple of months previously, he and his girlfriend were walking through the mall when they saw her mother selling raffle tickets for some charity. The prize was a new MG sports car. At his girlfriend's insistence, he had bought one and stuck it in his pocket, then forgotten all about it. That morning, the organizers had phoned to say that he had won. For his part, he had a hard time even remembering what they were talking about. Now Paul was convinced that this was a sign from God.

Paul actively studied the Faith for some time, but eventually his girlfriend gave him an ultimatum—if he wanted to continue in his relationship with her, he would have to stop all this Bahá'í 'cult' stuff. Soon after this, he discontinued associating with all Bahá'í activities. When I think back on this story now, I shake my head—although Bahá'ís believe it is for God to test his servants and not vice versa, it seemed like God really opened all the doors for this guy. But it was not to be.

1967 MGB GT convertible

32. The Pilgrimage[74]

My twenty-first birthday was coming up, so my father had, unbeknownst to me, applied for a pilgrimage for me to coincide with this very special birthday. This was a fantastic gift! I would start my adult life off with a trip to the spiritual centre of the earth—Israel. I had built up a lot of vacation time at work, so I planned to do my own 'Grand Tour'[75] and visit most of the major museums of Europe on my way to Israel. It's important, for this story, to note that, in my youth, I lived predominantly by intellect and reason, and was somewhat emotionally cool and aloof. This was the way I approached this tour of Europe, and this was the way I approached my pilgrimage. I visited both of the main classical capitals (Athens and Rome); then moved on to the main centres of the Renaissance and the Reformation; finishing in London, the home of modern science and the Industrial Revolution. I revelled in the advancements man has made in philosophy and technology over the past three millennia. Finally, it was time to go to Israel, the spiritual centre of the world, the primal point of genesis for all this outward development.

---

74   See Pilgrimage in the Glossary.

75   The Grand Tour flourished from about 1660 until the advent of large-scale rail transit in the 1840s, and was associated with a standard itinerary. It served as an educational rite of passage for young European aristocrats.

In a similar way, the first eight days of my pilgrimage were an intellectual adventure, especially visiting the archives building. (A museum containing many of the sacred relics of the Faith.) The beauty of the Shrines of The Báb and Bahá'u'lláh and the surrounding gardens was enchanting, but the sky didn't open, and spiritual ecstasy didn't pour down upon me from heaven. The few precious days and hours of my pilgrimage were almost over when I discovered a problem with my return airline ticket. So I had to go to Tel Aviv and get my return travel arrangements straightened out. This meant that I would miss most of the last day of my pilgrimage. That afternoon, I took the train back from Tel Aviv to Haifa, arriving at about sunset. I knew they closed the Shrines at about eight o'clock, and it was already past seven. As I was way downtown at the train station, I was going to be lucky to get there before it closed, and I wanted to pray in the Shrine one more time before my pilgrimage was over.

I took the bus to the top of Ben Gurion Avenue, at the foot of Mount Carmel. There were pedestrian stairways at various points up the mountain. (This was long before the current terraces were built.) I rushed and rushed, climbing straight up toward the Shrine of the Báb. By the time I got there, the attendant was just locking the door. I was so out of breath from climbing that I could barely speak, but I managed to gasp, "Can I just say one more prayer before I go?" He said, "Go in there and pray, and take your time. There's someone in the Shrine of 'Abdu'l-Bahá anyway, and I'm waiting for them." I thanked him and went into the Shrine of the Báb, turned the lights back on, knelt down on the carpet, put my forehead on the threshold, but I couldn't pray because I was still so out of breath. As I was kneeling there quietly, all of a sudden, this far-away, unearthly chanting filled the chamber—the beautiful prayers and verses just washing over me.

Now, I had heard that, on that pilgrimage, there was a woman whose voice was renowned throughout Persia as one of the most beautiful chanters. The Persian pilgrims talked about her almost like she was a pop star. What I didn't know was that it was her in the next room, in the Shrine of 'Abdu'l-Bahá. Time seemed to stand still as I knelt there, wrapped in the ecstasy of her heavenly chanting. When she finished praying, I knew I should finish also, because the attendant was waiting for her so he could close up the Shrine. I think I may have said a rushed prayer, but it would have been superfluous anyway because of the beauty of the verses that had just been chanted.

Looking down at the lights of Haifa, Israel, at night

As I was walking away, they turned out the lights on the Shrine and gardens, so the paths were dark. I walked over to the railing in front of the Shrine of the Báb, and I looked down on the city of Haifa, which was sparkling like a box of jewels with all its lights. As I stood there, quietly looking down at the beauty of the lights along the bay, I said to Bahá'u'lláh, "Please bless my life to the service of Your Cause." I just said that, spontaneously, as a heartfelt, sort of logical thing. But suddenly I was overwhelmed by the smell of roses from the gardens and a strange feeling like my logical mind was looking down on me standing by the railing. I thought to myself, "Something strange is going on here." This dissociation was unsettling enough, but at the same time some powerful, uncontrollable emotion was trying to rise to the surface. The thought suddenly occurred to me that I'd better get back to my hotel—fast!

I rushed back down to my hotel—about two or three long blocks east along Hatzionut Avenue. I hurried down the hall, and I was trying to get my keys to unlock the door, but the highly charged emotion, that was trying to burst out like a volcano, befuddled me, making it almost impossible. I knew that I had to get into my room fast, and, as soon as I got the door unlocked, I burst in and started to cry—loud, uncontrollable sobs. The sound came louder and louder. My logical mind was watching me, kneeling there on the floor, from above, and frantically saying, "Oh, this is terrible! What will people think is going on? I've got to stop this!" I grabbed my prayer book, and tried to say a prayer, but that only made matters worse. All I could do was watch myself on the floor, sobbing uncontrollably. I thought to myself, "What am I going to do? I've got to do something or the management or somebody is going to be in here demanding to know what's going on." The whole time, there was this powerful smell of roses and sandalwood incense. I don't remember exactly how it ended. I think, that after some time, I was able to re-associate and finally managed to get a grip on myself. But I didn't go back to my usual self. Something about me had changed—I couldn't say what exactly, but I was changed by this experience.

The next day my pilgrimage was over, so I had to get up really early to arrive at Tel Aviv airport in time for my flight back down to Africa. I seemed to be my normal self again and gave no further thought to the events of the previous evening. Because of the change to my travel plans, I had to fly on South African Airways instead of BOAC.[76] This meant that I couldn't fly straight south over Africa to Southern Rhodesia because of South Africa's then apartheid regime, but rather had to travel across southern Europe to Lisbon, Portugal, and then around West Africa through Tenerife, Canary Islands; Luanda, Angola; Johannesburg, South Africa; and then back up to Salisbury. It was a trip of about twenty-five hours, including layovers on the ground. When I got home, I was completely exhausted and slept, virtually continuously, for several days.

On about the third day back home, I began to notice there was a strange change in my perception of reality. Everywhere I looked, things had meanings within meanings within meanings. Everything seemed connected in this very holographic way. It's hard to explain, but the ramifications of every act we do, every word we say, positive or negative, ripples through to all things in creation, moving both forward and backward in time. I could see that the reality we live in is embedded in this spiritual matrix. We perceive it as a physical sphere of lineal time and space, but in reality it's all interconnected spiritually. All this information was flooding in my mind and it was just too much all at once. My ability to capture and make sense of it—to understand it—was utterly lost.

Slowly this changed perception equalized, and 'normal reality' came again to the fore, but now I understood that this reality was just a more user-friendly interface for humans, at our level of development and capacity, to interact with. It hides a much deeper and more complex reality underlying all

76   British Overseas Airline Corporation, a predecessor of
      British Airways.

things. Somehow, I had the feeling that this new understanding was a sign that my quiet prayer, while overlooking Haifa, was accepted. This change in perception was, for me, a necessary preparation for a life of service to the Cause of God.

Well, I guess everybody has a different pilgrimage experience, but, to say the least, my pilgrimage experience was life-transforming.

33. The Perils of Private Practice

After I had received my NTC III Architectural Technologist Diploma, I found that I was a hot item. As I mentioned before, trained technologists were in short supply in Rhodesia back in the '60s and early '70s. Also, as the Rhodesian civil war began to heat up, fewer and fewer people were inclined to move their families there. Consequently, a poaching competition soon broke out, in which companies began to entice technologists away from each other.

I had finished the design for the temporary domestic terminal and was beginning to turn my attention to the new international terminal, when I was approached by John Jackson, a chartered architect with his own practice. He had recently lost both his technologists and was in dire need. One had recently had a baby, and the other had moved to South Africa. Mr. Jackson had heard of me through one of the other technologists in the department and approached me, explaining his situation. Although I had really learned a lot and enjoyed working with the Department of Public Works, I was looking for something new. Mr. Jackson's offer was a step up, so I decided to go to work with his firm.

When I arrived, the office consisted of Mr. Jackson, Mazie, and a servant. May, who everyone called Mazie, was a bubbly, chatty young lady in her early twenties, who gave the immediate impression of a flighty dingbat, but who was, in fact, a very able receptionist, bookkeeper, secretary, and girl Friday. It seemed to me that she was keeping the whole enterprise afloat. Our office was on the seventh floor of one of the tallest office towers in Salisbury. All of the other tenants on our floor were dentists' offices. Most of their clientele were children, so we had to keep our door closed, because the drilling and bloodcurdling screams made the whole floor sound like it was a torture chamber in some medieval castle.

There was a backlog of projects, so I set to work, full speed, from day one. Most of these projects were residences and leasehold improvements for small businesses. This was quite a change from the large projects that I had worked on in government, but they offered a greater chance to be more creative. New projects were coming in, and it wasn't long before Mr. Jackson came into the office, all smiles, and said he had received a call from the Department of Public Works. They were asking if we would be willing to take on a project for them—yep, it was the Nuffield school lab conversion project! They had tracked me down—I felt like Br'er Rabbit fighting the Tar-baby.[77]

Mr. Jackson and I were both very busy, and we really needed that second technologist, so the search went on. Back when I worked as the computer for the surveyor general's office, a few of us would often go to lunch together. We had a favourite spot—because every day this drop-dead beautiful, long-haired blonde with a micro miniskirt would come out of her office and walk by. Imagine my surprise when Mr. Jackson walked in with her and announced that he had found a second technologist. Her name was Christine. She was married to a lawyer and had been working as a drafting technologist for a civil engineering firm, but was really more interested in

---

77 Uncle Remus stories by Joel Chandler Harris, featured in Walt Disney's film *Song of the South*.

architecture. This hire really reduced the backlog and gave us the time to produce some interesting and innovative work.

By this time, I had developed an increasingly debilitating case of agoraphobia[78] and liked to work alone in my office with the door closed. Mazie had made good friends with Sherry, a cute dental hygienist from down the hall, who would pop in from time to time and say, "Hi, Geronimo!" That would send me scurrying, red-faced, into my drawing office. I had mentioned my First Nation background to Mazie, and she had obviously told Sherry. I'm sure she was not being mean and was probably flirting with me, but I was socially non-responsive by this point.

Although this agoraphobia did not interfere with my work, I found it difficult to move about in public, and impossible to stay in situations with large numbers of people. For over two years, I cloistered myself in my room. But when I look back on that episode now, I realize what a great bounty it was. It was during this time that I intensively studied the Writings of the Faith. I especially devoured the letters of Shoghi Effendi. It was like a two-year intensive university course, and Shoghi Effendi was my professor. Never again in my life would I have the freedom to study the Faith so intensively, and the benefit of that study has been of inestimable value in my life and in my teaching work.

There is a saying among architectural technologists, when they are asked what the difference between an architectural technologist and a chartered architect is. They say: one designs and details buildings, and the other plays golf with prospective clients. This may sound trite, but, the fact is, in order to keep a small architectural office going, a substantial amount

---

78   An anxiety disorder causing fear and avoidance of places or situations
      that might cause panic or the feeling of being trapped.

of networking time is required to ensure a constant stream of new projects comes into the office. One day, Mr. Jackson came into my office and said, "I have a nice, interesting project for you." One of the dentists on our floor wanted to build a new home. He said he wanted it to be approximately 275 m², with three bedrooms plus den, and the only design criteria he gave was: he wanted anyone who saw it to know it had been custom designed by an architect, and not chosen from a catalogue of tract houses.

During this time I was developing agoraphobia and preferred to spend more and more time alone.

This was an amazing project, because usually the client dictates pretty closely what they want. I had already learned to say, "Just show me the picture from the magazine," right up front, so that I didn't have to draw several concepts, trying to guess what they had in mind. This project, however, was a clean slate, and I could let my imagination run wild. I took out some butcher paper sheets and began broadly sketching some outlandish ideas—just to get them out of my system, and to see if something promising popped up. One idea, using ferroconcrete shells to do some intersecting arches and domes, looked interesting, and I began developing that concept a little further, just to see if it would lead anywhere. Just then, Mr. Jackson walked in and asked if I had come up with anything. "No," I said. "I'm just throwing down ideas to see if anything leads in a good direction." He looked over several of my sketches and was also attracted to the ferroconcrete idea. He began playing with the original sketch and was becoming even bolder and more outlandish than I had been. We stopped and looked at this sketch, then I added two large Mickey Mouse ears and we both laughed. Mr. Jackson suddenly became serious. "Damn!" he said. "This," pointing to the sketches, "is why I became an architect. Now I spend all my time trying to keep this business afloat, and it's killing me!"

I felt sorry for Mr. Jackson. He was a skilled and talented architect, but he just never got much creative time on the drawing board. Such, it seems, is the nature of private practice. I stayed with his firm for just over a year, then circumstances changed in my life and I headed back to Canada.

34. When All Else Fails . . .

As the Nine Year Plan progressed, the Universal House of Justice sent the National Spiritual Assembly of South Central Africa a letter, asking them to work hard for the establishment of a certain number of local Spiritual Assemblies in the newly independent nation of Zambia[79], with the aim of having that country elect its own independent National Spiritual Assembly by the following Riḍván.[80] Apparently, this decision caused consternation with some members of the community, because the removal of Zambia would put a big gap in the middle of the regional National Assembly area, and Nyasaland would then be separated from Southern Rhodesia and Bechuanaland. One insolent individual even went so far as to say, "Don't those guys in Haifa even have a map of Africa?" But despite the apprehension with this decision, our National Spiritual Assembly, wishing to be obedient to the House's request, put much of its resources into publishing literature in the local Zambian languages, and asked the pioneers to concentrate their teaching trips on Zambia. By the end of the Bahá'í year, the requisite number of local assemblies had been formed, and the new National Spiritual Assembly of Zambia was elected.

To the amazement of everyone, a few months after this, Zambia cut ties with all its neighbours except Mozambique. The borders were completely closed, and, when they finally

---

79   Previously known as Northern Rhodesia.
80   See Riḍván in the Glossary

reopened, access was very restricted. But, as Zambia now had its own independent National Assembly, the Faith continued to develop without pause or delay. I asked my father, "How did the members of the House of Justice know that was going to happen?" He replied, "They didn't. But God did." This was a revelation to me. I realized that I didn't really understand the nature of the House of Justice.

I had always thought that the brilliant Bahá'í electoral process[81] that brought us the membership of the Universal House of Justice would naturally bring to the fore individuals that were intelligent, intuitive, and well-read. These individuals would give us the best chance to find the appropriate direction forward. However, I was beginning to see that decisions derived through prayer and proper consultation were above and beyond the ability of any of the individual members that made up the body itself. A mysterious power guides the Faith at this level. Bahá'u'lláh states, *"It is incumbent upon the Trustees of the House of Justice to take counsel together regarding those things which have not outwardly been revealed in the Book, and to enforce that which is agreeable to them. God will verily inspire them with whatsoever He willeth, and He, verily, is the Provider, the Omniscient."*[82]

I realized then that all the sacred scriptures of the Jewish, Christian, and Islamic faiths promising the coming of the "Kingdom of God on earth" and calling this the "Day of God," had a very real and practical meaning; that an important aspect of the Faith is that this **is** the Kingdom of God! Usually, after the Manifestation of God[83] has ascended, mankind is left pretty much on their own until the next Manifestation. But

---

81   See Bahá'í electoral process in the Glossary.

82   Bahá'u'lláh, *Tablets of Bahá'u'lláh*, p. 68

83   See Manifestation of God in the Glossary.

now, for the first time since God went with the children of Israel into the wilderness as a column of smoke during the day and a pillar of fire by night, mankind is again under the continual guidance and protection of God.

Hand of the Cause Dr. Muhajir, far right,
chatting with some of the participants

The force of this remarkable inspiration was evident to me again, a few years later, when the National Spiritual Assembly of Rhodesia (By this time each of the individual nations that formed the former regional National Spiritual Assembly of South Central Africa had their own independent National Spiritual Assemblies.) analysed its progress thus far in the Nine Year Plan, and concluded that, without doubling the number of pioneers, there was no way we could win our assigned goals. We wrote a letter to the Universal House of Justice stating this conclusion and asking for advice. Their reply was rather embarrassing. They asked us to reread their letter to us at the beginning of the Nine Year Plan. When we did, we noticed that the House, right from the beginning, had shown us how the Plan could be won. They said that we should train indigenous travelling teachers and send them out to the remote areas of the country. Instead, we had been relying on the few pioneers we had, to handle this work. By doing it our way, we soon outgrew our available human resources, and our progress had stalled.

In addition to their letter, the Universal House of Justice sent Hand of the Cause Dr. Muhajir to help us set up the travelling teacher-training institute. With the help of these well-trained travelling teachers, Rhodesia was able not only to meet, but to surpass, its goals for the Nine Year Plan. It appears that the old adage is true—when all else fails, try following the directions! This is especially true if the directions come from the Universal House of Justice.

35. The Good Campaign Manager

One of the jobs of the pioneers was assisting new Bahá'í communities to elect their local Spiritual Assemblies. In the remote areas of the country, the small villages (kraals) governed themselves as they had since time immemorial. The local tribal area had a hereditary grand chief, and each village had a kraal head. These kraal heads were appointed by the grand chief, but the community had grumbling rights, and an unpopular kraal head usually didn't last long in the job. Serious situations were handled by a tribal council, which consisted of the grand chief and several kraal heads consulting together. The idea was to reach consensus, but the grand chief always had the final say.

When a village had more than nine adult Bahá'ís, the pioneers came in to explain what a local Spiritual Assembly was and how it was chosen. This presented some difficulties, of course, because the concept of a formal, organized administrating structure was completely foreign to them, as were the concepts of democracy and voting for those in leadership positions. However, they participated, in mild amusement, as the pioneers set about helping them through this mysterious process.

Those few who could read and write were appointed as tellers. They were given a list of the Bahá'ís in the community and the community members went up, one at a time, and whispered the names of the people they wanted to vote for. The teller made a check against that name and continued until nine had been given, when the teller told them to stop. Then the next member came forward.

Trouble usually began when the results were announced, as some would say, "Wait a minute, I didn't vote for him!" or "Hey, I voted for so and so; how come they aren't on the Assembly?" To this, the pioneer would try to explain how the results of plurality voting were arrived at—but usually to zero comprehension. In fact, this didn't matter too much anyway, as the elected members didn't know what they were supposed to do, and, in all probability, would never meet as a formal Assembly. This was, in most cases, a good thing, as all this strange activity would take place under the watchful and suspicious eye of the kraal head, and he would not take kindly to anything that would undermine his authority or cause disunity or contention among the village residents.

Some pioneers would complain about the futility of this exercise, but I was enthralled by its historic perspective and excited to be a part of it. I could foresee that, one day, all these villages would have properly functioning Assemblies working hard to promote the spiritual, social, and economic vitality of these communities. But for now, these were the first few baby steps leading to that goal. Being a pioneer and helping with this process was a once-in-history opportunity, and I felt privileged to be allowed to participate in it.

Also, every year, the pioneers would come out and gather the Bahá'ís from several nearby villages to elect their representative to the National Convention in Salisbury. The local believers quickly learned that, unlike the elected local Assembly members, the chosen delegates would get an all-expense paid trip to the big city. So this was a far more eagerly anticipated event, and several inappropriate Bahá'í election behaviours had to be discussed and discouraged.

When the delegates arrived at the National Convention, the role of the National Spiritual Assembly was discussed. This was even more mysterious than a local Assembly, as many of the delegates from remote areas didn't know what a nation was, let alone that they were, by default, citizens of one. Also, this may have been their first time out of their tribal area, and they did not know anyone whom they might vote for.

My father had served on the National Spiritual Assembly for years. But, as it happened, my father and I have the same name, and I had turned twenty-one the year before. The friends in my community knew me as 'Junior', as that's what my dad called me. In the surrounding communities, my dad was known as 'Uncle John', and I was known as 'Johnny'. The year before, when the delegates had voted for John Sargent, the tellers weren't sure which John Sargent the votes were for. In the end, they assumed the votes were for my dad, but made a mental note to be sure to clarify the issue the following year.

Appropriately, at the next year's convention, the head teller informed the delegates that there were two John Sargents, and they had to make it clear which John Sargent they were voting for. Following this comment, there was a general air of confusion, and the delegates looked around in a questioning manner. The member of the Continental Board of Counsellors for Africa, who was attending our convention, saw that the delegates were confused and rose to further clarify the issue. "Junior has the same name as his father," he stated and turned around to write on the blackboard. "His father's name is John Sargent Sr., and his name is John Sargent Jr.," he continued, stressing the Sr. and Jr. "You have to clearly write on your ballot John Sargent **Sr.** and John Sargent **Jr.**," he concluded, underlining the Sr. and Jr.

I was not a delegate and was attending as an observer, at the back of the room, but, as the Counsellor took his seat, I turned to my friend Don Fouché and said, "Did the Counsellor just tell all the delegates that they must vote for my father and me?" Don looked back and said, "That's what it sounded like to me."

Sure enough, when the votes were counted, the delegates had dutifully written John Sargent Sr. and John Sargent Jr. on their ballots, and we had the highest number of votes in the election. I was a member of the National Spiritual Assembly of Rhodesia at age twenty-two, but I've always said it was because the Counsellor had been such a good campaign manager.

National Spiritual Assembly of the Bahá'ís of Rhodesia, 1971.
Note top row bracketed by John Sargents.

36. Apparently It's Time to Go

Apart from my increasing agoraphobia, everything seemed to be going well for me in Africa. Despite this affliction, I was still able to travel-teach, and now I had a responsible role as a member of the National Spiritual Assembly. In addition, by the grace of God, I was working in my chosen field of architecture, which was going well, and which I really enjoyed. The road ahead seemed clear and productive until, suddenly, I had a vision that changed everything.

Change was already happening. My dad had gone to the International Bahá'í Convention in Haifa, Israel, in 1968, and had met Aili Honkanen, who was a member of the Finnish National Spiritual Assembly, and single. Afterwards, they continued to correspond, until my dad proposed marriage, and she came to live in Rhodesia. Once they were married, they moved to a home of their own, and left me as sole caretaker of the National Bahá'í Centre.

It became my custom, just at sunset, to walk around the gardens and feel the fresh evening breeze. This particular evening, the jasmine was in bloom and the air smelled so sweet that, as I walked, I closed my eyes to imagine myself back in the Bahá'í gardens in Haifa. As I did, the savannah of Africa disappeared, but, instead of being in Haifa, I was standing in a wheat field in Saskatchewan. I quickly opened my eyes and I was back in Africa. That was odd. So I closed my eyes again, and there was that same wheat field. This time, I noticed that a strong wind was blowing. I could clearly see the shape of the wind as it undulated through the crop. The heads of the grain were full and ripe and ready to harvest. But, as grain farmers know, if the wind blows too hard, the stalks of the wheat can break, and, when the grain is lying down, it's hard to harvest. In that case, a lot of the crop can be lost. When I opened my eyes again, I knew what that vision meant. The wheat represented the First Nation peoples of the Prairies and that they were spiritually ready to receive the message of Bahá'u'lláh, but they must receive it soon, or the winds of tests would make it very difficult to reach them later.

This vision had come completely out of the blue, but it instantly instilled in me a strong resolve: "I've got to get back to the Prairies to consolidate the work that we started all those years ago!" The next day, I went down to the travel agency and bought a one-way ticket to Toronto. Then I hurried up to my office and handed in my resignation. Mr. Jackson was stunned. He didn't want me to leave, but asked if I could please delay a couple of months to give him time to find a new technologist. When my father heard about my decision, he was very disappointed. We had pioneered to Southern Rhodesia together, and he strongly believed that pioneers should leave their bones at their post. Now I felt unsure of the wisdom of my decision, both because my father was not in agreement with me leaving my post; and because Mr. Jackson was so distressed at having to find another technologist.

But then, three or four days later, my dad phoned me up. He said, "Junior, I've been thinking about you going back to Canada to work with the First Nation peoples, and I'm beginning to think that would be a very good idea." With that encouragement, I was fortified in my decision and continued with arrangements to come back to Canada. I decided to delay a couple of months to give Mr. Jackson time to find a replacement. Also, apart from the general feeling of needing to be back in Saskatchewan to continue the work we had started at the end of the Ten Year World Plan, I had no idea how that was going to happen.

On departure day, I arrived at the airport early and walked over to review the progress on the construction of the temporary domestic terminal that I had helped design. As I cast a critical eye over the work completed so far, I heard my dad coming up behind me, saying, "I thought I would find you here." He stood beside me for a time, and together we scanned the construction. At last he remarked, "The work is not finished." I was silent for a moment and realized he was speaking metaphorically. I put my hand on his shoulder. "No . . . it isn't. But my part of the work is." He smiled and nodded. "Come, let's get you on that airplane." A number of the friends had come to see me off, and, as I reached the top of the air stairs, I turned and waved one last goodbye to a chorus of best wishes from the observation deck. Many of the friends portended that I would be back, but I felt, in my heart, that the period of time I was to work in Africa had ended, and that a whole new arena of service was opening up before me.

Because I had delayed my departure a few months, I was able to attend the Reykjavik Oceanic Bahá'í Conference, in Iceland, on my way home. The National Spiritual Assembly of Rhodesia asked me if I would represent our Assembly at the Reykjavik Conference, as my last official act before resigning. I readily agreed, and the secretary of our National Spiritual Assembly wrote to the conference organizers, and said that they were sending, as their official representative, John Sargent Jr. I really didn't think anything more about it until I got there and started registering. My name seemed to ring a bell, and they said, "Oh, Mr. Sargent, we have a special representative conference package for you here." They handed me the package that had a special yellow badge, with a ribbon on it, that said: 'Representative of the National Spiritual Assembly of the Bahá'ís of Rhodesia.' I thought, that's nice—but I didn't give it a second thought.

Denny Fatheazam, Don Fouché and Gift Musarura
come to wish Junior bon voyage

When I walked into the main hotel lobby, much to my surprise, the first person I saw walking towards me was Angus Cowan. I hadn't seen him for years, but he hadn't changed a bit. I, however, was quite a bit different from the fourteen-year-old kid he had last seen. But, almost instantly, I could see that he recognized me, and he caught his breath. He looked at me, and then his face kind of squiggled up in a questioning way and he queried, "Junior?" I enthusiastically greeted him, "Yes, Angus, how are you?" "It's so good to see you!" he responded, then stopped and looked at my conference badge. "How come you got a yellow . . ." and his voice trailed off. I looked down where he was pointing and responded, "Oh, I'm representing the National Spiritual Assembly of Rhodesia here." And he just went like . . . I don't know what it would be, but he was just so shocked—stunned. He stood there for a second, and then he folded his arms across his chest and kind of rocked gently forward and back, with this beatific smile on his face. And I was standing there, and I was getting nervous because he was looking at me like this, and I was thinking, "What the heck?" I was madly, in my mind, trying to think of something to say to break this sort of awkward moment, when I finally realized that he wasn't looking at me at all. He was looking at 'Abdu'l-Bahá's prophecy, that the First Nation peoples, when they fully recognized Bahá'u'lláh, would become so enlightened that they'd shed light on all regions. I think, to him, this little First Nations guy, coming back from Africa as a member of the National Spiritual Assembly, was like the realization of that vision, right before his eyes.

The confirmations only seemed to continue. On the second day of the conference, I was going up the stairs to the conference room level, when I ran into someone I had seen recently in Rhodesia. "Oh, are you coming back from Africa?" he enquired. "Yeah," I replied. "I'm heading home to Six Nations Reservation in Ontario." "Really?" he said in surprise. "There's a Bahá'í here, at the conference, who is pioneering to Caledonia, near Six Nations, and I think it would be good for you to meet him." Apparently, this man and his wife had been working with the Six Nations Reserve community for some time, but were finding it very difficult. They had not made very much progress, and I think they were feeling overwhelmed. Suddenly, my friend pointed. "Oh, there he is now. His name is Dan Kelly. You should go introduce yourself." So I walked over and I introduced myself, and we talked for a few minutes. Soon he noticed my badge. "So you're on the National Spiritual Assembly of Rhodesia." To which I explained, "Well, I'm coming from Rhodesia, but I'm actually leaving my pioneer post, and I'm heading back home." "Oh," he said, "Where's your home?" "I'm from Six Nations Reserve in Ontario," I said. The shock almost knocked him over.

A few weeks later, after I had returned home, Dan introduced me to his wife, Helen. Both Helen and Dan continued to support and work with the Six Nations Bahá'í community for many years. I, on the other hand, let everyone know that my real reason for coming back to Canada was to do consolidation work on the prairies—or so I thought. About a month after I returned to Canada, my dad forwarded me a letter from the Rhodesian Government. It was call-up papers to serve in the Rhodesian Light Infantry. This was quite illegal, as, under international law, foreign nationals are not required to serve in the armed services of other countries. However, the civil war in Rhodesia was not going well, and it looked, to me, like they were calling up everybody and their brother. I had left just in time to avoid forced conscription. So it seems that God, in giving me that vision, may have had a different reason, or at least another reason, for getting me the heck out of there.

37. Reset to Zero

After leaving Iceland, I planned to make a few stops on my way to Toronto. First, New York, then Windsor Locks, Connecticut, to visit my grandma and grandpa Sargent, and then on to Chicago to visit the Bahá'í Temple.[84] Unfortunately, when I got to Windsor Locks, I discovered that the airline had lost my luggage, and all I could do was leave a forwarding address for when it finally arrived. All I had was the clothes I was wearing and my travel wallet. It was a zipped case about the size of a classic day timer with my money, traveller's cheques, airline tickets, passport, and prayer book inside. It seemed as if I was being stripped of all my earthly possessions, and that I was starting completely afresh back in North America.

In Chicago, I took the airporter bus downtown and caught the 'L'[85] up to Evanston station. I believe that is still the end of the line. On the way, the train passed through a very depressed area of the city: block after block of what looked like a war-torn landscape of garbage and burned-out buildings. Eventually, this gave way to more middle-class suburbs, and finally to the upper class neighbourhoods to the north of the city. These stately homes, with their manicured gardens and mature trees, dressed in autumn reds and golds, gleamed in the late September sun. I got off the train and began walking the three or four blocks

---

84   See Mashriqu'l-Adhkár in the Glossary.
85   The 'L' is the nickname of the elevated commuter trains in the Chicago area.

down to the Temple. It was a warm, glorious day, with a light, salubrious breeze wafting through the trees, and I never felt so 'alive.' I suddenly threw my hands into the air in exaltation, but . . . something wasn't right. I looked at my right hand, then over to my left hand. Fear gripped my stomach and I whirled around on the spot—WHERE WAS MY TRAVEL WALLET!?

I rushed back to the train station and arrived just in time to see the train heading back south down the line. At the last second, I caught the number of the train and rushed over to the ticket booth. I quickly explained my situation to the agent, and he called ahead to the next station. Minutes slowed to hours as I awaited the results of these inquiries. Eventually, the agent returned with a frown on his face, and said that the engineer had walked through the train and found nothing. I sat there quietly for a few minutes, contemplating my situation.

I had no money, no ID, and no airplane tickets home. Those things were on a train heading into a desperately poor part of Chicago. All of those things had value on the black market. And, even if a Good Samaritan found them and wanted to get them back to me, it would have been impossible—the only contact information enclosed was for Rhodesia, Southern Africa. They would have to mail them there. But I was here, and I needed those things now.

I don't know how long I sat there going over all my options—which numbered exactly zero—before I got up and wandered back toward the Temple in a daze. The dome of the Temple may have gleamed gloriously in the afternoon sunlight, but I don't know, because I didn't notice anything until I found myself in Foundation Hall (There used to be a large auditorium and public information centre in the basement of the Temple.), and someone said, "What happened to you? You look like a dying duck in a thunderstorm." I looked up to see an ebullient older gentleman, who was a little too full of joie de vivre for me to take at that particular moment. When I briefly told him what had happened, he cheerfully replied, "Well, just say a little prayer, and I'm sure everything will be all right!" I stared at him incredulously as my mind raced— say a little prayer and everything will be all right?! I am an unknown person with no money or ID, stranded in a city of eight million people with nowhere to go, nothing to eat, and no shelter to go to, and this guy wants me to say a little prayer! What can God do? I've screwed things up so thoroughly that GOD COULDN'T HELP ME EVEN IF HE WANTED TO!

Bahá'í Temple in Wilmette, Illinois

"Thank you," I said, and walked off toward the sanctuary of the Temple upstairs. I sat in silence, near the centre of the nearly empty auditorium, and looked way up at the Greatest Name[86], high above in the dome. My prayer book was in my

---

86   The Greatest Name is 'O Thou the Glory of the Most Glorious' in Arabic calligraphy.

travel wallet, so I said the 'Remover of Difficulties,' 'God Sufficeth,' and 'Oh God, My God,' short prayers that I had memorized, over and over again. Finally, after some time, I just had a quiet little talk with God. "I know this is all my fault. There is no one to blame but me. I know I should have been more careful, knowing how important those things are. You see me sitting here before You with nothing—absolutely nothing. Please take pity on this, Your servant, and show him the way."

I didn't even have a Kleenex handy, so I had to wipe away my tears with my sleeve, as I stood up and walked slowly to the exit. I was just heading out the door, when the guide said, "Hey buddy, are you a Bahá'í?" I nodded in the affirmative. "I've got to use the little boys' room. Could you hold the fort while I'm gone?" I said sure, and he proceeded to show me the ropes. "Everyone gets a pamphlet. If they have no shoes, we have slippers here. If they have no shirt, we have t-shirts there. And no food or pets—except assistance dogs—allowed. Got it?" "Got it," I said and sat down in his chair. After what seemed like a long time—but I didn't care, because I had nowhere to go and nothing to do—he came back. We chatted generally for ten or fifteen minutes, and then I got up to go.

I walked out into the gardens and looked around indecisively, thinking, what to do now? For no particular reason, I headed back down to the Foundation Hall. In those days, there was a small reception room off to the right as you entered the basement, and a long, wide corridor down to the public information centre. There was no one in the corridor, and my footsteps echoed off the walls. A short way down that corridor, again off to the right, was a little office with a Dutch door. (The top half could open independently, and the lower half had a little counter on it.) As I walked by this office, an impatient young man suddenly stuck his head out and shouted, to no one in particular, "Is there a John Sargent here?" "Yes, that's me!" I said in surprise. He stared at me in disbelief for a moment, and then asked, "Did you lose a small case with your passport and prayer book in it?" Now it was my turn to look shocked. "Yes, I did! Where is it?" "It's at the Travel Mart and you had better hurry. They will be closing soon." "At a Travel Market?" I asked. "Never mind, I had better take you," he said as he grabbed his coat and locked up the office.

There was an old travel trick which Bahá'í pioneers used to use to travel the world. If you bought a one-way ticket to anywhere, the last stop would not let you off the plane unless you posted a bond ensuring you could buy a ticket to get back home again. So pioneers who intended to stay indefinitely would buy a ticket for one stop farther than their intended destination. Once there, they would apply to change their visitor's visa to a work visa, and send for a refund for the unused final leg of their journey. Just as I was leaving Rhodesia, a recent pioneer came up to me and asked if I was going through Chicago on my way home. "I bought my ticket at the Travel Mart in Evanston. Could you take this unused portion to them and ask them to mail my refund to my address here in Rhodesia?" he asked. "Sure, no problem," I had said. But I had forgotten all about it.

When we reached the Travel Mart, there was a kindly, old gentleman waiting there with my travel wallet. I was so relieved and happy I would have hugged and kissed him if it weren't for my British/Mohawk reserve. "Where did you find it? How did you find me?" I asked. He smiled and said that he lived in Evanston and was on the same train as me. As he was leaving the train, he noticed that I had left my travel wallet on the seat, and he had retrieved it for me. But, before he could reach me, I was lost in the crush of the crowd leaving the train. When he searched the wallet for ID, he noticed all the contact information was for Salisbury, Rhodesia, except for an old airline ticket issued from the Travel Mart in Evanston. The Travel Mart had the record of the purchaser of the original ticket, but nothing under my name. Then the travel agent noticed the Bahá'í prayer book, and suggested they call over to the Bahá'í Temple to see if the owner of the wallet might be there—easy as pie.

I asked the agent if I could sign over one of my traveller's cheques to the gentleman, as a thank you, but he absolutely refused to take any reward. I thanked him again, profusely, and we left the agency.

I think God likes it when He does the impossible and/ or gets His timing down to the second. As the guy from the Temple and I left the shop to get back in the car, we smiled at each other knowingly—this had been God's work, not ours. We both knew that, when he got that phone call, his intention was to yell out into the empty hall, "Is there a John Sargent here?" and then quickly return to the caller and say, "Nope. No one by that name here."

38. Mysterious Invitation from 007

The main reason I had come back from Africa was that I wanted to help with the consolidation work with the First Nation Bahá'ís on the prairies. However, an additional benefit was the possibility of getting a degree in architecture from a Canadian University. In many ways, these were mutually conflicting goals. But I had no plan for how I was going to accomplish either of these objectives, so I needed to get settled back in Canada to devise one.

I first went home to Six Nations and moved in with my grandparents and my cousin Don. Don is the closest to me of all my cousins, and we grew up almost like brothers in our younger years. He had just graduated from university with a degree in English, when he decided to leave the States for Canada because of his objections to the Vietnam War. At first, many family members grumbled at what they saw as his 'freeloading' off Grandma and Grandpa. However, as my grandparents and their siblings got older, the family was more and more relieved that he was there to help the old folks out. Don was a wonderful caregiver and support. His handyman, Jack-of-all-trade skills became an indispensable help to all the grand aunts and uncles as they grew older. Don also eventually got to use his degree in English, as he is currently president of the Six Nations Library Society.

At that time, there were six Bahá'ís living on the reserve, so I made the seventh. I had never met them before, as I had become a Bahá'í in Wyoming and had pioneered to Africa from there. They were, of course, very glad to see me, as they too were unaware of my existence. This meant that we only needed two more to make our Assembly, and we began to devise some teaching plans. I indicated that we really needed to find three more Bahá'ís, as I was planning to head west to work in the Prairies. Although I had written to the Bahá'í National Centre to get my Canadian Bahá'í credentials, I otherwise had kept a low profile, and I thought that, other than the friends on Six Nations, nobody knew I was back in Canada.

Although I was anxious to get out west as soon as possible, I nonetheless travelled into Toronto to see about enrolling in the Architectural Program at the University of Toronto. As I already had a diploma in architectural technology, I thought I might get advanced placement into third year of the program. That would mean that I could get my degree in two years and then head out west to help with the consolidation work on the reserves. As it turned out, it was already late October, and I was too late for the January intake. This meant I would have to wait until the following September's class, at the earliest. This pushed my planning ahead another full year. I was impatient at this delay, but this still seemed like the best approach to my objectives. God, apparently, had other ideas.

One of the duties I took on at grandma and grandpa's was to walk down to the road and collect the mail. On this particular day, there was a letter addressed to me. As I walked back to the house, I noted the return address: L. Smith, St. Albert, Alberta. This was puzzling. I knew no one in Alberta and I was sure there was no one in Alberta that knew me.

As we opened the mail over tea, I exclaimed, "What the heck?" "What is it?" my grandmother asked. "This must be some kind of joke," I said, as I racked my brain trying to think who would be pulling such a weak prank on me. "James Bond wants to have dinner with me at the Royal York Hotel on

Friday night." "Let me see that," Don said as he came around my side of the table. I handed him the letter and he read it aloud. "Dear Mr. Sargent; Jameson Bond would be pleased to have dinner with you at the Royal York Hotel in Toronto @ 7:00 pm Friday Night October 22. Please call 416 555-0321 to confirm your availability. L. Smith." Don also looked confused. "You're right, it's likely some kind of joke," he said. "It's probably the suicide helpline number or some kind of promotion." "What's really odd," I said, "is that the phone number is for the Toronto area, but the return address is for Alberta." "Yeah . . ." said Don, as he stared blankly into the distance trying to fathom the significance of that. "Come on, call the number; that's the only way we're gonna get to the bottom of this," Don suggested.

I dialed the number expectantly, anxious to see who was going to answer on the other end. The phone rang twice and connected—"Bahá'í National Centre, Ginny speaking. How may I direct your call?" That was the last thing I expected, and I just sat there and didn't respond. "Hello?" "Yes, hello," I said and then asked, a little reluctantly, "is James Bond there?" "No," said Ginny. "Professor Bond is coming in Thursday morning for the National Assembly meeting. Can I give him a message?" "Yes, please," I responded. "Tell him John Sargent is available for dinner on Friday evening. I can meet him in the lobby of the Royal York. I am a short, heavyset young man, and I'll be wearing a navy blue raincoat with a light blue 'Bahá'í' button." "Fine, I'll be sure he gets that message," said Ginny, as she signed off.

So there really was a James Bond, and he did want to have dinner with me—but I still didn't know why. Friday, I took the train down to Toronto and met Professor Bond and a young Ojibwa women named Vicky Boucher, at the appointed time and place. We had a lovely dinner together, as Jamie explained that the National Spiritual Assembly of Canada had established an Indigenous Teaching Committee to help consolidate the work among the First Nation friends on the Prairies. They were looking for additional members and were wondering, if the National Spiritual Assembly asked us, would we be willing to relocate to Edmonton to serve on such a committee. I guess, because of my procrastination, God had to send his 'secret agent' to come and get me moving.

Professor Jameson Bond, former member of the
Canadian National Spiritual Assembly

Two weeks later, I was again standing on the train platform in Toronto, this time to board the 'Supercontinental' out to Edmonton. As I waited to board, I wondered briefly where I was going to live and work, but these concerns seemed of no consequence. Ever since that vision in Africa, I had felt like a leaf blown on the breeze of God's will. Now, here I was, on my way to assist with the consolidation work in the First Nation communities on the Prairies, just as that vision had presaged.

39. Two Over the Cuckoo's Nest

When I first went out to Edmonton to serve on the National Indigenous Teaching Committee, in 1972, I stayed with Jamie and Gale Bond. However, as soon as I had landed a job, I moved to the nearby suburb of Sherwood Park, where I was able to help them preserve their Assembly. At first, I roomed in the basement of a home, while looking for someone to share an apartment with.

Another member of the Sherwood Park Community was Joy, a pure, sweet, young Bahá'í who worked as a nurse at the Fort Saskatchewan Centre for Addictions and the Criminally Insane. She was a perfect example of 'Abdu'l-Bahá's request that we only see the good in others and ignore the negative. She said that there was this beautiful Indian man who was soon to be released from the Centre and would be looking for an apartment. While he had had a troubled past, she was sure that all he needed was a good influence in his life. So, it seemed to her a perfect match that we should share an apartment.

On the appointed day, Joy picked me up and we headed out to the mental hospital to pick up Rodger. The movie '*One Flew Over the Cuckoo's Nest*' hadn't come out yet, but she introduced me to this humongous Indian man who looked just like Will Sampson, who played Chief Bromden in that movie. After an awkward introduction, we got out the newspaper and set off to find an apartment. There wasn't much to select from, as Edmonton and area were undergoing a huge oil boom, and people from all across the country were flooding in to find work. Joy would wait in the car, as Rodger and I went in to try to rent an apartment. After several, "Sorry, the last apartment is already taken," responses, we had exhausted the list. However, I suspected that something else was going on, so we went back to one of these apartment buildings and sent Joy in instead. Surprise, surprise! She immediately secured us one of those 'already taken' apartments, and we were off to the 'Sally Ann' to get pots, pans, dishes and cutlery.

So Rodger and I set up housekeeping in a nice, unfurnished, two-bedroom basement apartment. I had my clothes folded on the floor of the closet, my books arranged along the wall, and my sleeping bag spread out on the nice plush carpet. But, unfortunately for Joy's plan, Rodger and I didn't interact much. In fact, we hardly saw each other. I would head out early, catch the bus into Edmonton, grab a bite at a restaurant near my work, and return home in the early evening. Most evenings, there was no sign of Rodger, who would come in sometime early in the morning. However, it wasn't long before he lost his keys, so he would buzz me at all hours to let him in—drunk.

One day, while dusting in the near-empty living room, I found a shiv in the radiator. As a matter of interest, I checked in all the other rooms, and, sure enough, there was one in all the radiators—even in my room! When Rodger got home, I questioned him about it. He said that, if someone came to kill him, he wanted to be able to defend himself no matter where he was cornered. I suggested, as an alternative, he just not let them in when they buzzed.

When month end came, he was broke and promised me that he would have the rent in a few days. A few days later, I came home late from Feast and found a strange man in convulsions, throwing up blood on the living room carpet, and Rodger unconscious in his bedroom. I called the paramedics, who came and carted them off to the hospital. Apparently, they had taken large doses of strychnine. When he came back from the hospital, I sat down with him and said that this was not working out. He still owed me last month's rent, and it had taken me a long time to get the blood out of the carpet. If we were not careful, we would lose our damage deposit. We agreed that if he didn't have what he owed me by the time the next month's rent was due, that I would have to give notice and give up the apartment.

I have to admit that I was fed up with Rodger's behaviour and was determined to follow through with this decision. Then, late one night, I was awakened by a moaning sound coming from his bedroom. He was saying, "God help me, God help me, God help me" over and over again, and my heart really went out to him—but what could I do? When the end of the month came, he had nothing. So I said, "That's it. Pack up your stuff and take off. I don't want to see you again unless you have the three hundred dollars you owe me."

After Rodger left, I gave notice, because money was tight and I couldn't maintain a two-bedroom apartment on my own. One dark and rainy Sunday afternoon, I did some laundry at the local laundromat, had a quiet meal at the greasy spoon in the nearby strip mall, and went to bed early. The next morning, as I headed out to work, I saw that I only had 15¢ left in my wallet, but I needed 40¢ for the bus fare into Edmonton. In a panic, I rummaged through the apartment looking for any spare change—nothing. Suddenly, I remembered that one of the Bahá'ís lived fairly close by, and, if I hurried, I might catch a ride in with her. I had to pass the bus stop on the way, and I noticed another passenger was still waiting for the bus. I hurried on to the friend's house, but no answer—she had already left for work. I hadn't missed the bus yet, but it didn't really matter because my bank was in Edmonton, so there was no chance to take a later bus either. What was I going to do?

As I wandered back home, I noticed the person was still waiting at the bus stop. I considered asking her if I could borrow a bus ticket; however, I hated to do this, as I felt it was against Bahá'u'lláh's injunction about begging. I weighed my options. I was desperate, so I asked anyway. "No I don't," was the curt reply. As I walked away, I finally had no recourse except to turn to God. I earnestly said the 'Remover of difficulties' and then stopped dead in my tracks—there, in the road, right in front of me, was a shiny silver quarter! With joy and relief I grabbed the quarter and shouted, "I'll pay you back!" turned and ran back to the bus stop just as the bus arrived.

Junior in front of his drawing board, Layton Design and Engineering, Edmonton, Alberta, 1972

While I rode into Edmonton, I felt so confirmed, so loved by our Creator. But also I thought it was odd I should yell, "I'll pay you back." That didn't make any sense. What a strange response.

I worked as an architectural technologist for a local engineering firm. We were extremely busy, as our firm specialized in walk-up apartments, and, because of the oil boom, accommodations were in very high demand. We were turning out apartments as fast as we could. Because we used an in-house design catalogue of standard apartment layouts and standard wall sections, the only creative parts of the process were the site layouts and building elevations. The engineers liked my work, and soon I was the 'elevator' of the group. The client would come in and say, "I would like a Tudor look or a Spanish look or a French provincial look," and I would turn our standard plywood box into a faux Tudor, Spanish, or French provincial looking apartment block. It was schlock architecture, but I found it to be a lot of fun.

I was working at my drawing board one day (This was before computer-aided architectural design.) when the company's receptionist came up to me with a very worried look on her face. She leaned over and whispered, "There's a huge Indian out front and he's looking for you." I got up and walked to the front. Of course I knew who it was, and thought, for a moment, that Rodger actually had my three hundred dollars, but that seemed highly improbable. "Hi Rodger, so you've got my money?" I asked cynically. "No," he said, with his eyes fixed steadfastly on the floor. "I've come to ask you if I could borrow twenty-five dollars." Annoyance came quickly up from the core of my being, but the tone of utter defeat in his voice stopped me from saying anything. "I need it for bus fare home," he said. "This city is killing me." Clarity came instantly. Now I knew what "I'll pay you back" meant, and

I also knew that this was finally something I could do that might really help him. I put my hand on his arm and said, "Sure, Rodger, I'll give you the bus fare. I think you're making the right decision to go home."

I never saw Rodger again, and I hoped that his decision to return to the reserve helped in turning his life around. I have felt reassured in my decision to give him the money (something I very seldom do for an addicted person), because I've come to the conclusion that God 'set me up.' Rodger had prayed earnestly to God for assistance, and God answers all our sincere prayers. He often uses us humans as His angels. But He knew that, in me, He had a particularly slow-witted angel, so He set up the 'can't make the bus fare into Edmonton' situation so I would be prepared to help Rodger when he really needed it.

40. The Car Cannibal of Muscow

The National Indigenous Teaching Committee met every Sunday at 'the Bahá'í House' in St. Albert, Alberta. It was called 'Bahá'í house' because two young Bahá'í couples and a single Bahá'í were living there, and it was the hub of many activities. The first task of the new committee was to build a nation-wide connection with all the regional teaching committees, and the second task was to get from them an assessment of the current status of First Nations teaching in their areas. One component of this assessment was to find those things that were working well. The assessment showed that, apart from a few hot spots, the work with the First Nation communities was at a low ebb, and that there didn't seem to be any promising methods being utilized. As a consequence of this information, the committee spent the better part of its first year rebuilding momentum for the First Nations work and consulting about the best approaches.

By the fall of 1972, we had re-established contact with most of our First Nation Bahá'í communities. About this time, we heard that, in Alaska, Jenabe Caldwell was utilizing a system he called the 'Nine Day Institute', with positive effect. The Canadian National Spiritual Assembly asked if a couple of facilitators could come to Canada to show us how it worked. In response, the Alaskans sent Lynn and Loretta King down, and they held a number of 'Nine Day Institutes' with both First Nation and non-First Nation attendees. The results were quite astonishing, and those attending left with revitalized spiritual direction in their lives. As a result, our committee decided to re-open the mothballed Fort Qu'Appelle Bahá'í Institute building, and to utilize the 'Nine Day Institute' methodology to re-invigorate the teaching and consolidation work in Saskatchewan.

Now we had to assemble the team that would operate the Institute. We were able to get Mark Caldwell, Jenabe's son, to help us set up the 'Nine Day Institute' program; Poova Murday, from South Carolina, to handle the outreach activities; a cook; and a facilities handyman. What we still needed was a co-ordinator to handle the day-to-day operations of the Institute. Although we had several promising leads, these all fell through. In the end, the committee decided that I should go down to be the co-ordinator. I agreed and made arrangements to leave my job and apartment. I had managed to save up some money, and that would allow me to act as co-ordinator for some time before I needed to find employment again. Although I had planned to take the bus down, Don Todd, a Dené[87] friend of mine, who was training to be a pilot, offered to fly me down. Flying down to Fort Qu'Appelle would give him the opportunity to log some good hours of flying time. So I agreed to go with him. He was able to get a plane that needed to be taken down to Regina. At the same time, he needed his car taken down so he could drive back. Dwayne Yanch was free and offered to drive it down for him.

Don had his solo rating, but he didn't have his IFR[88] rating yet. That meant that we needed to start out early to be sure we reached Regina before nightfall. Our flight plan was to fly southeast to Lloydminster, on to Saskatoon, and then south to Regina. The plane we were ferrying was an older Fleet

---

87   A First Nation tribe from the Northwest Territories.
88   Instrument Flight Rating, needed to fly at night and in bad weather.

Canuck made of metal rod and canvas and looked to me like one step up from a kite. It was a good thing that Don didn't need his IFR rating to fly, because the plane didn't have many instruments anyway. The fuel gauge was a cork on top of the fuel in the tank, with a bent wire against a gauge. As we flew, we encountered a stiff crosswind from the south, so the little plane was being tossed about quite a bit. As we were coming into Lloydminster, we were just about to land when a gust of wind hit the plane, and we made a perfect three-point landing in the field, parallel to the runway. After Saskatoon, we headed south, right into a strong headwind. We flew and flew, but we weren't getting very far very fast. I noticed that the cars on the highway were travelling much faster than we were. It was starting to get dark, and we were still some distance from Regina. Both of us had noticed that the fuel gauge had stopped moving, as the cork was no longer in contact with any fuel in the tank, but neither of us mentioned it. I wasn't really worried, however, as we had already landed in a field once on this trip. Finally, we landed in Regina, out of gas, in the dark, and with no landing lights. As our little stealth plane taxied through the dark, the tower crackled in, saying, "Would the pilot report to the flight control manager immediately!" Anyway, this method of getting to Regina was more interesting than taking the bus, but the bus would probably have been faster.

When I finally got to the Fort Qu'Appelle Institute building, it was in the final stages of being readied for the project. I met with the Institute Committee, which had been appointed by the National Spiritual Assembly from friends in the area, and we began to contact potential projecteers who could volunteer some time to the project. Poova was already there, and he was an excited, impatient ball of energy. To begin recruitment, I called a potential projecteer but she was temporarily indisposed, so I left a message indicating she could call us back collect. Poova was not at all happy with my laid-back manner, and he felt we wouldn't get anyone to come with that attitude. "When Linda phones back, let me handle it," he said. Soon the phone rang and Poova shouted, "Linda, oh Linda, we need you! We love you! We can't do with . . . yes, operator, I'll accept the charges." And thus it was that the grand project had begun.

We were able to get a number of volunteers for the project, and Mark Caldwell had arrived from Alaska. The first order of business was to put the projecteers through a 'mini institute' to get them up to 'spiritual speed' to begin the outreach program. While this was going on, I was faced with a big problem. The First Nation communities we would be working with, in southern Saskatchewan, were spread over an area of approximately 100,000 km^2, and we had no means of getting our project teams out, or of ingathering the First Nation friends back to the Institute. When I raised this with the committee, they contacted the National Spiritual Assembly, who made it clear they were not able to purchase or insure any vehicles for us. Our only option was to find friends able to loan vehicles to the project. This prospect did not look too promising. We decided to say some earnest prayers for a resolution to this crucial problem.

In the meantime, I did a quick assessment of what we had. The mother of Doreen Fox (one of our projecteers) needed her car during the week but could make it available to the project on the weekends. Cyril Spicer had brought his 1968 Pontiac station wagon with heavy duty suspension, and that looked like one good car we could depend on. Hilaire Hamonic had brought an old Chrysler with him; however, on the way down, his hood had blown off and smashed his windshield—so there was that. And that was just about it: one full-time vehicle;

one part-time vehicle; and one—yikes! Don Todd, seeing my dilemma, drew me aside and said he would be willing to sell me his car at a reasonable price to help with the project. We worked out a deal, and, even though I didn't have a driver's licence, I became the proud owner of a 1968 metallic-turquoise Corvair Monza SS with white leather upholstery.

One of the local Bahá'ís said that there was a car cannibal up at Muscow[89], and that he might be able to fix Hilaire's car at a reasonable price. When we got there, the mechanic said that he had several Chryslers in the yard and that he should be able to fix ours—no problem. A few days later, we went to get the car and it was looking perfectly serviceable. We now had three-and-a-half cars. While we were standing there, I saw a 1962 Ford Fairlane that looked to be in good condition, and I asked the mechanic how much he wanted for it. "Oh," he said, "the transmission is gone on that one, but I have a couple more in the yard, so I guess I could throw together one workable vehicle between the three of them." He quoted me a very good price and we had a deal. We finally had four-and-a-half vehicles, which I thought would be sufficient for our needs. By now we had developed such a good relationship with the car cannibal of Muscow that we went to him for all our automotive needs. It was almost as if he were a member of our project team.

Now, with a corps of charged-up volunteers and a fleet of sorry vehicles, held together with baling wire and duct tape, we were able to begin pursuing the project's objectives. Unfortunately, the purchase and repairs of the vehicles had used up most of the money I had intended to see me through the project. However, I was able to continue to function as

---

89   Muscow, Saskatchewan is an unincorporated locality 6 km south of
     B-Say-Tah village, on highway 210.

co-ordinator, because the project itself provided me with food and shelter, so everything was still a go. Through the fall and winter, with a constantly changing array of volunteers, the project was making good headway, and the level of activity had rejuvenated many of the First Nation friends on the reserves we were working with. The 'Nine Day Institute' methodology was working wonderfully, and those who came to the institute were being spiritually enriched.

The car cannibal at Muscow, Saskatchewan

41. **Blood in the Dust**

[Flash forward]

Not many years ago, when my daughter, Celeste, was attending Maxwell International Bahá'í School, my wife, Anne, and I lived in the Cowichan Valley, just outside Duncan, on Vancouver Island. The Bahá'ís in the Cowichan area decided to rent the local theatre to put on a play for the Ascension of Bahá'u'lláh. We had some outstanding local talent, and the production shaped up nicely. Most of the friends in the Cowichan Valley and some youth from the Victoria area systematically went door-to-door to hand out invitations to the play. Anne and I had gone with different groups, and, when I returned home, I found Anne sitting in the kitchen with hydrogen peroxide and some gauze, attending to a wound on her arm. But, to my surprise, she was squeezing the wound as if trying to remove some foreign object. "What happened?" I exclaimed. "Oh," she said. "I was bitten by a dog while trying to hand out invitations." "Is something stuck in the wound?" I asked. She laughed sheepishly and said, "No. I was trying to squeeze some blood out, but, try as I might, I haven't gotten one drop." I instantly understood, and we both laughed. She was referring to a quote by Bahá'u'lláh that states: *"Say: O ye lovers of the One true God! Strive, that ye may truly recognize and know Him, and observe befittingly His precepts. This is a Revelation, under which, if a man shed for its sake one drop of blood, myriads of*

*oceans will be his recompense. Take heed, O friends, that ye forfeit
not so inestimable a benefit, or disregard its transcendent station."*[90]

[Flash back]

I had been the co-ordinator on the Fort Qu'Appelle institute project for seven months now, and the constant stream of
little crises that attended the project had slowly been wearing
away on me. For starters, I was broke, and couldn't even buy
little necessary toiletries like toothpaste or aftershave. But the
real burden was the social condition of the reserves we were
working with. I could never have imagined the severity of
the tests represented by the winds I had seen blowing in my
vision. Alcoholism had swept the First Nation communities
like the 'Angel of Death,' destroying individuals, families, and
whole communities. Child neglect and abuse was rampant.
Incest, violence, and illness were commonplace. And acci-
dents and suicides made funerals a regular community event.
We had learned, early on in the project, that no teams were to
go out to the reserves the day of, and a few days following,
the issuance of the welfare cheques. It was just too dangerous.

I went out to visit one elder who had become a Bahá'í, back
during the Ten Year World Plan, only to find her, beaten and
starving, in her home. Her son had beaten her up to force her
to sign over her welfare cheque so he could continue his binge.
I brought her back to the Institute so she could get some nour-
ishment and regain her strength. But this was an exception.
We simply did not have the resources to begin to address the
magnitude of the social ills we faced. On another occasion, we
visited a home, in the middle of winter, to find four children,

---

90   *Gleanings from the Writings of Bahá'u'lláh*, p. 5

ages eleven years down to a baby, left for days without food or heat. We went to their uncle, who lived nearby, and asked him to take some wood to their house for them. We then went to a nearby gas station/convenience store and bought a couple of boxes of cereal and a gallon of milk so the kids would have a little something to tide them over. When we returned, there was no sign of the uncle or the fuel he had promised. We had to get back to the Institute, but we were very worried for the welfare of these kids. These are only a few of the countless situations faced by the projecteers as they went out to these reserve communities.

At the same time, those who came in to the 'Nine Day Institute' found a spiritual haven and shelter. We hoped that this would strengthen them to face the difficulties they would find when they returned home. But, in most cases, they simply sank back into the moral morass. I was particularly distressed when one attendee begged me to let him stay at the Institute. He fell at my feet, grabbed my legs, and bitterly sobbed, "Please do not send me back home." My heart was broken, but what could I do? We had no resources to act as a refugee camp for those seeking shelter from the appalling social conditions on the reserves.

I didn't realize it then, but all these situations were having a devastating effect on my mind and emotions. I was living in a constant 'slightly out of touch with reality' depression. Another aspect of the project was becoming apparent. It was proving hard to find people able to come in to the Fort Qu'Appelle Bahá'í Institute for a full nine days. In the end, this proved to be the 'Achilles heel' of the project. Still, I doggedly pushed forward, but it began to look to me like we were only providing a band-aid to the hemorrhaging wounds suffered by these desperate communities.

Firewood cutting 'bee' on Pasqua Reserve, Saskatchewan

Riḍván was coming up, so the National Spiritual Assembly asked the committee if the projecteers could help form the local Spiritual Assemblies in those First Nations communities that had nine or more adult Bahá'ís. One of these reserves was Nut Lake.[91] This reserve was quite a bit north of our area of operation, but I took a team up to see if we could make contact with any of the Bahá'ís living there.

After asking around, we managed to find the home of one of the Bahá'ís. There was an air of tension about our visit, and I asked the friend if we should leave. He said, "No, but today is election day for the Band chief and council—if they can find anyone sober enough to vote. This can often be a violent time

_____

91   Now known as Yellow Quill

on the rez." Just then, two pickup trucks, full of men with rifles, pulled up outside the house. They burst in without knocking and demanded to know who we were. We told them that we were just visiting with some friends, but they weren't buying it. "No you're not. You're those 'bahoos' trying to influence the outcome of today's elections!" he shouted. "Get out of here. Get into your car. And get off this reserve before we decide to shoot you." I started to explain that Bahá'ís were not interested in politics, but I could quickly see these guys were not interested in explanations—just action. So we got up and were escorted out to our car. We travelled in convoy off the reserve: one truck in front and one behind, until we reached the boundary of the rez. As we departed, we heard some gun fire, I guess to ensure we didn't try to sneak back on.

There was complete silence in our vehicle as we drove south. You could cut the tension with a knife. Finally, I said, "Almost exactly ten years ago my father was driven off Nut Lake Reserve at gun point. I guess this is sort of becoming a family tradition." Slowly, one of the projecteers began to laugh. Suddenly, we all broke out in uncontrollable laughter for several minutes—until most of the tension had dissipated. When we got back to the Institute, our trip to Nut Lake became the focus of general conversation. Alex Poorman, whose mother was from Nut Lake Reserve, happened to be at the Institute that day, and was distressed to hear that they would treat visitors in such a surly way. He had lots of relatives on that reserve and volunteered to go up and help them form their Assembly himself. I offered to go with him, but he said it would probably be wise if he went alone. "Okay," I said. "I'll get an oil change on the Corvair, fill it up with fuel, and you can take that."

We took the Corvair to the service station first thing in the morning, and by ten o'clock it was ready to go. I wished Alex a safe trip and we said a 'Remover of difficulties' together, and he was off. At about one o'clock we received a call from Alex. The bung had fallen out of the oil pan on the Corvair; all the oil had leaked out, and the engine seized a few kilometres north of Wadena. He indicated that he was going to hitch a ride to Nut Lake, but that we should probably make arrangements to recover the Corvair as soon as possible. Although the mechanic swore up and down that it was checked, it was obvious that, when the service station changed the oil, they had only replaced the bung finger-tight, and it had jiggled loose after a short while. They refused to take any responsibility, but I knew they felt guilty when they offered us the use of their recovery dolly and two Jackalls, free of charge. The only problem was that none of our vehicles had a tow hitch, so we took Hilaire's car up to the car cannibal at Muscow, and he quickly put a hitch on for us.

It was just after noon the next day when Hilaire and I headed north to recover the Corvair. We knew we were getting close when we saw the unmistakable line of oil down the road. There it was, pulled over on the gravel shoulder. We needed to jack it up using the two Jackalls, drive the dolly under the front tires, and then jack the car down into the two wheel wells provided. All of this went fairly smoothly until it was time to lower the car. Everyone knows, and a yellow warning label is clearly attached to the handle, that you must bring the handle of the Jackall up next to the jack stand before you switch the ratchet to lower the vehicle. Otherwise, the full weight of the vehicle will act as a lever and instantly snap that handle up against the stand, breaking your fingers if they are in the way.

The daylight was beginning to fade, and we didn't know how long the hazard lights would flash before the battery gave out, so we had to get a move on. Everything was lined up, so I quickly threw the ratchet into the lower position. Even as I was pushing it, I realized my mistake, but it was too late. I instantly looked at the handle, but it was already in my face. I took two steps backward and fell face down on the gravel shoulder. I don't know if I went unconscious or not, but all I could hear was ringing in my ears. My muscles didn't seem to want to work, so, when I tried to roll over, all I seemed to manage was to squirm in the dust. I was aware that blood was filling my left eye, making it hard to see. When I did manage to roll over, I saw Hilaire standing over me, and I could see from the expression on his face that the situation was not good. I managed to crawl over to the car, and I leaned up against it. I think Hilaire was talking, but I couldn't make out what he was saying. Oddly, I was in no pain. In fact, I felt detached, almost silly. Hilaire helped me into the car, and he quickly finished up, and we drove into Wadena. The blood was pouring out of my left brow, down my face and all over my shirt, so I put my hand tightly over the wound to staunch the flow. There were no medical facilities in Wadena, so we pulled into a service station, and I went into the washroom to wash off the caked-on blood and dirt from the road. When I had finished that, the situation actually looked a lot better. I took several wet paper towels, held them tightly to the wound, and we took off for the hospital in Fort Qu'Appelle—two hours south.

By the time we made it back, I was in pain. It felt like my skull was cracked open right across my brow. When we saw the doctor and I told him the story, "Boy are you lucky to be alive right now," he said. If I hadn't looked to see the handle coming, it would have probably hit me in the temple, and that would have killed me instantly, but, because it hit me in the brow, I was saved. "That's the hardest part of your head," he said. He also told me that I had done the right thing to keep pressure on the wound. The skin had already adhered on either side of it, so I didn't need stiches. He put on a butterfly bandage covered by a dressing, and held them in place with a gauze bandana. Finally, he gave me some pain medication and a prescription for more, which I could fill in the morning.

In the morning, I looked and felt a mess. I had two black eyes, and there was a heavy, blood-filled bruise under my left brow. To cap it off, I was broke and couldn't afford the pain medication. With the pain and decreased cognitive function, I was wandering around in a daze, not sure what I was supposed to be doing. Then Russell Lee, one of the Institute Committee members, came in and hustled me out to his car. "Get in," he said decisively. "We're going to fill that prescription of yours." On the way back to the institute, I asked if we could stop at the post office to see if I had any mail. To my surprise, my income tax refund cheque had come, and I had a little money again. I don't remember any of this time very well, but I went to the bus terminal and bought a ticket back home to Six Nations. I don't even remember if I met with the Committee or said goodbye to anyone. I just got on the bus and headed east. In retrospect, it seemed to me, receiving that cheque, at that particular moment, was like God saying—it's time for you to take a break. The only thing I remember of that trip home was that, while waiting to transfer buses in Winnipeg, one of the station's notoriously aggressive panhandlers sat next to me and offered me a swig of his whiskey. Although I declined, I guessed that I must have looked pretty down and out if even the panhandlers were taking pity on me.

So ended my stint as co-ordinator of the Fort Qu'Appelle Bahá'í Institute. Just as I had seen in the vision that night in Africa, I had stood in that wheat field and felt the full force of that mighty gale. But, in the end, I felt completely powerless to stem the tide. All my efforts seemed to have come to naught. The one thing I was able to take away from that experience was the memory of lying face down in the dust, with the blood pouring down my face. In retrospect, that was one of the more significant moments in my life—however, I have often wondered if Bahá'u'lláh's quote applied to injuries that were self-inflicted.

42. **My Days in Big Steel**

When I returned home to Six Nations Reserve from Fort Qu'Appelle, I was a bit of a wreck. I was broke, and I was suffering the after-effects of my accident. I needed to get a job, but I also needed to spend a couple of weeks recovering, especially the black eyes—not a particularly good first impression for a potential employer. When the black eyes had faded, and I had updated my résumé, I turned to job-hunting in earnest. Grandma subscribed to the Hamilton Spectator, so I began following the help wanted ads. Hamilton was Canada's heavy industry capital, and its huge plumes of acrid smoke were a sign of employment and wealth. But I had no idea that I was about to be involved with cleaning up some of that mess. Soon, I had an interview with a civil and structural engineering company in downtown Hamilton.

I met with the senior partner, Archibald Atkinson, and the interview went extremely well. Archie was very interested in First Nation's culture, and, when he found out I was from Six Nations Reserve, I think I had the job, even before he looked at any of my work. The firm consisted of four partners, and they called the company Atkinson, Parazater, Lostraco, Bannerman Engineering Ltd. For weeks after I got the job, people were happy for me, but when they asked where I was working, all I could say was, "I have no idea!" A year later, they merged with a company of four electrical and mechanical engineers and changed their name to Group Eight Engineering Ltd., which, I thought, was a good marketing move!

Archie was a kind, active man, in his late sixties. He had been a naval architect, but, when this work had moved overseas, he retrained as a structural engineer. He was like a father figure for the three other younger partners. He was an avid collector of First Nation's pottery and jewellery and was good friends with the Smiths on my reserve. Bun Smith was famous for her pottery, and her husband, Orville, was a silversmith. Steve Parazater, the next senior partner, was a younger, serious, no-nonsense sort of guy, who had developed a wide network of movers and shakers within the City of Hamilton, and was able to attract a lot of business to the firm. Tony Lostraco was a gregarious, animated Italian, who had previously worked for Dofasco Steel. A majority of the work we did was for this company. Glenn Bannerman was the youngest partner, and was the only civil engineer of the group. Glenn liked to do most of his own work, and I had the impression he felt he was in competition with the technologists, rather than being in charge.

We had four technologists in the office, but, unlike the situation in Rhodesia, we didn't work for specific engineers. Eugene Evans, the lead technologist, would assign projects based on who was doing what at the time. Personally, I liked the projects in the steel mills the best. This was the first time I had worked in heavy industry. These huge plants had been built around the turn of the twentieth century and had been modified so many times I don't think anyone really knew what made things work and what were vestigial remnants of the past. Now, as the new anti-pollution laws were coming into effect, these plants were once again undergoing major modifications, this time to try to curb the blatant dumping of every kind of toxic chemical into Lake Ontario and the atmosphere. These modifications were not only good news for the environment, but also for our firm, as it meant plenty of interesting projects for us.

Back at the turn of the twentieth century, mills belching clouds of toxic waste were a sign of industry and wealth.

The facilities and equipment in these mills are truly impressive, and they operate at such extreme pressures and temperatures that humans seem like insignificant gnats next to them. For example, there was a hot blast main pipe that channelled superheated gas from the Cowper stoves to the blast furnaces, and, because of a fatal accident, it needed to have an emergency shut-off system installed. Tony and I worked on the design, which included a shut-off valve in the three metre diameter refractory brick-lined pipe. As no metal surfaces could be exposed to the hot (1000⁰C) gases, it made for some innovative design challenges for the refractory brick lining.

Another tricky project was controlling emissions from the recycling-oxygen blast furnaces. Post-consumer steel was collected for reprocessing, and a large portion of this was made up of dead automobiles and trucks. These were flattened, chewed up in a rotating shear, and dumped into a charging hopper, along with refrigerators, washing machines, etc. At periodic intervals, these were dumped into the oxygen blast furnace. Instantly, all the volatile materials—upholstery, plastic, etc.—would burst into flame, releasing a toxic cloud into the atmosphere.

Obviously, this situation had to be cleaned up. The first step was to design a light-weight collector to sit on the roof of the existing mill building. To do this, I needed to clamber around in the trusses above the blast furnace to take the necessary measurements. This required great care, because, not only would it be good not to fall into the furnace, but also not to be asphyxiated by the toxic fumes. Every time the furnace was charged, hot toxic fumes would fill the upper part of the mill. A safety officer went with me to ensure I was properly tied off, and to monitor air quality. Every time the charging warning buzzer sounded, we would have to scramble out a roof hatch. There would be a loud whoosh as the combustibles were consumed in the furnace, and then we would wait until the meter indicated the air was safe before we could enter the hatch again. Although architecture was my first love, I really enjoyed the adventure of this work.

Another area we worked on was building a desulphurization station. When making steel, one impurity that must be minimized is sulphur. To remove this element, the molten iron is mixed with a magnesium/lime reagent, which combines with the sulphur and separates it from the iron. This process was being done in torpedo railcars out in the yard, which released all manner of sulphur by-products directly into the air. We needed to build a building for this process, which would make it possible to collect the gases and process them through a series of scrubbers and filters. Dofasco had purchased one of the pavilions from Expo 67, and it had been lying disassembled in a field for the past five years. They wanted us to use these pieces to make the new structure. It was a bit of a puzzle to turn a World's Fair pavilion into a heavy industrial desulphurization station, but it worked well.

Growing up on Six Nations, we did most of our shopping in Caledonia or Brantford, so to go to Hamilton was considered an adventure in the big city, or the 'Big Smoke' as my uncle called it. There was a certain satisfaction for me, as an adult, to go back and help clean up some of that smoke.

43. Hell—How Bad Could It Be?

Of all the stories I'm relating here—this is the hardest to tell. Not because I can't remember the details, or that it is difficult to put the words down on paper, but because words are simply incapable of conveying the impact of this dream on my soul.

In the Writings of Bahá'u'lláh, He compares His revelation to an ocean. All the previous Manifestations were constrained in what they could reveal by the limited capacity of mankind to understand. As Jesus said, "*I have yet many things to say unto you, but ye cannot bear them now. Howbeit when he, the Spirit of truth, is come, he will guide you into all truth.*"[92] Well, the Spirit of Truth has come and—Wow! His revelation, comprising over a hundred texts (books, tablets, letters, etc.), is a wonderland of concepts, ideas and verities.

When I was young and studying the Faith, I loved nothing more than to play in this wonderland. But all my play was intellectually driven, and, while there was plenty to satisfy the mind, there were also many perplexing and seemingly paradoxical concepts which troubled me. However, whenever I ran into a roadblock of understanding, I would pray to God for assistance, and, usually within a short time, an event or events would happen in my life that gave me insight into the very problem I was grappling with. For example: when

---

92   *King James Bible*, John 16:12, and 'Abdu'l-Bahá, *Some Answered Questions* (2014) p. 123.

I was in high school in the United States, I read Bahá'u'lláh's statement, *"Say: True liberty consisteth in man's submission unto My commandments, little as ye know it."*[93] I was perplexed. How could liberty be attained through submission? This didn't make sense. It was contradictory. It was—un-American! I therefore prayed for enlightenment on this topic.

Being the chubby little half-breed in the class, I was often the target of bullying, and so, sometime soon afterward, I was cornered by some guys determined to give me a wedgie. I managed to avoid that indignity but was roughed up in the process. I yelled at them to, "Stop this and grow up!" One of the assailants laughed and said, "We can do what we want. It's a free country." Illumination dawned—unfettered personal liberty was not the absolute virtue it was advertised to be. Its only logical outcome is anarchy. Only when mankind is internally constrained by the inculcation of the commandments of God can a society function in a truly free environment.

This became a spiritual habit then: whenever I didn't understand something, I would pray and wait expectantly for the answer. I was able to learn a lot through this process. However, in my early twenties I came upon what was, for me, one of the hardest ideas to conceptualize. It was the relationship between free will and predestination. I would engage in endless discussions with anyone who was even mildly interested in such conundrums, to hear their ideas on this and related concepts. The issue came to a head when I read Bahá'u'lláh's statement, *"He should forgive the sinful, and never despise his low estate, for none knoweth what his own end shall be. How often hath a sinner, at the hour of death, attained to the essence of faith, and, quaffing the immortal draught, hath taken his flight*

---

93   Bahá'u'lláh, *The Kitáb-i-Aqdas*, p. 63

unto the celestial Concourse. And how often hath a devout believer, at the hour of his soul's ascension, been so changed as to fall into the nethermost fire."[94]

When I combined this startling concept, in my mind, with the idea that God knows the end of all things in the beginning, I became troubled. Although I have free will, God already knows what my end will be. Here I am, struggling to understand God's Will and doing my best to try to follow it, and yet, He may be 'up there' shaking His head sadly and saying, "Nice try, John, but it's all for naught."

As time went on, these ideas began to fester in my mind. My relationship with God took on an adversarial quality, and I began to see the whole concept of creation as an unfair game. God makes the rules, He knows the outcomes in the beginning, and we are trapped in this game with no power to control it, and no power to get out of playing. Creation, both in this life and the next, began to seem to me like two cells of the same prison. I was an inmate and there seemed to be no way out. A deep spiritual depression began to settle into my life, and I became profoundly unhappy. I became so upset with God, that I never even thought to pray for a resolution to this conundrum.

Eventually, in desperation, I reached such a low point that I decided to say nine *Tablets of Ahmad*[95] just for some relief of my suffering. When I had finished, I waited expectantly, but no spiritual enlightenment descended upon me from heaven, and I felt so far from God that even my prayers could not reach Him.

---

94   Bahá'u'lláh, *The Kitáb-i-Íqán*, p. 194

95   A prayer of Bahá'u'lláh that has a special significance and power in times of tests.

A few days later, I said my evening reading and prayers in a perfunctory fashion and went to sleep. Soon, I was dreaming of my days in Edmonton and service on the National Indigenous Teaching Committee. These meetings usually took place at 'the Bahá'í house' in St. Albert, and I knew its layout perfectly. In the dream, we were meeting at night, and I had to go to the washroom, so I got up from the group and headed down the lighted central hallway. The bathroom was the door on the right, half way down the hall, but there was a bedroom door on the left first. As I passed that door, I noticed that it was open about six inches—but there was something very strange about it. At first glance I couldn't figure out what it was, so I turned aside and walked into the darkened room. Instantly, I was awake with the sound of the most agonizing scream echoing in my ears!

I was sitting upright in the dark with my heart pounding. Did I scream aloud, or was it just something I had heard in the dream? My hands were cold and clammy, and I felt sweat breaking out on my forehead; I was in a condition of spiritual shock. Then, a realization suddenly dawned on me—I COULD SEE GOD! He was all around! His warm, life-giving love was an all-pervasive presence—surrounding, nurturing, and sustaining every created thing. I began to weep uncontrollably—my grateful tears raining copiously down my cheeks. Yá Bahá'u'l-Abhá, Yá Bahá'u'l-Abhá, Yá Bahá'u'l-Abhá,[96] I repeated over and over and over again. My free will had been completely stripped from me. God was there, comforting me in His loving embrace. But I no longer cared about free will and predestination or any argument, verity or truth. I just wanted to be in the reality of God's love—nothing else mattered. I never wanted to be separated from Him again.

---

96   O Thou the Glory of the Most Glorious!

I don't remember how long I sat there weeping and praying, but it was weeks, nay months, before I regained a sense of 'normal' reality and the presence of God faded again behind the veil of creation. But my relationship with God was permanently altered. I no longer found discussions of the various arguments and proofs or the analysis of obscure intellectual paradoxes of any interest. God's love is the only thing that matters—at all—both in this world and the next.

"But what happened in that split second when you entered that room in your dream?" you ask. Well, this is the part that is hard, if not impossible, to explain. I had begun to view the creation of God as a prison. I was unhappy to be an inmate. I had prayed to God for a resolution to this spiritual depression. Well, God simply left the door open. "You want out—there's the door."

What is outside of God's kingdom is too horrible to possibly explain. I can use the words, but they simply cannot convey the meaning—there is absolute purposelessness!

Words like hopelessness, despair, sadness don't even begin to touch that place. Words themselves and any meaning they may contain are crushed into non-existence—even the idea of meaning itself has no place there. But don't get the idea that this is a place of blissful annihilation. It is not. It is an active, evil force. For the human soul cannot sustain, even for a second, the horror of the despair of that place.

Also, being there changed my whole conception of God. Before this event, I thought of God like Michelangelo's painting of Him on the ceiling of the Sistine Chapel—a large powerful-looking man with white hair and beard. However, I instantly saw that God is a force—Almighty, All Powerful, and irresistible. It is as though absolute purposelessness is the natural state of non-existence and is a crushing, powerful, and immovable force. But God stands against this force and pushes it back. Within His Kingdom there is meaning, there is purpose, there is love.

Because of my discontent, God allowed me to wander out from under His protecting shelter, but only for a second, and then He snatched me back from oblivion and held me so tightly in His loving embrace I could see nothing but Him, until the agitation of my soul was comforted and my fears were calmed. I now knew what hell awaited them that turned away from God, and I was abhorrent of it. I had new insight into Bahá'u'lláh's Hidden Word: *"O son of being! My love is My stronghold; he that entereth therein is safe and secure, and he that turneth away shall surely stray and perish."*[97]

---

97   Bahá'u'lláh, *The Arabic Hidden Words* #9

44. Poorman's Pop

I was home at my grandmother's, one day in mid-June, when the phone rang. It took me a moment to orient to the caller on the other end of the line, but I soon realized that it was a Bahá'í friend calling from the Poorman Band Office in Saskatchewan. She said that the Band Council had decided to host an annual powwow on the reserve, and they were wondering if I could come out to help them. She went on to say that, at a recent rodeo on the reserve, the temporary refreshment stall had been an unmitigated disaster: there had been no accounting; the purchases had missed the consumers' preferences by a wide margin; and the stall storage area had been broken into and a large quantity of merchandise had been stolen. So she was wondering if I could come out and run the refreshment stall for their powwow.

I was amazed that they would ask me to undertake this task, because, at the time, I was living on Six Nations Reserve some 2800 km to the east. But, at the same time, I was flattered that they felt I was trustworthy enough to take on this responsibility. I said I would be honoured to help out in any way I could, and asked when the powwow was scheduled. They said that it was planned for the 1st of July long weekend, which was only two weeks away, but I had nothing else planned for that weekend, so I said that would be fine. They also asked if I could come out a few days early and sleep in the band office, where the goods and supplies were being kept, for security reasons. I said that I would and that I would see them soon.

This was going to be a long trip and a big job, so I asked my cousin David Boren, along with Kevin Martin, a Bahá'í youth from the reserve, to come along with me for the trip, and they agreed. It was a cool, overcast day when we left Six Nations, about noon, and headed north over the Great Lakes. By about one o'clock in the morning we were passing Wawa, Ontario, and heading out for White River through trackless boreal forest. There was a sign as we left town that said "No Services for the next 90 km." It was a spectacular, warm, starry night and the Milky Way shone brightly in the clear moonless sky. We were somewhere in the middle of that long, desolate stretch of road, when another flash of light caught my eye. This one was the overheating warning light on the dash. It flashed again, and then came on steadily. I pulled the car over onto the shoulder of the highway and saw steam coming out from around the hood. When things had cooled down a bit, we were able to open the cap and shine the flashlight down into the radiator—not a drop of moisture in sight. Although I was a member of CAA, the nearest telephone was at least 45 km in either direction. (This was long before cell phones existed.)

I was tired anyway, so I suggested we get some sleep, and maybe someone would pass by when it got light. I tried for ten or fifteen minutes to get to sleep, but with no luck. I just kept thinking of ways to fill the radiator again. Finally, I said, "Guys, we need to find a stream and a beer or pop bottle so we can refill the radiator." Kevin took the flashlight and went across to the ditch on the other side of the highway, while David and I walked along in the dark on the near side of the highway, dragging our shoes side-to-side in the grass, hoping to hit something. David said, "Aren't you afraid a bear might come lumbering out of the forest?" He couldn't see the disgusted look on my face as I said, "No—not until you mentioned it." Time was going by, and we were getting nowhere, so I silently said a 'Remover of difficulties.' Just then, David yelled, "Oh yuck!" and jumped back, leaving his shoe stuck in the mud. I could see, by the reflection of the stars, that the ditch was filled with water for some distance. Just then, we heard a shout of triumph from Kevin on the other side of the highway, as he had found a beer bottle and came racing across to try and find us. It took us some time to fill the radiator with only one bottle. I don't know why the radiator fluid had leaked out, but we had no further problems until we returned home, where I had it flushed and a sealer poured in. I guess the mud and detritus from the ditch had sealed the leak for the rest of the trip.

We arrived at Poorman Band Office about ten the following morning, and were warmly welcomed by Elsie Poorman and some of the Band Councillors. It was Thursday and 'camping day' would start the next day about noon, so we went out to the powwow grounds to see if we could help set up. The arbour was set up in the rodeo grounds, and our refreshment stall was around behind. It consisted of about five meters of serving counter with four folding tables just over a meter behind that, all under two very large, olive green tarps that were nailed to a header above the counter and spread out flat behind. I looked at this arrangement and asked one of the helpers, "What's with all the tarp?" He said, "That's for all the pop. We have 200 crates coming tomorrow morning at ten." I said, "Are you sure?!" That would be nearly five thousand bottles of pop!" He said, "It's a three-day event and we are expecting between five hundred and six hundred people." I was beginning to see the magnitude of the job ahead of us!

*Kevin Martin and my cousin David Boren at the Bahá'í temple
in Wilmette, on our way back from Poorman Reserve*

That morning, we helped set up the porta-potties, but by
noon it was over 35° C, and the sun was beating down relent-
lessly. All the set-up activities had ground the bone-dry soil
into powder, and little dust devils would whirl around any
further disturbance. Everyone decided to stop work until
things cooled down in the evening, and we headed back to
the band office. That afternoon, we took an inventory of all
the merchandise for the refreshment stall. Then I left the guys
and headed into Punnichy to get about $50 in dollars, quar-
ters, dimes, nickels, and pennies, for 'float.' While I was gone,
Kevin and David helped inventory the 'give away items.' I
didn't realize this, but the powwow was, in many ways, based
upon the potlatch ideal, and was not designed to make a profit,

but, on the contrary, was to demonstrate the generosity of the host band. There were piles of blankets, household goods, and miscellaneous gifts that would be given out to the participants at various times during the powwow.

That evening, Kevin and David went out to help set up the lights and the sound system, while I kept guard on all the stuff in the band office, and tried to figure out the logistics of systematically moving through all that pop. The pop crates[98] would form the structure of the storage area, and the two large tarps would be draped over them. The Band had ordered a truck-load of ice for the campers and the refreshment stall, and we had three large washtubs to put the ice and pop in. It looked like we were all set.

The next morning, we went out and rolled up the tarps and blocked out the areas where we would stack things. We explained the plan to the pop truck driver, who smiled in a slightly bemused way that worried me, because he had done this many times before, and he didn't say, "That's a good plan." When the pop was stacked, we got some help to unroll the tarps over the pile, and this made a neat, little covered area that would be our post for the next three days. As the day rolled on, we made several trips to the band office to bring car-loads of the other merchandise to the stall.

That afternoon, again, the temperature soared, and, as the first campers began to arrive, the kids immediately headed to the refreshment stall for some pop. At first, we told them that we would be open first thing the next morning, but, as people kept coming, we decided to get everything set up and go right into business. We got ice and filled the tubs, broke out a selection of pop, and set out the chips and candy. However,

---

98 Pop crates in those days were heavy wooden boxes with metal cleats in the corners to enable them to be stacked.

when we opened a box of chocolate bars, we could feel they were just a squishy mess under the wrapper, so we placed the chocolate bars in the ice with the pop. The sun beat down on the dark green canvas tarps, and the temperature in the stall rose higher and higher. Finally, David said, "If this keeps up, the pop is going to start exploding!"

Uh oh! We needed to get some air circulation in the stall, before the temperature became absolutely unbearable. So we opened up the tarps at the back of the stall and took five empty pop crates and slid them on top of the stacks, but under the tarp, to allow freer air circulation. As we did, the metal cleats on the top of the crates began tearing into the canvas, so we flipped the crates upside down. While we were doing this, one of the crates got stuck, and, as I tried to free it, the sharp metal cleat cut a deep gash into the index finger of my left hand. I had a first aid kit in my car and bandaged up my finger, but, as the wound was near the middle knuckle, it meant my left index finger was permanently pointing straight out, and it would make it hard to work. As I walked back to the stall, I saw all those crates and sighed. "Two hundred heavy crates to move, and I'm already a broken-winged bird. What have I got myself into here?"

By ten o'clock that night, we closed everything down. David and Kevin would sleep in the stall, and I would sleep in the band office to guard the remaining merchandise and the give-aways. The next morning, I asked if anyone had any ointment to put on my wound, but nobody did, so I cleaned it up the best I could and redressed it. I counted out the 'take' from the night before, and, after recovering my 'float', still had several hundred dollars. I asked the Band secretary for a safe place to put the money as it came in, and she gave me the key for the top drawer of her desk. I headed out to the powwow grounds to enjoy the free pancake breakfast that the band provided. We set up the stall, but business was slow until the Grand Entry for the dancers, about one o'clock, when the relentless heat was back and everyone was thirsty, especially the dancers. A nice, ice-cold pop seemed to be on everyone's mind, and we were worked off our feet refilling the tubs with ice and pop, moving crates back and forth, and giving refunds for the bottles. Two or three kids kept coming back with more and more empties, and, at first, we thought they were going around the grounds picking up any empties they found, until we caught them crawling under the tarp and stealing the returned empties. We now not only had to attend to our customers, but keep an eye on our back too. Every hour or so the cashbox would be filled to overflowing, so I would take the cash back to the band office and lock it in the secretary's desk.

When we closed, about eleven that night, all three of us were completely exhausted. I looked at the stacks and was alarmed to see that we had already emptied 130 crates of pop! That meant that we only had 70 crates left to last for two more days! I talked to the organizing committee, and they agreed that we would need at least 100 more crates. Someone also pointed out that we were almost out of ice, and, at the rate it was melting, it would probably be all gone by morning. The secretary said she would order more of both in the morning, and I drove back to the band office for the night. My left index finger was really aching as I took off the dirt- and pop-soaked bandage, and I noticed that it was bright red and swollen. I cleaned it up the best I could and redressed it, but I was running out of bandage materials from my first aid kit. I awoke early Sunday morning with a headache and what I thought was a slight fever. I looked at my left hand and noticed that it was all red and swollen. I asked the secretary if they had a first aid kit, and, after a moment's thought, she said there may be one in the kitchen. She came back with a fairly comprehensive kit, including bandages and some Ozonol ointment. So I cleaned the wound, applied a liberal dose of the ointment, and bandaged the finger again.

Things were moving slowly out at the powwow grounds, so the guys and I pulled back the tarps and moved a hundred cases of empties off to the side to make room for the new load of pop, which was scheduled to arrive about eleven a.m. When the ice truck came, it was just over half full, and the driver said we were lucky to get that. Being a long weekend, and with a heat wave over the province, beer, pop, and ice were in very short supply. When the pop arrived, we unloaded a hundred full crates and loaded the hundred crates of empties back on the truck. The driver reiterated what the iceman said: that this was the last of the pop until the bottling plant opened again next week. The day proceeded pretty much as the day before, but we thankfully ran out of chocolate bars toward evening, which meant that we wouldn't be facing a complete meltdown if the ice ran out. But I was increasingly not well, and, despite the oppressive heat, I would go into violent chills and had to sit behind the stacks with one of the guy's sleeping bags wrapped around me until they abated. By closing time that evening, we had less than fifty crates of pop left and practically no ice. I was so exhausted that, when I got back to the band office, I just flopped onto my sleeping bag and fell into a fitful sleep.

Monday morning dawned and I ached all over. I had a high fever and my left hand was dangerously swollen. I set out for the powwow grounds for what was going to be one of the hardest days of my life. The last of the ice had melted overnight, and a slight breeze had kicked up, and, periodically, the whole powwow grounds would disappear in a cloud of dust. Often, I would just sit behind the pop stacks and say the healing prayer over and over again. Up front the crowds thinned, as we only had hot pop to sell. Still, by closing time, there were only five or six crates of the less popular varieties left. We stayed over one more night to guard the empties and to do the final accounting. The refreshment stall had pulled in over $4,000, which was a lot of money in those days.

I don't remember the trip home, as David did most of the driving. Kevin drove part of the way, but he didn't have a driver's licence, and I never would have allowed it if I had been thinking clearly. We got home about a quarter to twelve in the morning, and I had David drive me straight to the hospital in Brantford. The doctor took one look at my finger, took a swab, and hooked me up to an antibiotic drip, while I slept in the emergency room. When I woke up, it was evening, and I felt somewhat better. The doctor was furious. He said I had a massive systemic staphylococcus infection, and asked why I had waited so long to have it seen to. He sent me home with a prescription for some heavy-duty antibiotics and a warning not to wait so long in future. However, this episode gave me a great analogy to use in my deepening work with the friends over the years. (See *The Procrastinating Patient*—next story.)

It was my pleasure to be of service to the Poorman community, for these people have always been so responsive to the call of Bahá'u'lláh. But I think, if I am asked to handle Poorman's pop again, I would give this opportunity to serve to someone else.

45. The Procrastinating Patient

One of the things that I have stressed in my teaching and consolidation work, both with the First Nations friends and with my own daughter, was the critical importance of reading the Sacred Writings of the Faith. The Revelation of Bahá'u'lláh is an ocean of knowledge and spiritual healing, that has the power to recreate the individual, as well as the whole of society—but most of mankind has failed to search for and reach this ocean.

Bahá'u'lláh says, *"Whoso hath searched the depths of the oceans that lie hid within these exalted words, and fathomed their import, can be said to have discovered a glimmer of the unspeakable glory with which this mighty, this sublime, and most holy Revelation hath been endowed . . . Happy is the man that hath attained thereunto, and woe betide the heedless."*[99]

To emphasize this point, I would often tell this little story:

There were once two old friends. One of them was not feeling well, and complained to the other that he had been out of sorts for several days. He had a headache and fever, and had not wanted food. His friend asked, "Haven't you seen a doctor about this?" The sick friend responded that he felt that doctors were expensive, and, in most cases, didn't help at all. But the well friend indicated that he had a very good doctor, and he could call for an appointment if his friend wished. So the sick friend went with his well friend to see this doctor.

---

99   Bahá'u'lláh, *Gleanings from the Writings of Bahá'u'lláh*, p. 10

When the sick friend came out, he was very enthusiastic. "You were right!" he said. "He is an excellent doctor. He examined me and was able to identify that a minor injury I had had a few days ago was infected, and now I had a systemic staphylococcus infection, and that, with proper treatment, I should be well in no time!" With that, the two friends departed.

Medications not taken

The next day, when the well friend went to see how his sick friend was doing, he was surprised to find him much worse. "I'm not so sure your doctor was that good after all," said the sick friend. "I feel much worse today." "I don't understand that," said the well friend. "Have you been following the treatment that he gave you?" The sick friend looked confused and said, "What treatment?" "Didn't the doctor tell you what you needed to do to get better?" asked the well friend. "No, he just handed me a slip of paper." "Can I see that paper?" asked the well friend, and he took it and read it over. "This is a prescription for the medicine you need. If you want to be better, you have to take this down to the pharmacist and have it filled." That afternoon, the sick friend's wife went to the pharmacy and had the prescription filled.

The next morning, the well friend was distressed to get a call from the sick friend's wife. She said his friend was fading fast, and that he should come along to take his leave of him. When the well friend got to his friend's bedside, he saw that he was not looking good at all. He then noticed the bottle of pills on the man's bedside table. "Haven't these pills been helping?" he asked, as he lifted the bottle to read the label. Shaking the bottle, he noticed that none of the pills seemed to be missing. "Have you been taking these pills as prescribed? The label says: take one pill three times a day with meals." "What!" said the sick friend. "I have to actually take those pills!" "Yes, of course!" said the well friend. "If you don't actually take action and internalize the medicine, you can never hope to recover from your ills." So the sick friend followed the treatment and was soon well again.

Now, how silly was that patient? We would never be like that—or would we? Bahá'u'lláh tells us: *"The world is in travail, and its agitation waxeth day by day."*[100] *"Witness how the world is being afflicted with . . . inveterate diseases. Its sickness is approaching the stage of utter hopelessness . . ."*[101] *"The All-Knowing Physician hath His finger on the pulse of mankind. He perceiveth the disease, and prescribeth, in His unerring wisdom, the remedy."*[102] HOORAY! We're saved. But are we? Is it as easy

100 Bahá'u'lláh, *Gleanings from the Writings of Bahá'u'lláh*, p. 118
101 Bahá'u'lláh, *Gleanings from the Writings of Bahá'u'lláh*, p. 39
102 Bahá'u'lláh, *Gleanings from the Writings of Bahá'u'lláh*, p. 213

as that? Or, are we being like that silly patient? The remedy lies in the Revelation of Bahá'u'lláh. Some of the friends never even check the prescription to see what they need to do to become spiritually healthy again. Some may actually go out and buy the books, and even lay them on their bedside table, But if they never read them—if they never put the teachings into effect in their lives—then the healing remedy cannot save them, much less the ailing society of which they are a part.

46. **A Lesson in Detachment**

While I was working for Atkinson, Parazater, Lostraco, Bannerman Engineering Ltd., my old friend, Don Todd, came to town. Don would appear and disappear at random, and you never knew when he would show up. One day, as we were talking, he looked up at my hat and said, "My, that's a real cool hat you've got!"

When I was out in Saskatchewan, one of the projecteers had given it to me. It was a brown, heavy-felt fedora with a flat brim. I called it my 'half breed' hat, á la 'Billy Jack.' Marie Piapot, the aunt of Buffy St. Marie, had said it was much too plain, and gave me a beaded hatband for it. It was the only thing of personal value that I had returned with from the west.

"Thanks," I said.

"Yes, that's a real nice hat," he continued. "I'd sure like to have a hat like that!" I realized that he was hinting that I should make a gift of it to him. I prided myself that I was not attached to material things, and felt moved to offer it to him. However, there was a vestige of selfishness deep inside, and I thought to myself, "No, I like this hat, and it's mine." So I said, "Maybe, when you're out west again, you can find a similar one." And changed the subject. I felt sort of ashamed, and struggled hard to justify my action.

A few days after Don had left town, I was working a bit late and had to hurry to get home and have supper before Feast. As I was getting into my car, I realized that I had forgotten my hat and turned around to go back and get it. However, I was running late, so I thought, "What the heck, it'll still be there tomorrow." I got in my car and drove off. The next morning, I was surprised to see two police cars parked haphazardly in the parking lot behind my office building. As I opened the rear door, a policeman stopped me and told me I had to use the front entrance. The rear stair was taped off and covered in glass and blood. "What on earth happened?" I asked. "There's been a break-in, and you'll have to use the other entrance," he repeated as he shuffled me out.

My friend Don Todd

When I got into the office, Eugene, my co-worker, came up to me and said, "Some goofball, eh?" "What happened?" I asked. "Some nut-job tried to break in by taking a four pound hammer and a cold chisel to the hinges on the aluminum door out back. Only problem was, he cut the top hinge first, and, as he was cutting through the bottom hinge, the door fell on him and smashed over his head. The cops want us to check and see if anything's missing, so just take a look around. I can't see anything's gone," he said, and wandered off.

We all checked around, and, in the end, nothing was missing. It seemed that his injuries were severe enough to end his misadventure before it had begun. For the life of us, we couldn't imagine what a thief would find of value in an engineering office, anyway. (This was in a period before office computers.) When it was time to go home, I went to the coat rack by the back door to get my hat, but—it was gone! Suddenly, I surmised what must have happened. The thwarted thief decided to leave, but how to hide his obvious and suspicious injuries? He saw the hat on the nearby coat rack, grabbed it, and made his getaway. My hat was the only thing taken in the robbery! The words of Bahá'u'lláh came quickly to mind. *"Say: Rejoice not in the things ye possess; tonight they are yours, tomorrow others will possess them."*[103] Still, I would have far preferred that Don have my hat, than to lose it in that fashion.

103 Bahá'u'lláh, *Gleanings from the Writings of Bahá'u'lláh*, p. 138

47. Mail-Order Husband

By the time I returned to Canada from Southern Rhodesia, I was just coming out of a deep agoraphobia. This condition had isolated me socially. I functioned well at work and in my service to the Cause, but, outside of that, I preferred isolation. I assiduously avoided what I perceived was the invasive and dangerous arena of unstructured relationships with people—especially people of the opposite sex. I had had a brief friendship with a young projecteer during my service at the Fort Qu'Appelle Institute, but that had ended in a rather ambiguous way, which only reinforced my apprehension of such relationships.

Although Bahá'u'lláh had recommended marriage to His followers, it was not obligatory, so I felt I was in no need of companionship and was perfectly happy to live my life alone. However, when I moved to Kingston, Ontario, to help manage construction of the Basic Health Sciences Building for Queen's University, I found myself in a community of about fifteen twenty-something single Bahá'ís. At first, I kept pretty much socially aloof from the community, and threw myself into my work. Then, one sunny Sunday afternoon, as I was sitting alone in my office recopying some rough notes that I had taken at a recent site meeting, I stopped and looked down at what I was doing. There was absolutely no reason to be doing this. The notes were perfectly fine just as they were. I said to myself, "Stop this, and go home." Then I just sat there looking out the window at the park. As I watched the people below, I felt a dull, aching pain in my chest, and became alarmed. "I'm only twenty-six; I can't be having a heart attack!" But, as I pondered the source of this pain, it occurred to me—I was lonely.

Junior and a co-worker review the schedule for the construction of the Basic Sciences Library for Queen's University, Kingston, 1976

I thought, "I just need to be with someone to talk to—but who?" Margaret Boland, one of the young Bahá'ís in the community, lived only a few blocks away, so I went to her house, and one of her roommates answered the door. I asked if Margaret was home, and she had me wait outside as she went to find her. When Margaret came to the door, I said, "Hi, I thought . . ." but no more words came out, and, although I frantically searched, no thoughts came to my mind. Margaret just smiled and said, "Come on in and we'll have some tea." I realised then that I was going to have to work harder at developing my social skills and at interacting more with the young people in the community.

At this time, I was serving with Pat Harding and Anne Shuster, two young singles in our community, on the Regional Teaching Committee, so I got to know them in a more formal and comfortable (for me) setting. But soon my project in Kingston was ending, and I moved back to my grandparents' house on the Rez. For a while, I thought I was completely hopeless, to have had such a great opportunity and let it slip away without finding a suitable helpmate. But soon I got busy with other things, and that episode in my life faded into the background. For one thing, I was made an assistant to Auxiliary Board[104] member Dr. David Smith, and was assigned to work with eleven local assemblies in the Niagara Region. At that time, the assistants were a new facet of the administration, and it was exciting to be part of trying to figure out how they were supposed to function.

As a kid, I was a fan of the TV show *Route 66,* and dreamed I could travel around like Buzz and Todd in a new Corvette, helping to solve people's problems. Now, as it happened, I had just bought a brand new Celica GT, and here I was travelling around trying to help the local Spiritual Assemblies with their growing pains. It seemed like I was living my boyhood dream, so the thought of providing space in my life for a wife and family faded quickly into the background.

As before, one of my jobs at home was to walk down to the road and get the mail every day. I personally did not receive a lot of mail, so when I got a letter with an unfamiliar return address, I was curious to see who it was from. It was customary, at our house, to read the mail over morning tea, and I must have fallen silent as I read and reread the

---

104   See Auxiliary Board and their assistants in the Glossary

letter over and over again to myself, because I suddenly became aware of my grandmother saying repeatedly, "What's wrong, Jackie?" I smiled weakly and said, "Some girl I know is asking me to marry her." My grandmother, Aunt Marge, and Cousin Don all started talking excitedly over one another. "Who is she?" "How long have you known her?" "Where does she live?"

I, of course, knew this young woman but had never exchanged more than a few words with her, and was completely surprised and perplexed at this proposal. Not only was marriage the farthest thing from my mind, I could not generate even the slightest feeling of romantic interest for this person. Still, I didn't want to hurt anyone's feelings, so I agonized over the reply. I managed to scribble down my feeling flattered by her attentions, and added a few lame excuses why this would not be possible, and sent off the letter. A couple of days later, when I went to the mailbox, I saw the now-familiar stationery and return address. This time, she was more forceful and pooh-poohed my lame excuses: indicating time was passing, pointing out neither one of us was getting any younger, and intimating I needed to get with the program! My grandmother just laughed, and my aunt and cousin teased that I was "caught—hook, line and sinker!"

This time I decided to be more forthright, but, still, I didn't want to hurt her feelings. So I prayed and thought seriously about just what were my real feelings concerning marriage and settling down. I got out my copy of 'Marriage: A Fortress for Well-Being'[105] and studied the quotes carefully. I prayed for guidance to do the right thing, then composed a heartfelt letter saying I was happy the way things were, and that I really was not contemplating marriage at this time. I sent this letter off

---

105 A study guide for Bahá'ís contemplating marriage.

and hoped that that would be the end it. But, just in case, I suggested Don go get the mail for the next little while. I got really nervous when, a few days later, another letter arrived, but, in this one, she said that, although she was sad to hear my decision, she wished me all the best. So that seemed to be the end of that. I just hoped that I had handled it in the right and honourable way.

A couple of weeks went by and no more letters came. I had just begun to relax, when Don came in with the mail and announced that there was a letter for me. With much apprehension, I opened it. We sat drinking our tea, when I exclaimed, "What the heck!?" "Is that girl still chasing you?" asked my grandmother. "No," I said. "This is another girl asking me to consider marriage!" "No," said Don. "You're kidding, right?" "No, I'm not," I said. "I don't know what the heck is going on here!" "Whatever it is, you should bottle and sell it," said Aunt Marge. "You'd make a fortune." This was just too strange to believe. And, in my experience, when something is too strange to believe, God is at work behind the scenes.

How could the same thing be happening twice in one month? However, there was one crucial difference—this second letter was from Anne Shuster, whom I knew from Kingston—and I liked Anne.

Anne had also thought she would find her life's partner in the Kingston community, after returning to Ontario from pioneering in the wilds of Newfoundland. But, like me, she didn't really connect with anyone. Anyway, not long after I had left, she moved to Merrickville, Ontario, to help form a local Spiritual Assembly there. The next year, after the post-convention conference, she gave a ride home to a young woman who was soon off to the small settlement of Rae (Behchokò), in the Northwest Territories, to likely marry a man she had never met. He was a Bahá'í pioneer to that remote community and had not been able to find a suitable wife there. By coincidence, she was trying to pioneer to the North. She had answered an ad for an au pair position in that same community, and the postman, who knew everyone's business in the small community, had made the connection and suggested he write to her and propose marriage. Anne was impressed with how that story unfolded, from each partner initially thinking the idea was crazy to finally, actually, considering marriage.

For days afterward, Anne was in a deep depression. How could this wonderful thing be happening to a girl ten years younger than her? The depression was a motivator, putting her in touch with her desire to be married. She had been busy pioneering, serving the Faith, and expecting some man to take the initiative, and it just wasn't happening. So she began praying long and hard about what to do. During these prayers, she decided to be pro-active and write to the National Pioneer Committee to see if there was a youngish, potential pioneer looking for a wife. But she struggled with how to word such an awkward letter 'honestly,' as she didn't really want to pioneer again, at this point, just find a like-minded man. As she grappled with this, my name popped into her head. So, instead of writing to the National Pioneer Committee, she sat down and wrote me a letter suggesting we investigate each other's character with an eye to seeing if we might make good marriage partners.

I'm sure God was playing the matchmaker here, and He realized that, in me, He was dealing with a real knucklehead. If I had received Anne's letter cold, I would certainly have rejected the offer. So He had to 'prime the pump', and get me thinking seriously about marriage again, before Anne's letter reached me. This time, I responded positively, though tentatively, and, through consultation and prayer, the rest is, as they say, history.

Anne Shuster and John Sargent on their honeymoon
at the Grand Canyon, Arizona

48. Angel at Eight O'clock

As I have said many times, I believe God uses us as His helpers, if we are attuned to His will. In the late eighties, I worked at the Native Desk at the Canadian Bahá'í National Centre, but we lived in Welcome, a small community near Port Hope, Ontario, which was about 100 kilometres east of the National Centre. Every morning, I fought the rush hour traffic along Highway 401 to come into work. This particular morning, I was breezing along and passed a Bahá'í I knew in his BMW. However, as I looked back in my mirror, I saw him slow down and pull over to the shoulder of the road. That was not a safe place to stop. Something must be wrong—perhaps he had run out of gas. So I thought I had better turn around and go back to see if I could help.

Turning around on the 401 is no easy task, however, as you have to continue on to the next exit, get off the highway, cross over, and re-enter the highway in the opposite direction, go down to another exit beyond where you want to be, and follow the same procedure to go back in the desired direction again. As I did this, I was passing the place where my friend had pulled off on the opposite side of the highway, and I noticed he was no longer there. I didn't know why he had pulled over, but whatever it was must be okay now, for he had gone on his way.

But again, I couldn't just turn around. I still had to continue on to the next exit. Just at that moment, I saw a man standing beside a vehicle pulled off on the shoulder of the road, desperately trying to hitch a ride. Since I couldn't help my friend, I decided I may as well give this guy a ride. So I pulled over and stopped. As I was going at highway speed, I came to a stop a little ways down the road and put the car in reverse, but this was not really necessary as the guy came sprinting down the shoulder so fast that he had opened the door almost before I had backed up at all. "Thank God! Thank God! Thank God!" he said as he got in. "What's the trouble?" I asked. "I ran out of gas right there, but I really need a ride to work!" he said.

Highway 401 north of Toronto. Not easy to turn around.

He explained that, for one reason or another, he had been late to start his shift twice that month; and his supervisor had threatened, that if it happened again, he would be fired. This morning, he was careful to head out extra early so as not to be late, but forgot to check if the car had enough gas. He had been on the side of the road for fifteen minutes, and no one had stopped to offer him a lift. Finally, in desperation, he prayed to God, "Please help me, I need this job!" "Just then you pulled over, like you had heard my plea." I said, "I didn't. But God did. So let's get you to work before you're late again."

49. The World Changes—A Patriarch Passes

As I mentioned earlier, I believed I knew this incredible secret, and I used to tell my classmates at school, "The whole world is changing because of the coming of The Báb 175 years ago." Just during my years, which have rushed by so quickly, I have seen a constant increase in the rapidity of that change. From horse and buggy days of no electricity or plumbing, in my early life on the rez, to cell phones, the internet, and incredible improvements in transportation and health care. In fact, as I sit at my computer writing this, I look around me and see that virtually everything in my home, from the non-toxic paint on the walls to the low 'e' glass in the windows, has changed over those years. At the same time, we are faced with challenges unmatched in former times: climate change, weapons of mass destruction, threat of global pandemics, and environmental unsustainability. As we read from 'Abdu'l-Bahá, all these changes are necessary, to challenge the increasing maturity of the human race. *"That which was applicable to human needs during the early history of the race could neither meet nor satisfy the demands of this day . . . The gifts and graces of the period of youth although timely and sufficient during the adolescence of the world of mankind, are now incapable of meeting the requirements of its maturity. The playthings of childhood and infancy no longer satisfy or interest the adult mind."*[106]

---

106 Abdu'l-Baha, *Foundations of World Unity*, p. 9

Two incidents from watching my daughter, Celeste, grow up have clearly imprinted this basic truth on my mind. When Celeste was five, it was time to enroll her in kindergarten. But she was quite perceptive, and, as Anne and I began talking up this new and exciting event, she became more and more apprehensive about what her parents were trying to sell her. When the day arrived, she became obdurate, and we practically had to drag her to the school. When we arrived at the kindergarten room and introduced Celeste to the teacher, she hid behind her mother with the biggest pout I had ever seen. But, as we talked to the teacher, she was looking around the room. The room had several play centres set up. One was a pile of giant Lego blocks; another an Indian village; and the one that really caught her attention was a play store with fake products on the shelves and a play cash register full of play money. Quietly, as we talked, she slipped away and began playing with the cash register. She found, it seemed, that kindergarten might not be so bad after all. That big room was perfectly set up to attract the interest and challenge the intellectual capacity of the five-year-old mind.

Now pan ahead thirteen years. Celeste was a senior at Maxwell International Bahá'í School, on Vancouver Island, and we decided that, during the spring break, we would travel to Ontario to check out several universities with her. After visiting several of the top schools in that province, we ended up at Trent University near Peterborough. We met a professor in the Environmental Sciences School, and he took us to one of the big open labs they have. While he talked about the program they offered at Trent, I watched Celeste become more interested as she gazed around the room. The professor was saying, "Over there is the electron microscope, and over here is the mass spectrometer and gas chromatograph." I was having déjà vu. The only difference was the kindergarten room was set up to intellectually challenge a five-year-old, while this room was set up to challenge the mental capacity of an adult.

Five-year-old Celeste and her very patient cat

In the same way, the world 175 years ago was set up to challenge the capacity of mankind in its youth; but now the world is changing, and we are being challenged to grow up before we wipe ourselves out! This change began in early April 1863, when, in the Riḍván Tablet, God said to Bahá'u'lláh, *"Canst thou discover any one but Me, O Pen, in this Day? What hath become of the creation and the manifestations thereof? What of the names and their kingdom? Whither are gone all created things, whether seen or unseen? What of the hidden secrets of the universe and its revelations? Lo, the entire creation hath passed away! . . . Verily, We have caused every soul to expire by virtue of Our irresistible and all-subduing sovereignty. We have, then, called into being a new creation, as a token of Our grace unto men. I am, verily, the All-Bountiful, the Ancient of Days."*[107] This momentous event was prophesied about two thousand years ago in the Book of Revelation: *"And I heard a great voice out of heaven saying, Behold, the tabernacle of God is with men, and he will dwell with them, and they shall be his people, and God himself shall be with them, and be their God. And God shall wipe away all tears from their eyes . . . for the former things are passed away. And he that sat upon the throne said, Behold, I make all things new."*[108]

My daughter, Celeste, had graduated from high school and was accepted into the Environmental Sciences program at Trent University, but she deferred her first year so she could do a 'year of service'[109] in Africa. My father was very excited. He had only seen his granddaughter twice: once when she was eighteen months old, and again when he stayed with us for a week when she was twelve. Now, she was going to Africa to stay with him for the better part of a year. He was emailing us regularly to tell us of all the exciting things he had planned for her during her stay.

Celeste was his only grandchild, but Anne and I had no idea how actively he had followed her development. Karen

---

107 Bahá'u'lláh, *Gleanings from the Writings of Bahá'u'lláh*, p. 29-30

108 *King James Bible*; Revelations 21:3-5

109 Bahá'ís have a program whereby youth can defer their university studies to offer a year of service to another Bahá'í community somewhere in the world.

White, a friend of ours on Vancouver Island, who had recently visited some of her family in Zimbabwe, said we should see Celeste's 'shrine' in my dad's study. Like all proud parents, we had sent Celeste's annual school pictures to him, as well as copies of the various scholastic, equestrian, and singing awards she had received over the years; and he had one whole wall plastered with all these mementos.

Big changes were happening in our little nuclear family. Celeste was heading off to Africa, Anne had decided to part-time pioneer to China, and I decided to keep the home fires burning and prepare for retirement. Anne was accepted into the diploma program, Teaching English as a Second Language, at Vancouver Community College, and I was now the Executive Director of the Alliance Tribal Council, with its offices on Tsawwassen First Nation. So we needed to make arrangements to leave Vancouver Island and move to the Lower Mainland. One long weekend, we returned home, tired after several days of house hunting in Vancouver, to find several urgent messages from Aili, my dad's wife, on our answering machine. I immediately phoned her back. "Junior, I'm so sorry, so very, very sorry," she sobbed repeatedly. "What's happened?" I asked. "Your father has passed away, suddenly, of a heart attack," she said.

She told me that the Bahá'ís of Harare had set up a display at a local book fair, and my dad had agreed to be one of those who manned the booth for a four-hour shift. When the next person was not able to attend, he agreed to take on his shift as well. Aili said that he really enjoyed this opportunity to introduce the Faith to the many attendees who stopped by the booth, but, by the end of the day, he was exhausted and retired early without any supper. He spent a very restless night, and, when he still was not hungry in the morning, Aili took him to emergency at the hospital. It was discovered that he had suffered a heart attack. After several days in the hospital, he was doing better and phoned Aili to bring some fresh clothes, as he was to be discharged in the morning. When she arrived the next morning, they told her he had passed away during the night.

I was, of course, completely shocked by this news. There had been no warning that his health was poor. And he had been so excited about Celeste coming. I had been really happy that Celeste was going to get to know her grandfather. He had found Bahá'u'lláh while wandering in the wilderness of Wyoming (of all places) and passed on this priceless heritage to our family. Now, just weeks before she was to leave for Africa, he had passed away. Aili begged us to let Celeste come, anyway, and visit the friends in Africa. And Celeste was definite about her desire to continue with her plans.

For the last quarter of a century, my dad and I had lived, literally, on opposite sides of the planet, and I had always felt that great distance. Apart from occasional, urgent telegraph messages and his annual long-distance phone call on my birthday, we lived our lives completely apart. Now, I suddenly felt his presence very near to me. Even to this day, I feel him close at hand, and I frequently call on him for help, and am amazed how he has responded to these requests.

I am deeply proud of him. How this 'black sheep' of Windsor Locks, growing up in the racially charged atmosphere of that time, had spent his life in service: first to the First Nation peoples of North America, and then to the peoples of Africa. Now, he had done what he had intended to do—leave his bones at his pioneer post. I think, as a comfort to me, a few days after I received news of his passing, Bahá'u'lláh put in front of me the following quote: *"They that have forsaken their country in the path of God and subsequently ascended unto His presence, such souls shall be blessed by the Concourse on High and their names recorded by the Pen of Glory among such as have laid down their lives as martyrs in the path of God, the Help in Peril, the Self-Subsistent."*[110]

John Sr. and Aili at a Bahá'í conference in Harare, Zimbabwe, 1996

---

110 Bahá'u'lláh, *Messages from the Universal House of Justice 1968–1973,* p. 102

50. China-ward

In 2000, Anne started pioneering to China. She taught English there for several six-month stints, and returned to Canada for the rest of the year. In 2002, during one of her stays in China, I went to visit her. Wow, what an adventure! I wouldn't have believed it if I hadn't seen it with my own eyes! 1.3 billion people going full tilt twenty-four hours a day—every day! Everyone, everywhere, confident in the 'new China'. A developer here in Canada thinks it's a big deal to build a twenty-five-story apartment building. In China, a developer thinks nothing of putting up two dozen twenty-five-story apartment buildings. All at once! All in an atmosphere that seems like complete chaos! But I'm getting ahead of myself.

I arrived at the new Hong Kong airport at 5:15 in the morning. The relative calm of early morning gently acclimatized me for what was to come. The technology was astonishing! The airport itself, and the airport train to Hong Kong, were technological marvels, and new road works, fantastic bridges, and high-rise buildings were everywhere. Even that early in the morning, the tropical heat and humidity were becoming apparent. At Kowloon Station, I transferred to the older KCR rail link, and headed for the Chinese border. By this time, the city was waking up, and the crowds and noise were becoming larger and louder. By the time I left the train at the Chinese border, I was being swept along the platform by a sea of humanity. I felt like an extra in a sci-fi movie about some future dystopia. Glaring advertisements competed for space with multilingual directional signs in neon, all within a glass and chrome world, while a disembodied, computer-sounding voice droned in the background—"psychotropic drugs are forbidden in the People's Republic of China, with severe penalties of life imprisonment and five million Hong Kong dollar fines." But all of this was only preparatory to what awaited me on the other side of the border in Shenzhen.

Twenty-five years ago, Shenzhen was a sleepy fishing village of about 10,000. Today, it is an exploding industrial and commercial centre with ± 5.2 million people! Anne had arranged for me to be met by Kam and Nadia, two of her friends, who were English teachers at the Shenzhen Foreign Language Secondary School. From the border it was an hour-and-a-half bus trip to their campus, all the way across the city. This was my first experience with Chinese traffic, and I can assure you, it rivals anything they have at Six Flags![111] The main road had three lanes in each direction, separated by an island, but the traffic seemed to travel six or seven vehicles wide in each direction. The vehicles included ox carts, bicycles, motorcycles, rickshaws, cars, minivans, buses, dump trucks with pups, and 18-wheelers, all moving at different relative speeds. Traffic signals seemed to be taken as suggestions only, and I expected to be dumped on the street with a mighty crash at any moment. Add to this a constant stream of pedestrians jay-walking perpendicular to the traffic from both directions, and you feel like you're in some frenetic video game. But, in my two weeks there, I did not see a single accident, and in the end, concluded that everyone in China uses the 'Force' to get from point A to point B. The last stage of the trip to the campus was on a motorcycle taxi, with my large suitcase balanced on the handlebars, and me on the back, clutching my other bag.

---

111 A chain of amusement parks in the United States.

Rushing through this type of traffic without the surrounding steel cage of the bus, or even a helmet—now that really gets the adrenalin going.

Everything everywhere seemed to be under construction. I had heard that architecture in China had become rather 'kitsch and gaudy', and, I must admit, some of it seemed that way, especially the quarter-scale replica of the Eiffel Tower in a downtown park. But I was glad there was no trace of the sombre, sterile architecture seen in other communist countries, but, rather an architecture that had a sort of youthful exuberance, and wonderfully unrestrained and creative playfulness about it. I was in my element!

After supper and a rest, Kam dropped me off at the new Shenzhen airport for my trip to Nanning. After a long wait in the airport, the incoming plane arrived about two hours late. I watched the passengers disembark and the ground crew service the plane. I also noticed that the flight crew had come out and were walking around the fairly new Airbus 319, kicking the tires and checking to see if any of the vital pieces had fallen off. Suddenly, one of them stopped, looked at one of the engines, and called for the service people to bring the tools. A mechanic on a bicycle pickup truck peddled out to the plane, opened a panel on the side of the engine, and, after a minute or two, took out a piece. I looked on incredulously as he placed the part on the concrete apron and proceeded to pound on it with a hammer. After several tries, he eyeballed it to be 'just right' and proceeded to put it back in its place. Just then, the boarding call was made. I stood, transfixed, apprehensively staring at the plane for a long time. Finally, I said a 'Remover of difficulties', and got in the boarding line-up.

I arrived at the Nanning airport at about quarter to one in the morning, and it was so good to see Anne. She was tanned, healthy, and happy looking. We took a taxi from the airport to her apartment. I was amazed to see that the same traffic chaos I had seen during the day in Shenzhen was going on in the middle of the night in Nanning, except that many of the vehicles had neither lights nor reflectors! May the 'Force' be with them!

Anne's apartment was on the second floor of an older, teachers' apartment building, on the campus of the Nanning Foreign Language School. This was a private secondary school for upper middle class students who were looking at careers requiring some English capability. I must admit my first impression of the smallish two bedroom apartment, with all hard surfaces and a bare fluorescent strip light, was not favourable, but I could see, by the way everything had been neatly put in place, and a fresh bouquet of roses had been carefully placed in a vase on the coffee table, that I was being lovingly welcomed to this little outpost in the heart of China. I was hot and tired, having travelled for about thirty hours, all the way from National Convention in Toronto, straight to Nanning; so I was anxious to call it a day.

My next surprise was that the shower occupied the same space the water closet and only used cold water. However, after some initial short, sharp breathing, the cold water actually felt good and lowered my core temperature enough to make going to sleep easier. I made a quick mental note to myself that the next time I took a shower, I'd remember to remove the toilet paper roll first! This one had swollen to twice its normal size and was completely ruined. Even in the middle of the night, construction continued on a sports complex across the lane, with the concrete mixer going gloppeda gloppeda whump whump whump as a lullaby for this tired traveller.

Anne had the week off for the May holidays, and so we were free to visit, be visited, and travel. We met the other foreign teachers, including Karen (a friend from Vancouver

Island) and her three young daughters. Anne also introduced me to some of the staff at the school, former students from Yong Jiang University, and some local friends. Two of these friends, a couple named Victor and Nina, were especially welcoming and were able to visit with us several times. When they heard that I was interested in architecture, they arranged to take us to an ancient village that was not defaced during the Cultural Revolution—when so much of the priceless heritage of China was wantonly destroyed. Victor worked for a company that had a subsidiary in Vancouver, and he was trying to get posted there.

The picturesque Guilin area of China

After a few days, China began to seem more rational to me, even inviting. I was able to relax on the buses and even not to be chicken crossing the road. (Ha, ha.) I really loved the fresh food they served; however, they liberally used heavy soybean oil on all their food, and this eventually caught up with me and sidelined me for a day. After that, I bought some Pepto Bismol and was more careful about what I ate. We visited museums and parks, and shopped, both in the narrow, crowded lanes

and in the huge Western-style department stores (looking for
Pepto Bismol and mouthwash). One evening, we were invited
to a reunion supper with several of Anne's former students.
They had a very nice apartment, with furniture like you would
find in the West, but they insisted they were poor and told
fantastic stories of the opulent apartments that government
officials and their children were building. China was literally
transforming around us, and these student talked with great
confidence about their and China's future.

For the May holidays the school had arranged a trip to
Guilin for the foreign teachers and their families, but things
had not worked out, so a shorter trip was arranged for the
following weekend. I think most of us in the West have, at one
time or another, seen a picture of the Guilin area of China, but
nothing prepares you for actually being there! It is about two
thousand square kilometres of karst topography, with unusual
mountain formations and caves. Guilin is a four-hour drive
north northeast of Nanning on a state-of-the-art superhigh-
way. I forgot to mention that everyone seems to drive with
a bunch of small bills scattered on their dash, and is required
to pay tolls at random points along the road, both in the cities
and on the open highway. (I could never see the rhyme or
reason as to the where or why for all these toll booths.) We
stopped briefly in Guilin for lunch and then pushed on for
another hour and a half to Yangzhou, which is a tourist resort
town sort of like Whistler or Banff, and where we had our
hotel reservations. We put our bags in our rooms and headed
to West Street (its actual name) for supper and some shopping.
It was a perfect, exotic night, and I could have sat for hours
in the little sidewalk café, sipping cappuccinos and watching the Western tourists on the streets and in the shops. We
haggled in the markets until after midnight, then headed back
to the hotel, and yep—construction going on right outside our

hotel window, and it was another gloppeda gloppeda whump whump whump lullaby.

We assembled early the next morning and headed out to catch a boat down the legendary Lijiang River. It was not hard to see why this was the birth place of classical Chinese art and poetry. It was unbelievably beautiful. We went to see one of the many famous cave complexes and, as the road had been recently washed out, had to wade across a swift mountain stream to get to the cave entrance. That afternoon, we drove back to Guilin, which is a growing city of over 300,000, with a strong tourist focus. It seems to really come alive as the sun goes down and you get the feeling you've entered Epcot Centre at Disney World. The karst pinnacles and prominent man-made structures come alive in multi-coloured floodlights, and the streets are taken over by a bazaar of small booths that seems to miraculously appear from nowhere. Dazzling floats, with pretty girls dancing to modern Chinese music, move slowly through the traffic, and every square metre of the buildings' surfaces were covered in neon signs. Eventually, we headed back to Nanning—tired, and with our senses fully satiated. As we travelled along, I got a chance to talk to the vice-principal, a charming woman who spoke excellent English, about her vision of the future of China. She saw a world of great opportunity opening up before her students. We arrived back at the school at half past one in the morning.

Anne had to go back to teaching for the first three days of the next week, so she pressed me into service as a guest lecturer. I told simple stories about the First Nations people of Canada, and then answered questions. I was very pleased with these students and their simple, straight-forward questions. Again, I saw the same exuberant, self-assured attitudes I had observed with the university graduates a few days earlier.

John and Anne on a slow boat in China

After several years, Anne had the protocol of the Chinese people down pretty well. She had framed some First Nations pictures as special gifts, and, on the last day I was visiting, she asked the principal, the Communist Party secretary, the vice-principal, the head of the English department, the foreign teachers' liaison, and a senior English teacher to a special supper at a local sidewalk restaurant. Some hours before the event, a very nervous foreign teachers' liaison came to Anne's apartment and asked me what I wanted from the school. Anne had prepared me for this meeting and explained that, by asking these important people to dinner and presenting them with gifts, it would appear I intended to ask for a favour in return. When I explained that I merely wanted to thank them for allowing me to visit their school and for all the support they had given to Anne, she was greatly relieved. The event went very well despite the rumbling traffic and pouring rain.

Everyone enjoyed the dinner, we all made speeches, and I presented them with our gifts. For my speech, in addition to the thank-yous, I paraphrased parts of 'Abdu'l-Bahá's talk about the future of China.[112] The impact of these words was profound, even through translation, and we left that dinner with a deep sense of unity and joy.

The next day was my last in China. Although Anne and I were still tired, we had to get up early to pack and greet the stream of visitors who came to say their goodbyes. My visit had only been two weeks, and it had come and gone in a flurry of adventures, yet the friendship I developed with many of these people was warm and deep. The foreign teachers' liaison came up to the apartment with a brightly wrapped gift for me from the principal, and said that the school limo was at our disposal to go to the airport. Anne, two of her students, and I went to the airport together, driven by Mr. Li Tan, the driver who had taken us to Guilin and with whom I had developed a friendship, although he spoke no English. My flight was called, and it was time for a tired and tearful farewell to Anne.

I didn't know it at the time, but I was already beginning to come down with the mandatory bout of Chinese bronchitis, and my head was pounding. I had seen a lot, and the excitement of the constant noise and hustle and bustle was now wearing on me. Canada was only twenty hours away, and I craved its calm quiet. But, as I sat in the plane and looked down on China, I marvelled at this 'other world' and its dynamic spirit, and knew for sure it was, as 'Abdu'l-Bahá had predicted, 'the country of the future'.

---

112 Words of 'Abdu'l-Bahá from the Diary of Mírzá Ahmad Sohráb, 3
     April 1917 - *Star of the West*, book 5, Vol. VIII, No. 3, P 37

51. Angus

When I heard of the passing of Angus Cowan, I pondered this news with sadness, but also with wonder that I had had the opportunity to know this beautiful soul. Ever since my dad and I became Bahá'ís, we had known and admired Angus Cowan. My dad and I first met Angus when we came to Canada during the Ten Year World Plan to help with the First Nations teaching work. He was our mentor and exemplar of how pure, disinterested love can touch the hearts of those he was sharing the Faith with. When we first met him, before we went to Africa, he was a member of the National Spiritual Assembly of Canada, but when I saw him on my return in 1971, I noted that he was an Auxiliary Board member. I felt that he fit this role perfectly, as he was so good at encouraging the friends to arise and serve the Cause. He was always keenly interested in the First Nations work, and so our paths crossed again and again over the years.

Patricia Verge, in her book *Angus–From the Heart,* did a fantastic job of bringing the story of his life to the attention of future generations, so I needn't recount any of that here. But I thought I would add two stories that were particularly touching for me.

One day, while I was serving on the National Indigenous Teaching Committee in Edmonton, I received a call from Angus. He was heading down to Wolf Point, Montana, for a Regional Indian Teaching Conference, and he wanted to know if I would like to go with him. Our committee was always looking for ideas and methodologies for bringing the Faith to the First Nation Peoples, so this seemed like the perfect opportunity to learn what the Americans were up to. He was coming from British Columbia, so he suggested I take the bus down after work, and we could meet in Calgary.

It was late afternoon on a hot July day as we headed south to Lethbridge. The sky was clear where we were, but off to the west were some low cumulus clouds, and off to the east were some high anvil thunderheads, lit up spectacularly by the late summer sun. As we drove, we talked about many things, but the First Nations work and the Bahá'í youth revolution were the main topics. After we left Lethbridge, we headed southeast on Highway 4 to the Coutts crossing into Montana. The last vestiges of the evening sun had lifted off the thunderheads, so they were now lit only by periodic lightning bolts. Angus asked if we could drive in silence for a while. I said, sure, and he asked me to hand him some objects from the glove box. To my surprise, he had a scarf, cap, and driving gloves there. He put them on and rolled down the front windows. The warm evening air rushed in as he put the 'pedal to the metal' and we flew down that long, lonely road. Angus loved to drive fast on the vast prairie highways, and he had a stack of speeding tickets to prove it. After a while, I looked over at Angus. He had this sweet, serene smile on his face. He loved working with the First Nations people, and I had the feeling that he was anticipating greeting the friends gathered at the teaching conference. It seemed to me he had the air of a lover rushing through the night to the arms of his beloved.

Many years later, Anne and I were living in Saskatoon, and I was working for the Saskatchewan Indian Nations Company, which was the economic development arm of the Federation of Saskatchewan Indians (FSI). Saul Sanderson was the Grand Chief of the FSI, and, under his leadership, it had dramatically increased in reach and scope. Saul also held a senior position within the Canadian Liberal Party, and many felt he would be the first First Nation person to be the Minister of Indian Affairs and Northern Development. His wife, Carol, was even more ambitious, and confided to me that she was sure he would be the first First Nation Prime Minister of Canada.

Jamshid Aidun, Jalál Nakhjavani, and Angus Cowan at the Native Teaching Conference near Silver Creek, Alberta, December 1979

Late one evening, just as I was contemplating heading to bed, the phone rang. It was my boss, Pat Woods, calling from Regina. He and Saul had a seven o'clock meeting the next morning with the minister of Indian Affairs, and the proposal which he was going to present to him, had been left at the office. Could I, please, go to his office and get the three copies of the proposal and bring them down to him, at the Imperial 400 Motel in Regina, by six o'clock tomorrow morning? Sure, I said, as I quickly tried to figure out what time I would have to leave to accomplish this task. It was a three-hour drive to Regina, and I would have to get up, get ready, and then go to the office and retrieve the needed documents, before I could set out. That meant that I would have to be up by two o'clock in the morning to make it. I went straight to bed, but, because I was worried I might sleep through my alarm, I didn't sleep a wink.

Everything went according to plan, and I pulled into the Imperial 400 Motel at ten to six in the morning. I waited in the café, as instructed, and had a cup of coffee. By six-fifteen I began to worry if I had heard the instructions correctly. Finally, at six-thirty, I had the desk call Pat's room—no answer. This was strange, but I had no choice but to continue to wait, so I ordered breakfast. My meal had not yet come, when who should walk in but Angus and his wife, Bobbie. I was distressed to see how frightfully thin Angus was, as he leaned heavily on his cane. I could see he was in considerable pain, and I almost burst into tears. But, as soon as he saw me, his face lit up in such a loving greeting that I couldn't help but smile. I had heard he had cancer, but the person who told me that said he was in remission. We had breakfast together and talked for almost two hours. We laughed, again and again, as we recounted our adventures during the Ten Year World Plan and his many exploits since then. He was now a member of the Continental Board of Counsellors,[113] and, in his usual humble manner, could not understand why they had chosen him for this important service.

---

113 See Continental Board of Counsellors in the Glossary

At about eight o'clock, Pat Woods walked in, and I invited him to join us. However, Bobbie said they had already stayed longer than they had intended, as they were on their way home to Invermere, British Columbia. We said an unsatisfyingly short and rushed goodbye, and they were gone.

I asked Pat what had happened. He said that the minister got tied up in Ottawa, and that he and Saul would take the proposal down to him later in the week. I started to hand him the proposal, but he said I should just take it back to the office. So I got in my car and drove all the way back to Saskatoon, grumbling all the way. I had gotten up at two o'clock in the morning and driven all the way down to Regina and back for absolutely nothing! "What a waste of time," I thought. However, when I heard, a few months later, that Angus had passed away, I realized that that trip had not been for nothing. Quite the contrary. Bahá'u'lláh, in His loving kindness, had arranged it so Angus and I could have that last special opportunity to say our goodbyes.

52. The Aborigines are Coming!

The Mahboubi family fireside[114] in North Vancouver was, for many years, one of the most vibrant in the Lower Mainland. The Mahboubis worked with Curtis and Sonny, two First Nation believers in their community, to host these once-a-month events. Several times, they had invited me over, as the speaker, and the upcoming Friday night was one of these occasions.

That Friday afternoon was sunny and warm, and I was having coffee out on the balcony of the townhouse complex where we lived, when I heard the phone ring. It was the secretary of the British Columbia Regional Bahá'í Council.[115] She related a long and complex story about a young aborigine in Australia, named Franklin Freeman, who had recently become a Bahá'í, and was traveling to Vancouver for some sort of cultural exchange event. An Australian member of the Continental Board of Counsellors had contacted a Canadian Counsellor to suggest that it would be good for the Bahá'ís in Vancouver to greet him while he was here. The Canadian Counsellor had contacted the National Spiritual Assembly, and they had contacted the British Columbia Regional Bahá'í Council, and that was why they were phoning me.

---

114 A Bahá'í fireside is an open house occasion, when seekers can hear about the Faith and bring any questions they may have.
115 See Regional Bahá'í Council in the Glossary.

"Could I please make contact with him while he was in town?" "Sure," I said. "When is he arriving?" "We're not sure," was the reply. "He may already be here." "Oh, okay. What hotel is he staying at?" "We're not sure of that either." "Oh, okay. What was the name of the cultural event he is attending?" There was a pause on the other end of the line, and then she said, "We're not sure of that either." "What was his name again?" "Franklin Freeman," she said triumphantly, as that was at least one fact we had to work with. "Okay, leave it with me and I'll try to make contact," I said, as I hung up the phone.

The Lower Mainland is a vast cosmopolitan metroplex of several million people, with hundreds of, if not a thousand, hotels, and with many dozens of various cultural associations. How the heck was I going to find Franklin in all that mess? So I decided to say a prayer. During the prayer, a quote from the House of Justice crossed my mind:, *"When the friends realize that the hosts of the Kingdom are waiting to rush forth and assist them . . . they will then no doubt arise with greater confidence to take the first step, and this, we know, will be aided and guided from on high, for the very act of striving to respond to God's call will bring in its wake countless divine blessings."*[116] So I got up and glanced heavenward, and said, "Okay you guys, I'm going to take the first step—the rest is up to you."

I got out the phone book and decided to call the Indian and Native Friendship Centre in Vancouver. They should know of any Aboriginal cultural exchange event going on in the city. However, all I got was a recording saying the office was closed for the weekend. Well, that was the first step, and—nobody home—game over. So, I closed the phone book. But, as the book closed, I caught a glance of a listing with the words

---

116   The Universal House of Justice, *Messages 1963 to 1986*, p. 359

'Cultural Festival' in the title. "What was that?" I said to myself, and quickly leafed back through the book to the page I was at before. The listing was for the 'International Cultural Festival Society', so I hurriedly dialed that number. The voice of a small child came on the phone and simply said, "Hello." This did not sound promising. Maybe I dialed the wrong number. "Is this the International Cultural Festival Society?" I asked. "That's my mommy," said the little voice. "Is your mommy there?" I asked hopefully. "No." "Will she be home soon?" "I'm not sure." "Okay, I'll call back later." "Okay," she said. Then added, "Do you want her cell phone number?" "Oh yes, please!"

As I dialed that number, I wondered how I was going to frame my request. As this festival had its own phone listing, it may be a large event, with various groups coming from all around the world, and the organizer may not know the names of all the individual performers—but, before I could think it through, a quick, harassed voice said, "Charlene here." "Yes, Charlene, my name is John Sargent and I'm looking for an Aboriginal performer named Franklin Free . . ." "Hold on a second," she interrupted. Suddenly, a thick Australian accent came through the line. "Frankie hee-ya." What? Stop! No! Not possible! I looked heavenward and shook my head in disbelief—two quick calls and I'm talking to Franklin Freeman on the line!?

I explained to Frankie that I was a local Bahá'í and that I was going to a fireside/potluck supper that evening, and was wondering if he would like to come along. He said, "Sure, but hang on a minute." He was gone a few minutes, then came back and said, "Yeah, we'd love to come." We? I quickly calculated; I could take four, in addition to myself, in my car, and said, "Oh, that's great! How many will be coming?" "Twelve," he replied. Twelve?! My mind raced. How was

I going to get twelve people from downtown Vancouver up to North Vancouver? Frankie noticed my hesitation and said, "No worries, mate, just give us an address and we'll take a taxi." So I gave him the address and hung up the phone. Now, I thought, I'd better warn Mrs. Mahboubi that twelve extra people would be attending her fireside.

Although the event was advertised as a potluck, Mrs. Mahboubi herself would prepare a delicious Persian dinner for everyone, and the guests would bring a little something for dessert. I quickly told her what had happened, and I could sense a little alarm in her momentary pause, but she said, "Fine, great, the more the better! See you soon."

Aborigine performer

When I arrived, the Aborigines had just come, seconds before, and there was a general happy hubbub of greetings. Frankie was the only Bahá'í in the troupe, and the leader was an elder named Major Summer. He was a short, high-spirited, old imp. Black as coal, with white woolly hair and beard that made it look like he was peering out through one of those artificial white Christmas wreaths. The event followed the usual pattern: we started with a prayer, had dinner, a short presentation on the Faith, and dessert with socializing until late at night. During dinner, Frankie asked Mrs. Mahboubi if they could perform later, and she whole-heartedly agreed. That meant that Frankie and one of the women of the troupe had to take a taxi back down to the hotel and get their 'ge-yhar' (gear). We had to move the dining table out of the way to make a make-shift stage, and Curtis, Sonny and I went out on the deck to make more room, and watched the performance through the screen on the patio door.

The troupe's performance was spectacular, and a happy feeling of love and unity permeated the gathering. As we sat quietly in the dark, I overheard Curtis whisper to Sonny, "This is our best fireside ever!" The feeling of confirmation overwhelmed me, and I just sat back serenely and turned my eyes toward the clear, star-studded sky, and, as the Universal House of Justice had promised, felt the torrent of divine blessings showering down on the assembled friends.

A footnote to this story is that, some months later, I heard through the grapevine that, after their return to Australia, Major Summer had also embraced the Faith.

Epilogue

I had been serving as an Auxiliary Board member for a number of years, during the important transition to fifth epoch[117] thinking and acting. As the Universal House of Justice put it, *"We come thus to a bridge between times. The capacities developed through a century of struggle and sacrifice by a handful of intoxicated lovers of Bahá'u'lláh must now be applied to the inescapable tasks remaining to the Formative Age . . ."*[118] As a result, the Auxiliary Board members spent much of their time travelling to communities and conferences to: help the friends understand the new methodologies; learn new skills; and encourage them to step out of their comfort zone to implement this new strategy. Although I really enjoyed all this activity, it was obvious my health was in decline. For me, this was the ultimate irony. I had spent the last forty years trying to bring the Faith to the First Nation Peoples of Canada, without marked success, and now, when we were on the threshold of approaches that had a good potential for success, I was rapidly losing my physical ability to participate.

At this same time, I was working as the Band Administrator for a First Nation community along the North Thompson River, in central British Columbia. This was a largely sedentary, high-stress job, and, although I thought I was coping mentally—physically, I was not. I was working at my desk, juggling two or three concurrent crises, when my phone rang.

117　See Tablets of the Divine Plan in the Glossary.

118　　The Universal House of Justice - Riḍván message 2000

The nurse in the health unit urgently informed me that a drunk was in the lobby threatening to assault the receptionist. I quickly ran upstairs to the health unit and turned the corner toward the lobby, when the whole building began to swirl around me. The last thing I remember was my head hitting the wall with a loud thud. When I came to, a couple of paramedics were struggling to get me on a gurney. Although I was told that this diversionary action, on my part, had ended the dispute in the lobby, it was my last official service for the band.

Celeste, Anne, and John visiting isolated believers in Haines Junction, Yukon Territory, 2009

When I got to the hospital, they ran several tests, and my doctor said I was a complete mess. My blood pressure was through the roof, my cholesterol was too high, my sugars were way out of control, and I was operating on pure adrenalin.

"You are a heart attack or stroke just waiting to happen," he said. "No more work for six months, and no driving," were among his instructions. My wings were clipped. I phoned Ann Boyles, the Continental Board of Counsellors member I was working with, and told her what had happened, and that, sadly, my health prevented me from continuing in the role of an Auxiliary Board member.

It took about a year before I felt I was well enough to work again. About this time, the Human Resources Officer for the T'kemlúps First Nation called and asked if I could do some temporary work for the band. He informed me that the band had had to fire its Chief Operations Officer, and that they were right in the middle of an important restructuring. (It seems Bands are always in the middle of an important restructuring.) I said, sure, and started back to work. There were dozens of loose ends that needed to be picked up, and I put in a couple of pretty hectic weeks reining in these loose ends and preparing a plan and schedule to complete the restructuring. After a month getting the plan in place, I asked the CEO, "Aren't you going to post the COO position?" "Why?" he said. "You're doing such a good job. Just carry on." When I told my wife, she looked at me incredulously, and said, "Are you out of your mind? This is exactly the kind of work that ruined your health the last time!" I said, "No, this will be different. Now the buck stops with the CEO, not with me." However, it turned out that, with this larger band, it was even more stressful than my previous position, and, after a year, my angina was back almost constantly. My doctor said, "Frankly, John, you are leaving that job. Either you will walk out or they will carry you out." I decided I had better walk out.

I was really not able to hold a high-stress job any more. But that was the only type of work I had done in the past decade. I had never really thought about retirement. I always thought

I would work till I dropped. Then it occurred to me—I had worked until I dropped! Now I realized the next time could be the last time. So there I was, retired at 61. But what was I to do with myself? I had always enjoyed a happy and productive life. Doing nothing was going to drive me crazy. Then I remembered that my daughter and sister had been pestering me to write down my stories. Although I had been reluctant to do this in the past, I now had the time. So, gradually, I began the process.

You have just completed reading the result, and I hope you have found some of these stories interesting and amusing. As I look back at these stories, myself, I am overcome with gratitude for the way the confirmations of God have continually rained down upon me. The prayer I prayed all those years ago, at the Holy Shrines in Haifa, to be allowed to serve the Cause, has been more than answered. My biggest regret is that I wish I had been a more intelligent, wise, and effective servant. In the end, I hope that these stumbling efforts have found some measure of acceptance in the sight of God.

However, I am comforted by these words of Bahá'u'lláh: *"Wert thou to consider this world, and realize how fleeting are the things that pertain unto it, thou wouldst choose to tread no path except the path of service to the Cause of thy Lord. None would have the power to deter thee from celebrating His praise, though all men should arise to oppose thee.*

Go thou straight on and persevere in His service. Say: O people! The Day, promised unto you in all the Scriptures, is now come. Fear ye God, and withhold not yourselves from recognizing the One Who is the Object of your creation. Hasten ye unto Him. Better is this for you than the world and all that is therein. Would that ye could perceive it!" [119]

---

119 Baha'u'llah, *Gleanings from the Writings of Baha'u'llah*, p. 314

Glossary

'**Abdul'-Bahá** – (Servant of Glory) Abbas Effendi, 1844–1921. The eldest son of Bahá'u'lláh, centre of his Father's covenant from 1892 through 1921, and authorized interpreter of Bahá'u'lláh's Writings. Spent most of his life a prisoner of religious persecution by the Ottoman Turks.

Alláh-u-Abhá – (God is Most Glorious) A greeting passed between Bahá'ís.

Amatu'l-Bahá Rúḥíyyih Khánum - Née Mary Maxwell, 1910–2000. Wife of Shoghi Effendi, the Guardian of the Bahá'í Faith. She was appointed a Hand of the Cause of God residing in the Holy Land.

Auxiliary Board and their assistants – Bahá'í Administration has two sides: one side is elected by the membership; the other is appointed by the Universal House of Justice. The senior institution on the appointed side is the International Teaching Centre, with its offices in Haifa, Israel; and in each continent a Board of Counsellors is appointed to direct the activities of the Auxiliary Board members and their assistants on that continent. These individuals provide advice and assistance to the membership and institutions in new and/or difficult situations.

Báb (the) – (The Gate) Siyyid 'Alí Muhammad, 1819–1850. The Herald of Bahá'u'lláh, and the author of His own Divinely Revealed Dispensation. Martyred by the Persian authorities, at the instigation of the Muslim divines.

Bahá'í Assemblies – The administrative affairs of the Faith are handled by a board of nine directors elected annually from and by the membership. Each local community of nine or more adult Bahá'ís elect a local Assembly, and each national community elects its National Assembly at an annual national convention.

Bahá'í electoral process – All adult Bahá'ís in good standing in a community are eligible to vote and be voted for a position on the local Spiritual Assembly. There are no nominations, and all those who are elected are expected to serve, unless compelling obstacles prevent them. Shoghi Effendi has provided a list of five characteristics which members of this body must possess. Each community member votes for the nine individuals who they think best combine these five characteristics. These votes are tallied, and the nine individuals with the highest number of votes are elected to the new local Assembly for the coming year. Once a year, at a unit convention (may contain one large community or several smaller ones), a delegate is selected to attend the national convention for the purpose of election of the National Spiritual Assembly.

Bahá'í Faith – One of the fundamental verities of the Faith is that God reveals His will for mankind through a succession of Manifestations, whom He sends at approximately one thousand year intervals. Each of these great Teachers reiterates the fundamentals of God's truth and prescribes laws suitable to the age in which they appear. Bahá'ís believe that Bahá'u'lláh is the latest of these great Teachers.

Bahá'u'lláh – (Glory of God) Mírzá Ḥusayn 'Alí, 1817–1892. Founder of the Bahá'í Faith. Revealed God's will for mankind in this age. Was imprisoned, tortured, and exiled by the Persian authorities, and spent most of His life a prisoner of religious persecution by the Ottoman Turks.

Continental Board of Counsellors – The Universal House of Justice appoints, on each continent, a Board of Counsellors, whose members help the national communities with implementation of the current plan and report back to the House on their progress. They also direct the activities of the Auxiliary Board members and their assistants.

Covenant – The principle underlying God's purpose for mankind in this day is the oneness of the world of humanity. In order to do this, it is necessary to safeguard His Faith from schism. To accomplish this, Bahá'u'lláh has entered into a covenant with his followers, that they follow the administrative structure set out in His Writings and in the *Will and Testament* of His son, 'Abdu'l-Bahá.

Hands of the Cause – During the early days of the Faith, The Báb appointed eighteen 'Letters of the Living' as disciples to help teach His Faith. During the ministries of Bahá'u'lláh, 'Abdu'l-Bahá, and Shoghi Effendi, these helpers were designated 'Hands of the Cause.' With the passing of Shoghi Effendi, it was no longer possible to appoint further 'Hands', and this institution came to an end on September 22, 2007, with the passing of the last living 'Hand of the Cause'.

Ḥaẓíratu'l-Quds – (The Sacred Fold) The headquarters of Bahá'í administrative activity, both at the local and national level.

Lesser Peace – Bahá'u'lláh predicted that humankind would soon enter into a political peace that would establish a period of security for the whole human race. This would be followed, in the future, by 'The Most Great Peace', where each individual would be so changed that the mere thought of causing harm to another person would be absolutely abhorrent.

Manifestation of God – The word 'manifest' means to show or reveal. Bahá'ís use the term 'Manifestation' to designate an entity specially created by God to manifest His will to mankind. Abraham, Moses, Buddha, Jesus, Mohammed, The Báb, and Bahá'u'lláh, among others, are considered such entities.

Mashriqu'l-Adhkár – (Dawning Place of the Remembrance of God) Bahá'í Houses of Worship at the local, national, and continental levels. These will, in future, be the centre around which community service and philanthropic activities revolve.

National Convention – An annual gathering, where regional delegates come together to elect the National Spiritual Assembly and consult on the affairs of the Cause in their country.

Pilgrimage – Bahá'ís are urged to undertake, at least once in their lives, a pilgrimage to the Holy Shrines of the Faith. At present, only those Shrines in Israel are accessible to the Bahá'ís. In the future, it is hoped that the Holy Shrines in Iran and Iraq will also be made accessible to the Bahá'ís.

Pioneer – The Bahá'í Faith has no clergy or missionaries. However, individual Bahá'ís can offer to leave their native land and move to other communities that may require their help. These individuals would become landed immigrants, find employment, and become regular members of the community. As the Faith has grown, the need for international pioneers has lessened, and the friends are now encouraged to 'homefront' pioneer, within their own country, to communities with few Bahá'ís.

Progressive Revelation – One of the fundamental verities of the Bahá'í Faith is that God progressively reveals His truth to humankind, in direct proportion to man's capacity to understand it. He sends His Manifestations to man at approximately one thousand year intervals.

Regional Bahá'í Council – In larger countries, a National Spiritual Assembly may subdivide its jurisdiction into various regions. A consultative body is elected by the members of the local Spiritual Assemblies in that region, to handle those administrative duties assigned to it by the National Spiritual Assembly. (In some countries the National Spiritual Assemblies still appoint the Regional Councils.)

Riḍván – The holiest and most significant of all Bahá'í festivals. It commemorates Bahá'u'lláh's declaration of His mission to His followers, during a twelve-day stay in Baghdád's Najíbíyyih Garden, in 1863. Bahá'u'lláh designated this garden the 'Garden of Riḍván' (paradise).

Shoghi Effendi – Shoghi Effendi Rabbani, 1897–1957. The grandson of 'Abdu'l-Bahá. He was the Guardian of the Bahá'í Faith, and sole interpreter of the Bahá'í Sacred Writings from 1921 to 1957. The Guardian and the Universal House of Justice are the central pillars of the administrative order of Bahá'u'lláh.

Tablets of the Divine Plan – During the dark days of World War I, 'Abdu'l-Bahá wrote a series of Tablets to the Bahá'ís of the United States and Canada, setting out the manner and methodology for the unfoldment of his Father's Faith. These have become known as the 'Tablets of the Divine Plan'. Using 'Abdu'l-Bahá's Tablets, Shoghi Effendi worked with Canada and the United States to actuate this plan. Eventually, these plans involved all the Bahá'í communities throughout the world. The Universal House of Justice continues, to this day, to carry forward the 'Divine Plan' by instituting a continuous series of teaching and consolidation plans. The `Divine Plan` is also divided into longer phases call `epochs`, which may contain several plans.

Universal House of Justice – This is the senior administrative body in the Bahá'í Faith. It is composed of nine members, who are elected to five-year terms at an international convention, where the National Spiritual Assembly members from around the world vote. The decisions of the Universal House of Justice are promised by Bahá'u'lláh to be inspired by God.

CPSIA information can be obtained
at www.ICGtesting.com
Printed in the USA
LVHW01s0718010618
579185LV00003B/4/P

9 781525 516672